Graham

Thank you for your
feedback and support.

Enjoy the book.

D1020131

ACCELERATING LEADERSHIP DEVELOPMENT

PRACTICAL SOLUTIONS FOR BUILDING YOUR ORGANIZATION'S POTENTIAL

Jocelyn Bérard

JB JOSSEY-BASS™
A Wiley Brand

Copyright © 2013 Jocelyn Bérard

Published by John Wiley & Sons Canada, Ltd.

All rights reserved. No part of this publication may be reproduced, stored in a retrieval system, or transmitted in any form or by any means, electronic, mechanical, photocopying, recording, scanning, or otherwise, without either the prior written permission of the Publisher, or authorization through payment of the appropriate per-copy fee to the Canadian Copyright Licensing Agency (Access Copyright). For an Access Copyright license, visit www.accesscopyright.ca or call toll free 1–800–893–5777. Requests to the Publisher for permission should be addressed to the Permissions Department, John Wiley & Sons Canada, Ltd., 6045 Freemont Boulevard, Mississauga, Ontario, L5R 4J3, or online at www.wiley.com/go/permissions.

Tables and figures copyright © Global Knowledge are used by permission of Global Knowledge.

While the publisher and author have used their best efforts in preparing this book, they make no representations or warranties with respect to the accuracy or completeness of the contents of this book and specifically disclaim any implied warranties of merchantability or fitness for a particular purpose. No warranty may be created or extended by sales representatives or written sales materials. The advice and strategies contained herein may not be suitable for your situation. You should consult with a professional where appropriate. Neither the publisher nor the author shall be liable for damages arising herefrom.

For general information about our other products and services, please contact our Customer Care Department within Canada at 1–800–567–4797, outside Canada at (416) 236–4433 or fax (416) 236–8743.

Wiley publishes in a variety of print and electronic formats and by print-on-demand. Some material included with standard print versions of this book may not be included in e-books or in print-on-demand. If this book refers to media such as a CD or DVD that is not included in the version you purchased, you may download this material at http://booksupport.wiley.com. For more information about Wiley products, visit www.wiley.com.

Library and Archives Canada Cataloguing in Publication Data

Bérard, Jocelyn, author
    Accelerating leadership development : practical solutions for building your organization's potential / Jocelyn Bérard.

Includes bibliographical references and index.
Issued in print and electronic formats.
ISBN 978-1-118-46411-3 (bound).—ISBN 978-1-118-46472-4 (pdf).—
ISBN 978-1-118-46473-1 (epub).—ISBN 978-1-118-46477-9 (mobi)

    1. Leadership. 2. Leadership—Evaluation. 3. Executive ability.
4. Organizational effectiveness. I. Title.

HD57.7.B47 2013   658.4'092   C2013-902911-7
                                            C2013-902912-5

Production Credits
Managing Editor: Alison Maclean
Executive Editor: Don Loney
Production Editor: Pauline Ricablanca
Cover Design: Adrian So
Composition: Thomson Digital
Printer: Courier

Printed in the United States of America

1 2 3 4 5 CRW 17 16 15 14 13

Contents

To Paul-Émile and Gaétane, you have been the best leaders and role models of my life. You made me who I am today.

To Lise, I couldn't have a better partner to realize my dreams. Your love, encouragement, support and positive attitude are remarkable. Thank you for all you do to help me succeed in life.

To Raphaël and Alexy, you are amazing! Because of you, I am very encouraged and enthusiastic about the future leaders of the 21st century. I learn a lot from you.

Acknowledgments

I love the saying "It takes a village to raise a child"—maybe because I am the eighth of a family of nine and I have two wonderful children of my own. But I love it mainly because it is so true. The whole village must be involved if the child is to have a good life. The teachers, the art instructors, the friends, the sports coaches and the extended family, along with the parents, all contribute to the success of this great family endeavor. It is the same for leaders: they can't make it by themselves; rather, leaders perform with and through others and receive help from other internal and external leaders and professionals, in so many ways. Leaders need a village too!

Guess what? The same goes for writing a book. There is no way I could have realized my dream of writing this book by myself. So many people contributed to its content and to the success of the work with clients that is illustrated in these chapters. I believe in teamwork, collaboration and leveraging the skills, know-how and experience of others to co-create better work. This is the approach I have taken here.

I had the pleasure to engage in great conversations with many senior leaders in Canada, Europe and the United States to get their "pearls of wisdom" regarding leadership. I want to thank them all for their contributions and their comments of great added value that appear throughout the book. They make the concepts speak with their real-life examples. Thank you sincerely to Dr. Jack Kitts from The Ottawa Hospital, Dan Pontefract from Telus, Alan Booth from Deloitte, Chris Hodgson from Scotiabank, John Duncan from the Royal Mail in the UK, Joe D'Cruz from University of Toronto's Rotman School of Management, Robert Hogan and Ryan Ross from Hogan Assessment Systems, Colleen Johnston from TD Bank, Stéphane Moriou from MoreHuman Partners, Margaret O'Neal from Purdue Pharma and Sylvia Chrominska from Scotiabank. I also want to thank Scott Williams, president of Global Knowledge Canada, and Brian Branson, Global Knowledge president and CEO, for their contributions through the discussions, and for their wonderful support and encouragement while I was writing the book. It is reassuring to have great leaders while creating a book on leadership.

Thank you so much to my amazing team at Global Knowledge. You are Kim Caughlin, Tom Gram, Marilyn Breen, Marsha Anevich,

Jeff Cole, Joan Taras, Suzanne Beaudoin, Jacqueline Boileau, Val Boser, Michelle Moore, Kevin Kernohan, Louise Chapman, Katharine Murrel, Sylvie Létourneau, Anita Bowness, Sébastien Houde, Heather Sperdakos, Maggie Li, Melissa Price-Mitchell, Mike Martel, Norma Thompson, Reed Carriere, Moe Poirier, Randall Vickerson, Adrienne Serrao, Lucie Guertin, Ross Rennie, Mary-Jo Williams, Kim Finkelstein, Lorraine Kirchmann, Georgia Phair, Priscilla Bahrey, Debbie Pearmain, Claire Beaulne, Rosemarie Bugnet, Nadja Corkum, Andrée Drolet, Pascal Karsenty, Sylvie Rimbach, Richard Robitaille and Debbie Carr.

And thank you to the many, many other fantastic associates in the Leadership and Business Solutions group at Global Knowledge who day in and day out support leaders' growth by designing, implementing and delivering award-winning leadership development solutions around the world. Your support, encouragement and dedication to quality work are inspiring. A special thanks to Tom Gram for your contribution to Chapters 4 and 14. With all of you I share my gratitude; it is an honor to be your leader.

This book would not be a reality without the tremendous contribution from two wonderful individuals. Thank you, Paul Brent, for spending numerous hours asking great questions, listening to me and patiently helping me put together my thoughts and ideas while creating the book. Thanks for the hard work and dedication. Let's go for another coffee!

And Ashley Pincott, thanks a thousand times for your brilliant work on the What the Experts Say sections of each chapter. The literature reviews you did allowed me to add a lot of value to the content and demonstrate how solid the practical solutions are. Thanks for your curiosity, tenacity and collaboration. And for the laughter!

I want to thank the wonderful Jossey-Bass and Wiley team for their support and high level of professionalism, including Jennifer Smith, Don Loney, Terry Palmer, Josie Krysiak, Pauline Ricablanca, Lukas Wilk, Brian Will, Jonathan Webb, Judy Phillips and so many other people involved in the creation and distribution of my book. Thanks, Don, for believing in me.

And finally, all my appreciation goes to my immediate family—the love of my life, Lise, and Raphaël and Alexy—for your patience while listening to me talking about the book and your constant encouragement. I am realizing all my dreams with you. *Merci de tout coeur!*

Introduction: The Business Performance Framework

Leaders are the ones who keep faith with the past, keep step with the present, and keep the promise to posterity.

—Harold J. Seymour

Why another book about leadership? It's a fair question. There are literally hundreds of business books that address the subjects of leadership and organizational change. As consultants to companies across North America and Europe, however, at Global Knowledge we have found there is a continuing demand for guidance on accelerating leadership development within an organization. That's what this book is all about: speeding up the process of leadership development. It's a multistep process that organizations can use to identify talent gaps, determine leadership requirements, select next-generation talent, develop the identified candidates, ensure their growth and acquire the tools they need to succeed.

Faced with increasingly complex and difficult business realities, managers from every area within an organization—be it sales, production, marketing, information technology or operations—are challenged to keep the business performing at as high a level as possible. Attracting, and more importantly developing and retaining, high-potential employees provides the lifeblood of any organization. It is these people who assume critical organizational roles, and retain and develop intellectual and knowledge capital.

Organizations do not operate in a vacuum, however, which is why Global Knowledge created the Business Performance Framework, to enable us to truly understand an organization's environment, business plan and strategy so that we can determine employee gaps that either exist today or will open up tomorrow. The framework allows for an understanding of a company's external environment (such as its competition, regulatory hurdles, speed to market, economy, technology and demographics); internal environment (such as its internal culture, change, systems, communication, retention and demographics); as well as its vision and business strategies.

Only after answering all the questions in the framework, in order to develop a working knowledge of the business, can we help an organization determine where the gaps are that it must fill to succeed. The question then becomes, does the business have the people it requires already in its talent pipeline, and if not, what can it do to accelerate the development of its high-potential employees and current leaders?

This is a reality that is recognized by Scotiabank, which, despite annual revenues of more than $19 billion and healthy profits, knows it is in the people business as much as the banking business. "It is actually not about the numbers," says Christopher Hodgson, the bank's group head of Global Wealth Management. "What sets our bank apart globally from other banks is our people and their skill sets, how we develop them and how we move them along to other jobs. The numbers help, but they come from the development of our people."

Speaking of people, organizations are arguably under more stress today than they have been since the Great Depression. The developed world faces a future of slow growth at best and a looming demographic tsunami in the form of its largest demographic group, the boomers, all rushing to retirement over the next ten to twenty years. Against this sobering backdrop, the requirement for companies to identify their high-potential leaders and develop them, as well as continue to develop current leaders, has never been greater.

It's an area of study that cries out for better research, documentation, structure and understanding, illustrated with real-life, tangible examples of what to do and—just as importantly—what not to do.

Organizations need to recognize that they are engaged in an everyday war for talent. Leaders and HR professionals from rival companies are attempting to hang on to their high-potential employees and attract all they can from others', including yours. "People who are very talented can always find opportunities in the marketplace," says Global Knowledge president and CEO Brian Branson. "So it is important to make sure that we as leaders in our organizations are not only trying to attract the right talent but making sure that we have the right opportunities and support infrastructure to retain that talent."

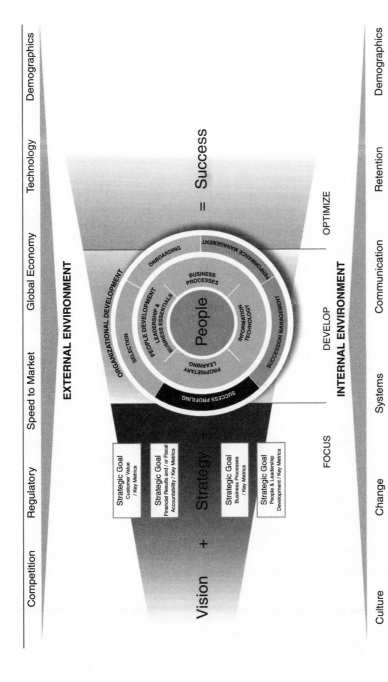

©2010 Global Knowledge Training LLC. All rights reserved.

Figure 0.1: Model of Business Performance

HOW THE BOOK IS ORGANIZED

The book is divided into three parts. The first, Leadership and Succession covers the best practices and most up-to-date research in the field with regard to succession management, leadership attributes and identifying future leaders. Part 2, Leadership in Action, is where the rubber hits the road. The chapters in this section cover skills and competencies that determine whether leaders are high functioning and successful or are simply placeholders in the organizational chart. Part 3, Leadership Best Practices, covers the role of the leader in aligning and cascading down the business strategy at each level of the organization and deals with issues related to transitions and the possible applications of new media technology.

I interviewed scores of executives and academic thought leaders from North America and Europe so they could share their expertise and experience on the key themes of the book: finding and nurturing leadership talent, ensuring their future development and making the necessary changes to create first-class organizations. In addition, the leading-edge work carried out by Global Knowledge—practical solutions that we have used in numerous organizations to help them identify leaders, accelerate their growth, improve their management skills and achieve better overall business results—informs this book.

Because this book is intended for two audiences, generalist readers (including people in leadership roles) and human resources professionals, each chapter comprises recommendations and effective practices and a summary of the relevant academic research. Readers who choose to skip over the What the Experts Say sections will still learn the practical and innovative strategies and practices to accelerate leadership development in their organizations. The first section of each chapter is based on personal and Global Knowledge collective expertise and know-how. But because I believe in the importance of learning from others who are doing excellent work and research on the topics covered in this book, I added those final sections, to complement and broaden the content of each chapter with a brief literature review.

One final note: although this book is about leaders and leadership, it must be stressed that producing better leaders results in more motivated and engaged employees throughout an organization. If you don't have great leaders, your organization may miss out on its chance to achieve greatness too.

PART I

Leadership and Succession

1

The Leadership Success Profile

Hire and promote first on the basis of integrity; second, motivation; third, capacity; fourth, understanding; fifth, knowledge; and last and least, experience. Without integrity, motivation is dangerous; without motivation, capacity is impotent; without capacity, understanding is limited; without understanding, knowledge is meaning-less; without knowledge, experience is blind. Experience is easy to provide and quickly put to good use by people with all the other qualities.

—Dee Hock

The first few chapters of this book lay out the theory and practice that organizations can use to recognize and develop great leaders. It is a process that includes defining the success profile required for leader-ship positions (What does it take to be successful as a leader in your organization?), identifying those high-potential individuals within your organization (Who are the future leader candidates?), diagnosing their strengths and specific development needs (What can they leverage and acquire to become better leaders?), determining how to accelerate their development by taking advantage of multiple development approaches and, finally, determining how to make sure development and growth are happening.

Most leaders today come to the position armed with a distinct skill set or expertise from some sort of technical background. Making the leap from that position to a leadership position, commonly called the leadership transition, is often misunderstood and underestimated. There is a world of difference between doing a particular job and managing people who are doing those same tasks. People get the idea from the world of sports and entertainment that it's easy to do: former players become big-league coaches and the likes of Clint Eastwood make the transition from actor to Oscar-winning director and producer. We tend not to notice that as many fail as succeed. In simple terms, the leadership success profile is a clear definition of what it takes to be an effective leader in a certain organization. Once it has been clearly defined, it will be used to diagnose the actual leaders (Chapter 3) or the high-potential ones (Chapter 2) in order to determine what to do to develop them (Chapter 4).

THE CRITICAL COMPONENTS

What does it take to be successful in a leadership role? A number of individuals both within and outside an organization may have the necessary qualities. However, until an organization determines exactly what specific combination of ability, background and personal makeup is required, launching a search to fill a leadership position or implementing a solution to grow leaders will prove fruitless. Through research and firsthand observation, we at Global Knowledge have identified a set of four key requirements that are critical components of the leadership success profile. These are:

- Competencies
- Knowledge
- Experience
- Personal traits/motivation

Acres of forest have been sacrificed to detail the volumes of academic research on the areas of competencies and personality traits/motivation in relation to leadership development. Perhaps surprisingly, very little research

Figure 1.1: The Triangle of Truth

has been done on experience and knowledge and their development. We refer somewhat tongue-in-cheek to the holistic combination that makes up the leadership profile at Global Knowledge as the "Triangle of Truth." An individual needs to have or acquire certain elements of all four components of the triangle as they relate to leadership.

The combination includes attributes that go well beyond what is generally in a person's résumé. A résumé, after all, lays out only what the person has done and perhaps describes some competencies. It does not describe that person's makeup.

The leadership success profile is not a schematic describing any one individual but rather a description of the requirements at the job or level in an organization (for example, vice-president or director level). The level-by-level approach is one that more and more companies are adopting.

Competencies (What I Can Do)

Competencies can be best described as a set of desired behaviors. For example, at one particular pharmaceutical company, the competency requirement for the vice-president of sales revolves around customer focus—providing internal and external customers with value. (See sidebar,

"What It Takes to Succeed as a Leader at TD Bank.") So just what does that look like in action? A typical behavior would be identifying, building and maintaining long-term customer relationships. Other behaviors that illustrate key competencies might be grouped under the heading "Things the individual is skilled at" or "Things the individual is required to have (or learn) to fill the role."

Knowledge (What I Know)

The knowledge necessary in the leadership success profile could be organizational knowledge or product knowledge, or knowledge of systems and business functions. It also could include knowledge of laws and regulations. This component of the profile could be roughly described as "This is what I know."

Experience (What I Have Done)

The experience component of the leadership success profile might be tagged as "This is what I have done"; this, too, is a key component of any potential leader's résumé. Rather than vague descriptions, such as "I have ten years of business planning experience," the experience component must be expressed in granular and specific terms, articulating the types of situations the candidate has experienced and exposed to justify a claim as a "good manager." Examples might include having led an advisory group of customers, or having addressed public relations challenges, such as a product recall or labor issue. In the finance arena, it could be a specific experience, such as having implemented a budget-tracking system and defended the variances.

Personality Traits/Motivation (Who I Am)

Why is it important to define personality traits when creating a success profile for a particular leadership role? The simple answer is that any individual's personality traits will influence their leadership style, which will go a long way to determining the leadership results of the person in that role.

WHAT IT TAKES TO SUCCEED AS A LEADER AT TD BANK

TD Bank has, like many other organizations, a leadership profile. But what is interesting to note is how it clearly made it behaviors-based, actionable and observable. Competencies, or profiles, should not be done to meet HR obligations. These words and definitions need to mean something for the line managers who will apply them, and they need to be the right ones for the organization.

The most important challenge for a leadership profile is to "make it happen" in a day-to-day fashion. For example, some leaders may say sarcastically, "The values and competencies are on the wall, but not in the hall!" At TD Bank, numerous efforts are made at all levels, including the executive level, to live the competencies and make them real. All executives must realize the power of what they say and do; they are visible and influential. So if they believe, talk and live the competencies, they are sending a very powerful message—one much more powerful than any official communication.

TD'S LEADERSHIP PROFILE

Make an Impact and Value Speed

Leaders at TD make an impact by:

- Getting things done.
- Valuing speed.
- Focusing on what matters.
- Owning results—not blaming others.
- Knowing the business from the ground up and customer in.
- Finding ways to outperform—not settling for average.
- Delivering superior results for all stakeholders in both the short and long term.

Build for the Future

Leaders at TD build for the future by:

- Having a vision and proactively taking action to implement it.
- Developing tomorrow's leaders.

(continued)

- Creating an organization that starts with the customer.
- Building organizational capabilities today that business will need tomorrow.
- Seeking continuous improvement.
- Creating a learning environment.

Inspire the Will to Win

Leaders at TD inspire the will to win by:

- Demonstrating passion for the business.
- Attracting and retaining great people.
- Bringing out the best in individuals and teams and making it fun.
- Showing perseverance and resilience in bad times.
- Recognizing and rewarding the contributions of others, both in little ways and more formally.
- Caring about people.

Act Decisively while Working Effectively in Teams

Leaders at TD work effectively in teams by:

- Being driven to win for the TD team.
- Making things happen by leveraging their partners.
- Using positive influence, not power, to deliver results.
- Showing trust in their business partners.
- Working well with people who are different than they are.
- Knowing instinctively how to engage the organization to make things happen.

Live Transparently and Respect Different Views

Leaders at TD live transparently by:

- Speaking candidly but with respect.
- Not rounding corners.
- Having no time for internal politics.

(continued)

- Respecting different views.
- Being grounded, authentic and genuine, and not taking themselves too seriously.
- Being willing to personally wear problems.
- Surfacing problems, fixing them and learning from them.
- Recognizing their own strengths and weaknesses.

Show Excellent Judgment

Leaders at TD show excellent judgment by:

- Making pragmatic decisions using a mix of intellect, experience and street smarts.
- Dealing with tough issues fairly, decisively and calmly.
- Making timely decisions, even in ambiguous, rapidly changing situations.
- Taking intelligent and prudent risks.
- Making decisions based on what's best for TD, not their ego.

Demonstrate Unwavering Integrity

Leaders at TD demonstrate unwavering integrity by:

- Doing the right thing to the highest ethical standards.
- Putting the interests of the organization above their own and their business unit's.
- Treating people with respect.
- Showing that actions speak louder than words.
- Acting as a role model publicly and privately.
- Demonstrating loyalty and responsibility to TD.

THE BUCKET LIST

The TD Bank profile is certainly a positive model, but there are many ways to define what it takes for a leader to be successful. Joseph D'Cruz, professor emeritus of strategic management at the University of Toronto's

Rotman School of Management, describes five "buckets" of competency that successful leaders need to develop:

1. **Management basics.** The first bucket consists of fundamental competencies such as planning, deployment, accountability and performance management, as well as continuous improvement as popularized by Japanese management approaches.
2. **Strategic outlook.** Frontline managers who are preparing to move to higher levels in the organization need to be coached to think strategically and assess their own abilities and capabilities.
3. **People skills.** D'Cruz argues that leaders must be able to manage people effectively—"that is the individual interpersonal stuff, such as having difficult conversations, performance management, as well as team management skills and even some self-management and self-regulation, seeing how your behavior impacts others."
4. **Analytical competence.** The fourth bucket is understanding data. The successful leader possesses a basic understanding of statistics and behavioral economics.
5. **Skill at negotiation.** "Every manager throughout an organization can be thought of in terms of negotiation," says D'Cruz. "Negotiating with the people who work for you, you are negotiating with the people you report to, you are dealing with peers of the organization." D'Cruz is a big believer in "interest-based negotiation," where both sides come away satisfied rather than endure a zero-sum negotiation in which one side tries to better the other.

Alan Booth, an associate partner at professional services firm Deloitte, highlights three core competencies for any leadership success profile. "It starts with intellectual horsepower, somebody who gets it, somebody who is a quick study," he says. "The second is maturity and resilience—someone who can take direct feedback, analyze it, learn from it and get back to work. The third is the ability to manage relationships with others: the ability to form them, the ability to leverage them and the ability to add value to the relationship."

Earlier in the chapter, the four essential leadership requirements that make up the Triangle of Truth were listed. Remember, though, that it's imperative to take a holistic view of the success profile for any given leadership position. In reality, most people's skills, experiences and traits cannot be configured into neat triangles. Sometimes, for example, people are "professional students," with a handful of degrees but little or no real-world experience working in an organization. A leadership success profile has these four components because, to be effective, leaders need the right balance of experience, knowledge, competencies and traits according to the position and the organization. To use another analogy, building a robust leadership success profile is akin to constructing a stable foundation for a house.

Hogan Assessments, a firm that provides a variety of psychological assessment tools that have HR applications, contends that every well-run organization needs to have a competency model encompassing four broad skill sets:

1. **Intrapersonal:** integrity, emotional stability and self-control
2. **Interpersonal:** the ability to build and maintain relationships together with compassion, empathy and humility
3. **Business:** a capacity to analyze data, allocate resources and forecast budgets
4. **Leadership:** vision, a gift for empowering staff and the ability to act as a good role model

---

HOW TO DEFINE AND EVALUATE LEADERSHIP

Leadership is typically defined in terms of the persons in charge. That is a mistake. Why? Leadership should be defined in terms of the ability to build and maintain a high-performing team. And when it is time to evaluate leadership, we should look at it in terms of the performance of the team relative to the other teams with which it competes. This is rarely done.

Source: Hogan 2003.

COMPETENCIES, EXPERIENCE AND KNOWLEDGE

The following section outlines just what is contained in a real-world leadership success profile for a Global Knowledge client. The sample profile provides the observable behaviors or actions that are required for successful job performance on the executive leadership team, organized by competencies, experience and knowledge.

The most important aspect of competencies is to make them relevant for the people who will use them: the job incumbent, the incumbent's leader and people in HR. It also has to be easy to understand. Can you see the person doing this behavior? If the language is too vague or esoteric, it will lead to confusion.

Competencies

- **Customer focus.** The ideal person for the job provides internal and external customers with value-added quality service, and identifies, builds and maintains long-term customer relationships that are of strategic significance and drive the success of the business. He or she takes accountability to provide service and resolve customer issues in a manner that exceeds customer and market expectations. As well, this person must use customer data and feedback to identify changes required and understand customer/market trends and adapt products, sales, processes and customer relationships.
- **Industry networking.** The ideal person for the executive leadership team is required to have prominence beyond the walls of the organization and is required to "develop and maintain relationships with competitors, stakeholders, government and regulatory organizations" and "identify valued relationships with key organizations related to the pharmaceutical industry." The individual is also required to "develop and maintain a planned network of relationships," use that network "to identify opportunities, gather market intelligence and resolve challenges" and "maintain high visibility for company in the industry and the community."
- **Resource management.** Because even the largest companies have limited resources, the executive-team member is asked to "prudently manage the company's financial, technology and space resources to achieve

16

business goals," and to develop budgets "to align with company strategy and revenue plans," while maintaining access to "resources and capabilities across the multiple companies" and "to monitor performance against plans and reassign resources as required."

- **Business processes (problem solving and decision making).** The individual is required to use logical processes to resolve issues by making decisions "based on principles, values and business cases"; to champion initiatives that have "significant potential paybacks but possible adverse consequences, based on an assessment of the risks and benefits"; and to integrate risk management into departmental and organizational planning.
- **Creativity and innovation.** The individual is asked to develop "leading-edge, new or improved ways of doing things," which requires him or her to, among other things, apply innovative solutions "to significant business issues, challenge current products and processes, create a culture that promotes and rewards creativity and innovation, [and] champion new ideas and facilitate their implementation."
- **People and leadership (collaboration).** The ability to work collaboratively is a major part of having what it takes for a spot on the company's executive leadership team, so the individual is required to work cooperatively and constructively with others to achieve desired outcomes, which include encouraging "idea sharing and debate from all areas and all levels" of the company while "soliciting and using ideas and opinions of others" and "assertively challenging others in a tactful and diplomatic way."
- **Courage.** Yes, courage is also required, because members of the executive leadership team are expected to take actions that may be unpopular but necessary. To do that, the sought-after individual offers "fact-based assessments of situations, offers [his or her] own perspective even when others disagree" and "sustains initiatives in the face of resistance and setbacks."
- **Coaching and developing others.** A top executive also needs to be a coach and is required to plan and support the development of employee skills for current or future job roles by helping others "in exploring and discovering new possibilities," creating a work environment "of empowerment, self-development and continuous learning" and reinforcing "the importance of development and learning as a business priority."

Experience

As a member of the executive leadership team, the individual also needs to have experienced or had exposure to several key business situations:

- **Leadership challenges.** The ideal executive-team candidate would have experience leading a regional advisory group of customers, working on a new product launch, addressing a public relations challenge such as a product recall or delayed product launch, developing local market knowledge through focused networking activities and representing the company in external professional or regulatory associations.
- **Business processes.** The individual is asked to have relevant knowledge or experience of the full product lifecycle by working in various company departments, allowing him or her to develop new techniques, products or services, lead a team through process change, deal with the impact of delays in operations and participate in negotiation of supplier agreements for a new product launch.

Knowledge

To be a member of the executive leadership team, the individual is required to have company-specific knowledge of its processes, systems, services and external relationships. It's a list that includes knowledge of the company's vision, its mission, strategy, departments and functions, finances, customers and people and external relationships.

THE IMPORTANCE OF PERSONALITY

I like to say when I work with leaders that their personality traits are the DNA of their behaviors. Robert Hogan's definition is that "personality concerns the characteristics inside people that explain why they do what they do" (Hogan 2012). Hogan then adds two dimensions to personality, depending on whether we are looking at it from the inside or the outside: "Personality should be defined from two perspectives. First, there is personality from the inside, which is called identity. This is the person you think you are and it is best defined by your hopes, dreams, aspirations, goals, and intentions—i.e., your values. Second, there is personality from the outside, which is called reputation. This is the person that others think you are."

In Chapter 3 we will review how to measure each component of the success factor. One of the key objectives is to identify if there is disparity between the person's identity and his or her reputation. The larger the gap, the bigger the problem.

Advanced research demonstrates that we can distinguish two aspects of personality traits, the enablers and the derailers—or what we might think of as the bright side and dark side of performance. The "bright side" refers to our way of relating to others at our best in "normal" conditions. Hogan says that the so-called dark side "reflects the impression we make on others when we let our guard down, or when we are at our worst." Derailers tend to show when leaders are stressed, in unusual situations or operating under pressure. Hogan likes to say, perhaps with a sliver of irony, that "the bright side concerns the person you meet in an interview; the dark side concerns the person who actually comes to work!" (Hogan and Kaiser 2005). Of course, these two sides of personality always coexist and affect your reputation as a leader.

The personality traits defined by Hogan as enablers, or the bright side, fall under the following headings:

- **Adjustment.** The Adjustment scale reflects the degree to which a person is calm and even-tempered or, conversely, moody and volatile. High scorers seem confident, resilient and optimistic. Low scorers seem tense, irritable and negative.
- **Ambition.** The Ambition scale evaluates the degree to which a person seems leaderlike, seeks status and values achievement. High scorers seem competitive and eager to advance. Low scorers seem unassertive and less interested in advancement.
- **Sociability.** The Sociability scale assesses the degree to which a person appears talkative and socially self-confident. High scorers seem outgoing, colorful and impulsive. They dislike working by themselves. Low scorers seem reserved and quiet. They avoid calling attention to themselves and do not mind working alone.

- **Interpersonal Sensitivity.** The Interpersonal Sensitivity scale reflects social skill, tact and perceptiveness. High scorers seem friendly, warm and popular. Low scorers seem independent, frank and direct.
- **Prudence.** The Prudence scale concerns self-control and conscientiousness. High scorers seem organized, dependable and thorough. They follow rules and are easy to supervise. Low scorers seem impulsive and flexible. They tend to resist rules and close supervision; however, they may be creative and spontaneous.
- **Inquisitiveness.** The Inquisitive scale reflects the degree to which a person seems curious, adventurous and imaginative. High scorers tend to be quick-witted and visionary, but they may be easily bored and not pay attention to details. Low scorers tend to be practical, focused and able to concentrate for long periods.
- **Learning Approach.** The Learning Approach scale reflects the degree to which a person enjoys academic activities and values education as an end in itself. High scorers tend to enjoy reading and studying. Low scorers are less interested in formal education and more interested in hands-on learning.

Hogan defines the following personality traits as derailers, or the dark side, that can put leaders at risk:

- **Excitability.** Marks those who appear overly enthusiastic about people or projects, and then become disappointed with them. Result: they seem to lack persistence.
- **Skepticism.** Marks those who are socially insightful, but cynical and overly sensitive to criticism. Result: they seem to lack trust.
- **Caution.** Marks those who are overly worried about being criticized. Result: they seem resistant to change and reluctant to take chances.
- **Reserve.** Marks those who lack interest in or awareness of the feelings of others. Result: they tend to be poor communicators.
- **Leisureliness.** Marks those who are independent but tend to ignore others' requests and become irritable if they persist. Result: they come across as stubborn, procrastinating and uncooperative.
- **Boldness.** Marks those who have an inflated view of their competency and worth. Result: they tend to be unable to admit mistakes or learn from experience.

- **Mischievousness.** Marks those who are charming, risk-taking and excitement-seeking. Result: they may have trouble maintaining commitments and learning from experience.
- **Colorfulness.** Marks those who are dramatic, engaging and attention-seeking. Result: they may become preoccupied with being noticed and lack sustained focus.
- **Imaginativeness.** Marks those who think and act in interesting, unusual and even eccentric ways. Result: they appear to be creative but may lack judgment.
- **Diligence.** Marks those who are conscientious perfectionists and hard to please. Result: they tend to disempower staff.
- **Dutifulness.** Marks those who are eager to please and reluctant to act independently. Result: they may be pleasant and agreeable but reluctant to support subordinates.

LAST THOUGHTS ON WHAT IT TAKES

Brian Branson, president and CEO of Global Knowledge, sees one critical characteristic of leadership that is often overlooked by organizations. "The most important leadership characteristic is integrity, ethics," he says. "If a leader doesn't have that, it doesn't mean he or she will not be successful, but people will ultimately realize that the leader lacks integrity and, at the end of the day, that creates tremendous risk—for talent retention, and real business risk." He recalls working as CFO for a competitor of WorldCom in the late 1990s and puzzling along with the rest of his management team about how its rival could have such superior profit margins. "I kept saying, 'I can't figure it out.' It turned out that they were not doing the right thing—that is why they had better numbers." WorldCom emerged to be behind one of the largest accounting frauds in U.S. history. "So, to me, integrity is the most important thing. If you don't have that, you don't have the foundation to build upon," Branson says.

Generosity in leadership is another key trait. "My first manager was such a significant influence on me because he gave credit to those around him. When he brought a client into the room, he would say, 'Bob did this for us, Betsy did this for us.' He never took any credit for himself. So what did that do? It may or may not have had an impact in the eyes of the customer. However, for the employees around the table, it motivated them. I wanted to work hard for that person because I knew that he recognized the commitment that I had and brought to the table. It was an important lesson for me in my first job out of college. I saw that you could be successful without heaping the praise upon yourself, and instead building up those around you."

Dr. Jack Kitts, CEO of The Ottawa Hospital, looks for three traits or attitudes when evaluating leadership candidates. "First of all, they have to be high energy. Nobody wants to follow a leader who is a downer," he explains. Also, "they have to have a passion for the organization; it has to be evident they really want that organization to be the best and succeed. And, finally, they have to have a positive focus. In every challenge there is an opportunity."

WHAT THE EXPERTS SAY
Going beyond Core Personality Traits
Research on the relationship between personality, motivation and leadership development has found consistent strong support for the Big Five personality traits—the foundation for all personality trait measurement tools.

The Big Five are often described as follows:

1. **Extraversion.** This trait includes characteristics such as excitability, sociability, talkativeness, assertiveness and high amounts of emotional expressiveness.
2. **Agreeableness.** This personality dimension includes attributes such as trust, altruism, kindness, affection and other pro-social behaviors.
3. **Conscientiousness.** Common features of this dimension include high levels of thoughtfulness, with good impulse control and goal-directed behaviors. Those high in conscientiousness tend to be organized and mindful of details.
4. **Neuroticism.** Individuals high in this trait tend to experience emotional instability, anxiety, moodiness, irritability and sadness.
5. **Openness.** This trait features characteristics such as imagination and insight; those high in this trait also tend to have a broad range of interests.

Each of the five personality factors are represented on a continuum. As an example, on one end we can find strong extraversion, with strong introversion on the other end. In society, people are somewhere in between the two polar ends of the continuum.

While endorsing the importance of the Big Five personality traits, two studies looked beyond the Big Five to examine work orientation and motivation as desirable traits needed for leadership, as well as precursors to the inclination to engage in leadership self-development. Studies by Boyce, Zaccaro and Wisecarver (2010) and Hendricks and Payne (2007) move away from traditional applications of trait theory to examine multiple individual differences, as predictors of leadership effectiveness and leaders' inclination to engage in self-development. In their empirical study of 400 undergraduate psychology students, Hendricks and Payne examine the relationship between the personality traits of goal orientation, leadership self-efficacy, motivation to lead and leadership development. The authors found that learning goal orientation was positively related to leadership self-efficacy, whereas leadership self-efficacy was positively related to both affective-identity and social-normative motivation to lead, suggesting that individuals with a high level of leader-goal orientation are more likely to want to lead because they like to lead and feel a sense of duty to lead. In their study of 400 junior military leaders, Boyce, Zaccaro and Wisecarver extend the findings of Hendriks and Payne to include motivation as a precursor to engage in self-development activities, finding that for leaders with low or moderate levels of motivation, an organizational support program positively influenced their engagement in self-development.

This research on personality and motivation and its relationship to leadership development has practical implications for organizations in predicting successful leadership through assessments of individual personality differences to support selection, placement and promotion decisions. Because personality traits tend to be established early in life and remain reasonably stable, this research also has implications for training leaders. Hendriks and Payne (2007) point out that the development of leaders may be more efficient if the Big Five, along with the factors of learning goal orientation, leadership self-efficacy and motivation to lead, are taken into account when selecting who receives leadership training and development. Furthermore, the authors suggest that trainers work to enhance the traits of leadership self-efficacy and motivation to lead during leader training because they tend to be more pliable than learning goal orientation and other stable personality factors. Boyce, Zaccaro and Wisecarver (2010) recommend that organizations screen and target employees with low self-development inclinations to receive structured organizational support that would motivate leaders to engage in self-development, and provide them with the resources and skills necessary to do so effectively.

Competencies

A review of the literature examining the relationship between core competencies and leadership found that it reflected the increased global nature of business environments. In her review of global leadership research, Jokinen (2005) attempts to combine the findings in an integrative framework that would contribute to a more comprehensive understanding of the effect that different aspects of globalization have on leadership development. The author reports that in order to develop a network of specialists, organizations are continuing to select for and develop leader competencies based primarily on human capital, and only secondarily working to develop and train general managers with a global mindset. She identifies characteristics of a global mindset that lead to global competencies, including bigger, broader picture thinking (leading to managing competitiveness); balancing contradictory demands and needs (managing complexity); trust in networked processes, rather than in hierarchical structures (managing adaptability); valuing multicultural teamwork and diversity (managing teams); and seeing change as opportunity (managing uncertainty). In addition, she identifies three main types or levels of global leadership competencies:

1. **Core competencies,** including self-awareness, engagement in person transformation and inquisitiveness
2. **Mental competencies** related to self-regulation, social judgment and cognitive ability
3. **Behavioral competencies** related to social and networking skills

More recently, in a review of five major leadership studies, published from 2002 to 2007, that surveyed executives, leaders, HR professionals and training managers across a wide range of industries, McCallum and O'Connell (2009) sought to raise the awareness of relational competence by attempting to clarify the role that human and social capital orientation competencies each play in leadership. This study represents a significant shift from past research that focused on the "hard" individual-leader competency growth, to give more attention to the "soft" relational context within which leadership takes place. An analysis of data from 150 to 5,000 respondents that identified critical competencies as either human or social capital revealed mixed results. Human capital competencies were classified as those that involved individual-level knowledge, skills and abilities (e.g., work experience, education, knowledge, skills and abilities). Social capital competencies involved relational ones (e.g., social awareness, self-management, forging commitments, fostering cooperation, coordination and networking, giving feedback and establishing trust). The results found that while there is still a tilt toward human capital rather than social capital in leadership, there is a growing trend toward the increasing awareness of and need to develop the latter, especially in light of the volatility and virtual nature of organizations.

Looking to future leaders, McCallum and O'Connell identify critical individual and relational leader competencies, including master strategist, change manager, relationship builder/network manager and talent manager. Other skills and qualities found to be important are cognitive ability, strategic and analytical thinking, decision-making skills, communication skills, influence and persuasion, ability to manage in a context of diversity, ability to delegate and manage risk, and personal adaptability. It is clear from the literature that effective future leadership will increasingly value and require both human and social capital competencies. The authors argue that the power of each is found more in their symbiotic relationship than in their individual strengths.

Most recently, a study by Gentry and Sparks (2012) samples a total of 9,942 practicing managers from over 1,550 companies in forty countries, with a minimum of twenty managers per country, to determine whether certain leadership competencies are universally endorsed by managers across countries as being important for success in organizations, or if the importance of the leadership competencies is dependent on cultural factors. Across the forty countries, more than two-thirds of managers (averaging 66 to 80 percent) believed that resourcefulness, change management, and building and mending relationships were each important for success in their organizations. Together, the literature reviewed on the importance of competencies on leadership development offers several practical implications for organizations. Gentry and Sparks argue that to be successful, organizations need to invest in training and development to address leader competencies, including being strategic and future-oriented in their management of material, human and financial resources; managing change by creating new systems; and mobilizing others to follow and focus on building and maintaining relationships through the establishment of a strong network of ties, internally and with business partners. McCallum and O'Connell suggest that social capital could be emphasized in leadership development by creating a more open systems mindset, drawing attention to the importance of relationships by capitalizing on coaching, mentoring and specific job assignments, and work at hiring for the long term.

Knowledge and Experience

Most major learning and development theories place experience at the center of the learning process. Successful experiences in leadership roles in a variety of frameworks (family, educational, social and work) serve to strengthen an individual's belief in his or her ability to be a leader. In a recent experimental study that compared a group of fifty soldiers perceived as leaders with a group of thirty soldiers perceived as non-leaders, Amit and colleagues (2009) examine the impact of early experiences on leaders' development. The quantitative part of the study found that leaders, more than non-leaders, remembered themselves as experiencing more influential leadership roles at school, enjoying social status at school and trying to change things in the school framework. A thematic analysis of the qualitative part of the study indicated that leaders report many more childhood experiences perceived relevant to the development of leader identity than non-leaders report. They also found that the development of leader identity through accumulated experiences leads to increased self-efficacy as a leader and to the acquisition of knowledge of influence, including self- and other awareness, situational awareness and diagnostic knowledge. The authors note that the diagnostic knowledge acquired through analysis of one's experiences provides individuals with the sensitivity to read situations as well as people's feelings and motivations, skills determined to be important in transactional-type leadership.

Another recent but later experimental study by Dragoni and colleagues (2011) extends and builds on the findings of Amit et al. (2009) by investigating the relationship between work experience and leadership. Through an investigation of the work histories and individual characteristics of 703 executives, the authors found that the accumulation of work experience was directly related to executives' ability to think strategically about their organizations and business environments, identifying cognitive ability as the strongest predictor of strategic thinking competency and finding consistency with other research that executives' extraversion was positively related to their accumulated work experience. Given that cognitive ability was identified as the strongest predictor of strategic thinking competency, hiring for executives with strategic thinking and decision-making competencies should lean toward choosing "smart" leaders over those with experience. However, the positive relationship between extraversion and accumulated work experience has implications for organizations in terms of selecting managers for further development. Extraverted individuals can be expected to be more proactive and motivated to learn and develop, and therefore will be likely to seek out various developmental opportunities, which in turn will lead to an increase in amassed work experience.

Organizations of all sizes and industries face tough challenges in preparing managerial personnel to assume future leadership positions. A study by Groves (2007) introduces a best-practices model for integrating the leadership development and succession planning process through optimal utilization of managers and a supportive organizational culture. Interviews with thirty CEOs and HR executives across fifteen best-practice organizations revealed that best-practice organizations effectively build their leadership pipeline by:

1. Developing the organization's mentor network by engaging managers in mentoring relationships with high-potential leadership employees.

2. Ensuring active manager participation in the organization's method of identifying high-potential employees.
3. Fully engaging managers at all levels in leadership development activities, such as teaching courses and creating project-based learning experiences (e.g., stretch assignments and action-learning projects) for high potentials.
4. Ensuring a flexible and fluid succession planning process by frequently updating lists of high potentials based on project-based performance, and basing succession decisions on a diverse pool of candidates.
5. Creating organization-wide forums (e.g., leadership academy) for exposing high potentials to multiple stakeholders, including senior executives and board members.
6. Establishing a supportive organizational culture through active CEO and senior management participation in development programs, performance appraisal and reward systems that reinforce managerial engagement.
7. Evaluating the effectiveness of leadership development practices through empirical studies that model program theory and assess knowledge, behavior and results outcomes.

Having a holistic view of what it takes to be an effective leader is critical. It does not take only one of two competencies: a combination of knowledge, experience, competencies and personality traits is absolutely necessary. Defining the success profile is setting the foundation to so many activities in talent management, such as learning and development, succession management, recruitment and selection, and performance management. Now that we have defined what it takes, let's see how we can identify those high-potential leaders for whom we will invest significant effort.

2

Identifying Leadership Potential

> I have no special talent. I am only passionately curious.
>
> —Albert Einstein

In athletic circles, the former Soviet Union was famous for its well-honed practice of identifying high-potential athletes at an early age, far earlier than most other countries. That was one of the reasons the former superpower consistently dominated the Olympic medal podium. A more recent, and powerful, example of identifying high-potential athletes occurred in Canada for the 2010 Winter Olympics. The Canadian government put in place years before the Vancouver Olympics a program called Own the Podium, in which young high-potential athletes were rigorously identified and trained extensively for the 2010 Games. Result: the best performance ever for the Canadian athletes, with twenty-six medals and a world record of fourteen gold medals won by a single country in the Winter Olympics.

One of the critical tasks for the leaders of any organization is to identify the leaders who will succeed them. Much as a professional sports organization sits down on draft day to determine which young athletes are most likely to grow into the superstars around which a team can be built, an organization's leaders are required to create their own draft list of candidates who can assume increasingly responsible roles in the organization.

"I have a sort of simplified competency executive model: IQ, EQ, XQ," says John Duncan, Human Resources group director with the Royal Mail in the UK, referring to the concepts of intellectual, emotional and execution quotients. "IQ is their intellectual horsepower; EQ, how self-aware are you and how do you manage relationships with others in all levels of the organization and externally? IQ is 'Are you smart enough to develop the strategy?'; XQ is all about execution: 'Can you get it done?' To those three I would add a fourth, AQ—adversity quotient. How resilient are you—how do you deal with obstacles, tough times and organizational setbacks?"

In most cases, just like those pro scouts and team managers, we are looking for future potential rather than current leadership ability. Many managers, however, look at potential leaders from a *performance* standpoint. That is to say, they are judged on what they have achieved—often by assessing their behavior against the organization's leadership competency or capability framework. It's a natural tendency; unfortunately, past performance does not present the full picture when it comes to assessing leadership potential.

So just what is potential, exactly, and what is the difference between future potential and past performance? How can leaders consistently determine potential? We define high-potential leaders as "high performers in their current role who have strong probability of being successful one or two levels higher in the organization, and for which specific development solutions need to be defined in order to accelerate their growth." It is great to be clear on a definition, but leaders and HR professionals involved in identifying high-potential leaders need more than that. Global Knowledge researched the concept of high potential, not only to define it more specifically but also to develop solid and rigorous practices and tools to better identify high-potential leaders. Leaders need to assess candidates against a set of standardized factors, which are the personal characteristics that make up leadership competence and success. There is no single attribute that makes a great leader. Leadership potential goes beyond an employee's record of academic achievement or résumé. It is a combination of powerful elements.

Our research, experience with clients, and discussions with practitioners led us to isolate six factors that predict the success of future leaders.

PREDICTORS OF SUCCESS FOR FUTURE LEADERS

Here are the predictors of success for future leaders that we have identified, and real-life examples of leaders who possess them in spades.

1. Cognitive Complexity and Capacity

Research suggests that successful leaders have higher cognitive, or intellectual, abilities than their less-quick-witted competitors. In order to deal with the new competitive landscape driven by globalization, technology, deregulation and democratization, current leaders must be able to rapidly make sense of tremendous amounts of information in shorter and shorter time frames and decision-making windows. Best described as having the ability to logically integrate or articulate multiple sources of data, and having the ability to look beyond the obvious in order to meet the demands of a situation, these high-horsepower thinkers thrive in confusing, fast-changing environments.

A great example of a leader with cognitive complexity and capacity is George W. Merck, president and chairman of Merck and Co. during the tumultuous period of 1925 to 1957. Following in his father's footsteps at the company, George W. set Merck and Co. on a path of pioneering drug research to create the model for the modern pharmaceutical company. It was his early recognition of the crucial importance of research and keeping the company focused on solving medical problems that transformed Merck and Co. from a small player into a $100-million industry leader responsible during his three decades at the helm of the drug company for countless medical breakthroughs, among them introducing cortisone, vitamin B12 and streptomycin to the marketplace.

2. Drive and Achievement Orientation

Success is, in part, the product of initiative and effort. Terms often used to describe this dual quality include "sweat equity" and "the school of hard knocks." Employees who demonstrate personal initiative, a passion for results and a desire to challenge the status quo are likely to be more successful leaders than their counterparts. Among the markers are grit (perseverance and passion for long-term goals) and personal initiative (taking an active and self-starting approach to work goals and tasks, and persisting in overcoming barriers and setbacks).

Ryan Ross, vice-president of Global Alliances at Hogan Assessments, uses the term "basic employability" to cover this attribute. "Are you showing up and getting the job done? Then we will look at whether you have what it takes to move up. Sometimes at Hogan we talk about the GSD—get shit done—factor."

As indicated, however, current performance alone does not predict potential. "It is the biggest mistake we see," warns Ross. "You need objective data to predict if somebody has the potential to move up."

Characterized by the ability to overcome barriers and setbacks to conquer an important challenge, or jumping on an opportunity whenever it presents itself, this dirt-under-the-fingernails type owes as much to hard work as any other innate ability.

A modern-day example of this type of leader can be seen in Nissan head Carlos Ghosn. He got his start as a plant manager to French automotive supplier Michelin in 1981. Within three years, he was named head of research and development for the company's industrial tire division. One year later, he became COO of Michelin's South American operations, based in Brazil, and in a few short years was appointed chairman and CEO of Michelin North America. He later joined French automaker Renault as executive vice-president and soon after became COO and then CEO of Japan's troubled Nissan auto company.

At Nissan, he was given the "mission impossible" task of turning the company around. He succeeded by defying Japanese business etiquette: he cut jobs and shuttered plants, and sold prized assets, such as Nissan's aerospace unit. Unpopular as those moves were, Nissan's annual profit more than doubled in the first year of his leadership, and the company quickly became one of the world's most profitable automakers. For the relentless change he forced on Nissan, Ghosn has been compared to another Westerner who drove sweeping changes on Japan, U.S. General Douglas MacArthur.

3. Learning Orientation

Learning-oriented leaders have a strong desire to improve themselves and others. This type of individual actively seeks, and is responsive to, feedback. These are people who enjoy challenges, and are willing to take risks and step out of their comfort zone in order to develop their skills and advance their careers.

Sylvia Chrominska, former group head of Global Human Resources and Communications at Scotiabank, recalls that her drive to improve led to her success at the bank. "I had two very good sponsors in the bank who were more role models to me than coaches, and they challenged me to work harder and want to learn more," she says. "When we have conversations about leadership potential, certainly that intellectual curiosity is important."

There is perhaps no better an example of this trait in action than that of iconic American artist Andy Warhol, who established the Factory studio in the late 1960s. On its face, it was a venture that was doomed to failure, except for the overwhelming influence of Warhol himself. Best known as a venue for celebrity-studded parties, it was the place where his team of workers would make silkscreens and lithographs in assembly-line settings. That motley collection of workers—adult film performers, drag queens, socialites, drug addicts and musicians, known as the Warhol superstars—helped him create his paintings, starred in his films and helped build the Warhol legend. As well as two-dimensional art, the Factory and its counterculture cast of workers made shoes, commissioned pieces, sculptures—whatever could be sold under the Warhol name. Trying different things, experimenting and thinking differently are just some examples of Warhol's desire to learn and to encourage others to do the same.

4. Personal and Business Ethics

Recent high-profile scandals have raised questions about the way leaders can shape the workplace, both negatively and positively (Colvin 2003; Mehta 2003). Evidence shows that an authentic and ethical approach to leadership is an effective way to achieve positive and lasting outcomes in an organization. Ethical leadership, viewed as being fair, honest and trustworthy, results in positive employee outcomes, including job satisfaction, dedication and willingness to report problems to management (Ciulla 1998; Brown, Treviño and Harrison 2005).

Individuals best defined by this factor describe success not just by results but also by the way that those results are obtained. Typically, they have the best interests of fellow employees or colleagues in mind during both good and bad times.

A recent example comes from Internet search engine giant Google, with its early and unofficial "Don't be evil" corporate motto. In part a jab at competitors' business practices, it became part of the official corporate policy and was included in the prospectus for Google's 2004 IPO, eventually morphing into a pillar of its ten-point corporate philosophy as "You can make money without doing evil." After the company's IPO, founders Sergey Brin and Larry Page, as well as CEO Eric Schmidt, requested that their base salary be cut to just one dollar. The trio has resisted calls to increase their salaries, and their main compensation continues to come from owning stock in Google. The Internet company has devoted significant investments to renewable energy initiatives and philanthropy.

Another living example of personal and business ethics in leadership is investor guru Warren Buffett, the Oracle of Omaha. An independent thinker who challenges the conventionally accepted way of looking at things, and armed with more conservative values, he is about as far from the flinty-eyed Wall Street titan as one can get. When Buffett became acting CEO of Salomon after its trading scandal in the 1990s, he told employees that if they lost money, he would understand, but if they were unethical, he would be ruthless. The selfless gift of his fortune to the Bill and Melinda Gates Foundation (rather than spending it or setting up a foundation in his own name) perhaps best illustrates his character.

5. Motivation to Lead

Just as people differ in their ability to lead, so too do they differ in their desire or motivation to assume a leadership position. These individuals have a natural tendency to emerge as leaders when presented with the opportunity. They are confident in their abilities and do not shy away from leadership. Hopefully, the desire to lead stems from a sense of duty or responsibility, rather than for personal gain (benefits, salary, status).

Individuals best defined by this factor are comfortable taking a stand and defending their ideas, and facing adversity head on. They may view the opportunity to lead others as an honor and a privilege.

A prime example of this sort of individual is Frederico Fleury Curado, CEO at Embraer. His strong belief in people and people development, and the way he sees employee satisfaction at the center of

Embraer's success, makes him a great example of a leader demonstrating the motivation-to-lead factor.

6. Social and Emotional Complexity and Capacity

This leadership factor refers to employees' ability to process emotionally charged information and use it as a guide in their thinking and actions. These employees are better at perceiving, using, understanding and managing emotions in themselves and others, and are the key components in what is defined as emotional intelligence (EI). Research indicates that managers with higher EI are better able to cultivate productive working relationships with others and to demonstrate better personal integrity. EI also predicts the extent to which managers engage in behaviors that are supportive of the organization's goals.

"I'm an introvert by nature," says Global Knowledge's Brian Branson. "So for me, as I began to move out of staff-level roles, I recognized that I needed to do a better job of being able to go into a room and engage with people. If I want to have a conversation, I need to ask some questions— [it's] like going on a date. Not necessarily having to be over the top, but [in order to] go into a situation that I'm uncomfortable in and talk to someone I don't know. Oftentimes, asking good questions and interacting efficiently can be very important for a leader in a business. If you can't engage in a proficient way, it can really undermine your credibility."

Individuals who display this leadership potential factor typically keep disruptive emotions and impulses in check when facing challenging situations. In any given interaction, they are attuned to both their own needs and emotions and those of others.

There is no better exemplar of social and emotional complexity and capacity than Marshall Goldsmith, a world-renowned thought leader on leadership development. The author or coeditor of thirty-one books, including the *New York Times* bestseller *What Got You Here Won't Get You There*, is an invaluable (and accessible) resource. Most of Dr. Goldsmith's interviews and published works are available for viewing and sharing online (free of charge) at the online Marshall Goldsmith Library. By the end of 2010, visitors from around the world listened to or downloaded over 5.6 million articles, columns, interviews, webinars, audios, videos and resource pages from this website.

THE NEXT PHENOM

No one can predict which athletes will win a medal at the Olympics, not even a few days before the event. Logically, it's even harder to predict five, six or seven years before the Games who has the athletic ability to take them to the Olympic level. But this is exactly what the Olympic coaches and program directors are doing. Past performance in their respective sports is certainly an indicator, and physical attributes as well; but this is not enough, because the young athletes are performing at two or three levels below the Olympic or professional level. So what else can be observed and assessed to predict the athletes' performance? Various characteristics and behaviors will be observed, but it seems that there are often variables such as the desire to win, the passion for the sport and the strong desire to constantly improve.

Alison Beard (2012) interviewed gymnastics coach Bela Karolyi about precisely these issues for the August 2012 issue of *Harvard Business Review.* Karolyi has used tough talk and bear hugs to coach nine gymnasts to Olympic gold medals. After victories with the Romanian team in the 1976 and 1980 Games, he defected to the United States. But because he spoke no English and had limited funds, he found himself cleaning restaurants to make ends meet, before eventually working his way back to coaching in international competitions. With his wife, Martha, he now runs the USA Gymnastics training facility.

For Karolyi, success is measured by the willingness to sacrifice in order to be the best possible. He demands of his athletes complete dedication, and puts the same demand on himself—to the point that he has not had a vacation with his wife in thirty-six years. He states that he was not very successful in his own athletic career, a fact he attributes to lack of coaching, which has also driven him in his pursuit of perfection—both for his athletes and for himself. "I realized that was what I would like to give: to elevate my students, to stand behind them and give them that boost to reach what I never reached," says Karolyi.

Karolyi identifies athletes with high potential through physical testing—measuring quickness, strength, agility and flexibility—but, just

(continued)

as importantly, by the students' mental makeup—intelligence, tough-
ness, discipline and competitiveness. Those who have those traits have
a significant advantage over those who don't. "I won't say it's not
improvable. It is. But those who already have it in their general nature
have a great advantage," he says.

A MEETING OF MINDS

In many organizations, an annual meeting occurs where the senior leaders
come prepared to discuss their high-potential leaders in their respective
teams. Impacting these types of conversation are multiple biases, such as
the halo effect, in which a critical strength so remarkable in an individual
will "cover" for a weakness of the same person, making him or her seem
strong in everything.

To impose some order and generate effective outputs, all the participants to such conversations should be oriented to the factors that will be
used to determine which leaders have more potential than others. Orienting
the senior leaders to the concept of potential—the factors that are good
predictors and how to use them—is a concrete way to materialize the
notion of reliability and improve the quality of the decision.

A very common approach used by leaders and HR professionals in
selecting their high-potential leaders is to use a Nine-Box Grid or an
alternate version of this grid. Essentially, the grid is a three-by-three-cell
table, with *performance* rated low, medium or high on the X axis, and
potential similarly rated low, medium or high on the Y axis. It is popular
mainly because of its simplicity and its incorporation on two axes of an
assessment of a subject's past performance and future potential. It is fairly
widely recognized that, to identify a high-potential leader, he or she needs
to perform in the current role. (See Figure 2.1.)

There are many benefits—and some drawbacks—to using the
Nine-Box Grid.

On the plus side, it is simple and effective. Leaders will understand its
use and merits. It will ensure that the leaders involved in the nomination
process are considering the past and current performance of the individual.

Labels and Definitions

	PERFORMANCE		
	Low	**Medium**	**High**
POTENTIAL			
High • Possesses a great deal of excess capability • Drive and desire to do more in current and future	• Consistently fails to meet targets • Too early in role	• Works consistently • Meets deliverables • Dependable • Meets most/all KPIs	• Consistently exceeds targets • Sets ambitious targets • Identifies ways to add value • Exceeds KPIs
	• Novice • New in role, may have moved recently • Need to provide support/monitor closely	• Has capacity to do more • Look to stretch/grow • Provide coaching/support to achieve greater results/outcomes	• Clear potential beyond current role • Look for new, mission-critical assignment • Capacity and ability for immediate advancement
Medium • May have some excess capabilities • Can be expected to progress normally	• May be new in organization/role • Monitor closely • May need to delve more deeply into nature of poor performance	• Solid citizen • May have capacity for more • Look to stretch/grow	• Great results • May have capacity to do more • May not be totally motivated or engaged • Engage in career-planning discussions
Low • Working at top of capabilities • Limited desire to progress • Has mastered current role	• At risk • Clear performance issues • May need to enact performance-improvement plan	• Solid performer • Well situated in current role • Should investigate possibility of driving toward more challenging goals	• Very strong performer • May have plateaued • May possess specialized knowledge and experience • May be comfortable in role • May be able to coach/train others

NOTE: KPI stands for "Key performance indicators"

Figure 2.1: Global Knowledge Nine-Box Grid

On the minus side, there's a chance that once the grid gets filled, the process ends. The raison d'être of the grid is to generate discussion among the leaders about the various high potentials (note that, in many organizations, candidates often are referred to simply as "potentials") who are being assessed on the grid.

Getting various perspectives on each high potential will help make the profile more complete, so the leaders know each of these "corporate assets" better. The assessment of one high potential conducted by his or her immediate leader may suffer from blind spots regarding performance or behaviors that would be revealed by involving other leaders from across the organization in the assessment process.

One of the most important risks—I would dare to say failures—that comes from using the grid is that, in many situations, the notion of performance is well understood but that of potential less so. What is meant by "potential" in the context of leadership development? Organizations need a common definition and consistent means to recognize and measure high potential. This is where the concept of reliability comes into play. There is a need to better define the notion of potential—and the six factors described below are the answer to that need.

The engagement of a team of leaders in the discussion and selection of the future leaders of the organization is a high-impact management gesture that reinforces the fact that it is a common shared responsibility of a management team to develop a pool of talent in order to support the organization's leadership talent pipeline.

The whole purpose of selecting high-potential leaders is to determine their development needs and to accelerate their development. So one of the risks of using the Nine-Box Grid is to have the leaders thinking the work is done when they have selected the high potentials according to their positioning on the grid. Remember, selecting high-potential athletes does not make them ready for the Olympics; most of the work begins after the potential has been identified.

The bottom right-hand box, which identifies employees who exhibit high performance but low potential, is as significant in its way as any of the others. Although the majority of the work done on succession management and the identification of high potentials is for leadership roles, there is a growing trend toward the identification of succession for professional employees. The term "professional employees" is used loosely here.

A professional could be a manager with a small team but with a very high degree of expertise in certain products, services or R&D initiatives. He or she could be an employee with a professional designation in accounting, law, engineering, and so on, or one who has accumulated years of experience and expertise within the organization and has very high value for the continuity of the operations.

The aging of the population is impacting the professional employees as much as it is the leaders, so attention needs to be given to protecting and transferring the knowledge and wisdom of these professionals. One of these days, the highly knowledgeable employees will pull out of the parking lot and never come back. Although the spot in the lot will be occupied the day after by someone else, this does not bring back the years of valuable accumulated experience, knowledge and wisdom. The future of succession management will see more frequent attention paid to the practices affecting the preservation of knowledge workers and high professionals, not just the high-potential leader.

DO WE TELL THEM OR NOT?

To communicate or not to communicate, that is the question that scares a lot of leaders.

Once a leadership team has selected high-potential leaders, should they communicate the decision to them or not? And if yes, what should they communicate? These are probably among the most sensitive questions senior leaders have to struggle with. The understandable fear is that the process will lead to the creation of an elite group of people who will be excited about the fact they are "in," and another, larger group of people who will feel left out and disappointed. As consultant and adviser to our clients, I always pay attention to the specific culture within the organization regarding the openness to share information. I have seen both ends of the spectrum: an organization in which the high potentials were not only informed but also involved in open group activities among themselves, and another, smaller organization in which the CEO asked all leaders to not communicate a single word on the succession management work I did with them. The trend in progressive and high-performing organizations is clearly toward more transparency (Conger and Fulmer 2003).

Although Global Knowledge remains flexible on this issue, we lean toward sharing more rather than less—transparency as opposed to opacity. Even if some risks exist, there are numerous advantages to communicating earlier rather than later with the high potentials who the organization wants to invest in their development toward more senior positions. These advantages include:

- **Increased engagement and retention.** High potentials are among your most highly valued employees. They are certainly more at risk of leaving or being recruited by your competitors than are the other employees. Letting them know that there are opportunities in your organization, and that you want to maximize their chances to be ready when openings occur, is a great motivator for them to stay.
- **Increased learning opportunities.** How can you discuss openly the various talent development activities they will experience (assessment, feedback, elaboration of an individual development plan, special assignments, various courses, etc.) if you can't tell them what their opportunities are and why they are doing these activities? That situation limits significantly what can be done and creates awkward situations.

The key questions are what to communicate and to whom. I believe high potentials should be informed that the organization sees potential in them and a discussion should take place concerning their career aspirations. If the persons are interested in such a discussion, the following guidelines will help determine what—and what not—to say:

- You want to invest in them and describe the types of talent development they may be undertaking.
- You should never make any promises of promotion, even though they may be readier when an opening comes. You can't, in fact, because you don't know how they will progress even if you invest in them, and you don't know what the conditions will be when it comes time to fill certain positions.
- You expect them to keep performing in their current role or any new and stretched assignments.

- You expect them to behave professionally. Demonstrating arrogance toward other leaders and employees not identified as high potential would be a big red flag. Humility is preferred.

When employees ask their leaders if they are part of the high-potential pool and the answer is no, it is best to be truthful. Employees deserve honest, specific and balanced feedback on performance and potential. Honesty is the best policy.

Simply stated, identifying high-potential leaders is a way to accelerate the development and preparation of future leaders because it helps HR professionals and executive leaders focus their effort and investment on the right people at the right time.

WHAT THE EXPERTS SAY
Leadership Potential

As mentioned above, a thorough review of the research and professional literature, our experience with clients, as well as discussions with practitioners, led us to isolate six factors that predict the success of future leaders. Let's look now at the theoretical foundations, the supporting theories and empirical evidence for each, and behavioral descriptors of each of these leadership potential factors.

Cognitive Complexity and Capacity

Numerous researchers on leadership effectiveness and leadership perception point to the importance of cognitive, or intellectual, abilities; this has emerged as a key characteristic of leaders in most literature reviews (see Judge, Colbert and Ilies 2004; Bass 1990). Rather than leading for efficiency and control, modern leaders are finding themselves leading for adaptability and responsiveness (see Achtenhagen et al. 2003; Volberda 1996). This new business reality places the leaders in a position where they have to assume multiple roles (e.g., enabling vs. administrative), effectively deal with ambiguity (e.g., articulately paint credible pictures and visions of possibilities and likelihoods) and achieve effectiveness (e.g., generate competitive strategies) in a variety of contexts or situations.

In a review of the literature on executive leadership, Zaccaro and Klimoski (2001) identify a number of conceptual models that focus on the requisite qualities of executive leaders: the conceptual complexity models, the behavioral complexity models, the strategic decision-making models and the visionary or inspirational models. The underlying assumption of these models is that cognitively complex individuals process information differently and perform certain tasks better than cognitively less complex individuals because they use more categories or dimensions to discriminate among stimuli and see more commonalities among these categories or dimensions (Hooijberg, Hunt, and Dodge 1997). On average, cognitively complex people search for more information and spend more time interpreting it.

Drive and Achievement Orientation

Research has demonstrated that success in leadership positions cannot be predicted solely by cognitive ability. Success is also the product of initiative and effort. Individuals differ in terms of the likelihood of initiating action and in terms of the intensity, direction and duration of the efforts exerted toward a goal. Specific behaviors can be identified by the qualities of grit and personal initiative.

Grit is defined as perseverance and passion for long-term goals. It entails working strenuously toward challenges and maintaining effort and interest over years despite failure, adversity and plateaus in progress. The gritty individual approaches achievement as a long-term goal that requires consistency of interest and perseverance of effort. Grit has been related to educational attainment, retention and performance (Duckworth et al. 2007).

Personal initiative is defined as taking an active and self-starting approach to work goals and tasks, and persisting in overcoming barriers and setbacks (Fay and Frese 2000, 2001). Instead of passively adapting to present conditions, individuals high in personal initiative will attempt to improve the situation to achieve positive results. In research, personal initiative has been related to problem-focused coping, job satisfaction and clear career planning (Frese et al. 1997).

Learning Orientation

A wealth of research has been published on organizational learning over the past three decades. Theorists generally see the learning organization as a way of keeping ahead of competitors and gaining an important competitive advantage (e.g., Slater and Narver 1995; Lahteenmaki, Toivonen and Mattila 2001). Therefore, successful companies need to facilitate the learning of their contributing members and build feedback loops into their management systems. In the marketing and organizational learning literature, three organizational values are associated with the predisposition of organizations to learn:

1. Commitment to learning
2. Open-mindedness
3. Shared vision (see Tobin 1993)

Initiating, implementing and supporting strong learning orientation policies and learning practices (e.g., mentoring) is ultimately the responsibility of each appointed leader. Learning-oriented leaders have an intrinsic desire to improve themselves and to foster and facilitate learning in others. Example of behaviors can be linked to the qualities under goal-orientation theory (see VandeWalle 1997; Button, Mathieu and Zajac 1996).

Within the work motivation literature, goal orientation is most commonly conceptualized as a set of dispositional tendencies that cause individuals to strive toward certain types of implicit achievement goals in performance settings (Hafsteinsson, Donovan and Breland 2007). Goal orientation is conceptualized as a three-dimensional construct consisting of:

1. Learning goal orientation or the desire to acquire new skills, master new situations, persist when facing difficulties and seek challenges (intrinsic motive)
2. Prove-performance goal orientation or the desire to prove competence and to gain favorable judgments about one's competence (extrinsic motive)
3. Avoid-performance goal orientation or the desire to avoid negative judgment about one's performance and to avoid the invalidation of one's competence (extrinsic motive)

Although all three goal orientations can predict success at different levels and in different contexts, only learning goal orientation produces a high level of intrinsically motivated effort exerted by individuals (Dweck 1999). In addition, learning goal–oriented mentors are likely to display idealized influence behavior by acting as inner-directed and mastery-seeking role models for their protégés (Sosik, Godshalk and Yammarino 2004).

Personal and Business Ethics

As an organizational reality, most employees look outside themselves for guidance; they often consider their immediate supervisor as an important source of guidance (Treviño 1986). As such, the definition and behavioral items of this factor were constructed based on the theoretical dimensions and assumptions put forward by the theories of ethical and authentic leadership.

Ethical leadership is defined as the demonstration of normatively appropriate conduct through personal actions and interpersonal relationships, and the promotion of such conduct to followers through two-way communication, reinforcement and decision making (Brown et al. 2005).

Authentic leadership is defined as a pattern of leader behavior that draws upon and promotes both positive psychological capacities and a positive ethical climate to foster:

1. Greater self-awareness
2. An internalized moral perspective
3. Balanced processing of information
4. Relational transparency on the part of leaders working with followers, fostering positive self-development (Walumbwa et al. 2008)

Empirical evidence reveals that authentic leadership is positively related to organizational commitment, extra-role behaviors, job satisfaction, job performance and follower satisfaction with supervisor (see George 2003; Gardner and Schermerhorn 2004; Walumbwa et al. 2008).

Motivation to Lead

It is well known that people differ in their ability to lead. However, people also differ in their desire or motivation to assume a leadership position (Chan and Drasgow 2001). Cognitive approaches to motivation suggest that there are important individual differences (i.e., within-person variation) that are capable of predicting direction, intensity and persistence of behavior. As such, a key stepping-stone in predicting leadership potential is identifying the individuals who have expressed a genuine interest in leading others or have demonstrated a natural tendency to emerge as a leader when given the opportunity to do so. This dimension is derived from research on individual differences in leadership development and leadership performance (e.g., Atwater et al. 1999), and more specifically on concepts such as motivation to lead and leadership self-efficacy.

Motivation to lead is defined as the tendency of a leader or leader-to-be to assume leadership training, roles and responsibilities (see Chan and Drasgow 2001; Paglis and Green 2002; Bobbio and Manganelli Rattazzi 2006). Contrary to cognitive ability, the assumption is that employees' motivation can change following leadership experience and training. It hypothesizes that high motivation is the result of positive leadership experiences and perceived leadership efficacy. Preferably, this desire to lead results from a sense of duty or responsibility and/or a genuine desire to lead others (i.e., liking/truly enjoying leading others to success), and not simply from a sense of personal gain (e.g., benefits, salary, status).

Leadership self-efficacy refers to an employee's perception regarding his or her general ability to lead (see Murphy 1992; McCormick 2001). Research has demonstrated that leadership efficacy is effective for predicting various leadership, group and organizational outcomes (e.g., Hoyt et al. 2003; Chemers, Watson and May 2000; Watson, Chemers and Preiser 2001; Murphy 2001).

Social and Emotional Complexity and Capacity

When interacting with others (e.g., leaders interacting with their subordinates), some individuals tend to demonstrate a greater capacity than others to process emotionally charged information and to use this information as a guide to thinking and behaviors (Mayer, Salovey and Caruso 2008). That is, these individuals are better at differentiating the personal and relational aspects of a social situation (e.g., emotions, value preferences, degree of interdependence) and integrate that information in a manner that results in increased understanding of the social situation.

It has been demonstrated that this ability to perceive, use, understand and manage emotion is necessary to effectively navigate the social world (Keltner and Kring 1998) and consequently contribute to optimal social functioning (e.g., Feldman, Philippot and Custrini 1991; Nowicki and Duke 1994; Savage 2002). These four basic abilities contribute to the higher order construct known as emotional intelligence (EI).

Perceiving emotion pertains to the ability to identify emotions in oneself and others, as well as in other stimuli. Using emotion involves the ability to harness feelings that assist in certain cognitive enterprises, such as reasoning, problem solving, decision making and interpersonal communication. Understanding emotion involves language and propositional thought that reflects the capacity to analyze emotions. Managing emotion pertains to the ability to reduce, enhance or modify an emotional response in oneself and others, as well as the ability to experience a range of emotions while also making decisions about the appropriateness or usefulness of the emotion in a given situation (see Mayer and Salovey 1997).

Research in social settings indicates that people with high emotional intelligence tend to be more socially competent, to have better quality relationships, and to be viewed as more interpersonally sensitive than those lower in EI (see Brackett et al. 2006; Brackett, Warner and Bosco 2005; Lopes et al. 2005; Lopes, Salovey and Straus 2003).

Research in work settings indicates that managers higher in EI are better able to cultivate productive working relationships with others and to demonstrate greater personal integrity (Rosete and Ciarrochi 2005). EI also predicts the extent to which managers engage in behaviors that are supportive of the goals of the organization (Côté and Miners 2006).

In addition to the research done by Global Knowledge, other authors and research organizations have identified leadership potential factors that are aligned with our findings.

The Corporate Leadership Council has proposed the following definition: "A high-potential employee is someone with the ability, engagement and aspiration to rise to and succeed in more senior leadership positions."

The council identifies the following factors indicating leadership potential: mental/cognitive ability, emotional intelligence, technical/functional skills, interpersonal skills, prestige and recognition, advancement and influence, financial rewards, work-life balance, overall job enjoyment, emotional commitment, rational commitment, discretionary effort and intent to stay.

Ram Charan, coauthor of *The Leadership Pipeline*, finds that those with high leadership potential have the capacity and inclination to see things in a broad context, seek information, exhibit drive, put their business on the offensive, synthesize data for decisions, balance inherent tensions, passionately pursue learning and growth, are intellectually honest and dissatisfied with the status quo, and have integrity and tell the truth.

3

Diagnosing Development Needs

Before you lead others, before you can help
others, you have to discover yourself.

—Joseph Jaworski

What do the physician and the language teacher do in common when they meet their patients or clients for the first time? They both perform a diagnostic exam by asking a series of questions, making observations and ordering tests. It would never occur to the physician to prescribe a solution without the diagnostic; neither would the teacher recommend a specific course without first gauging the learner's relative mastery of the language.

Companies similarly need to know what raw talent they have in their bullpens, to switch to a sports analogy, but that's just the beginning. They need to identify what each high-potential leader has and doesn't have. A critical task of the organization, therefore, is to define the set of activities that will accelerate the future leaders' development and get them ready to lead. To do that effectively and efficiently, organizations need to identify each high-potential leader's strengths so they can leverage and develop them in areas where they are weak.

This process naturally follows on after an organization has defined and documented the leadership success profile. From that base, the organization can perform a comprehensive diagnostic to determine the strengths and development needs of high-potential leadership candidates in every category. This process allows for the creation of a personalized and effective development plan.

So how does an organization (or consultant) carry out a leadership diagnostic? Thankfully, there are apps for that, or at Global Knowledge, three assessment tools that we regularly use to measure the components of the success profile. These are the Multi-Rater Survey, a Knowledge and Experience Inventory and the Hogan Personality Assessment tools.

1. THE MULTI-RATER SURVEY

Essentially, the Multi-Rater Survey, also called a 360-degree assessment, provides multiple perspectives on observed behaviors in order to identify specific competency development needs. The power of the 360-degree assessment (which draws on information taken from direct reports, peers, managers, and possibly vendors and customers, and the individual being assessed) is that it provides an objective, unassailable assessment of a leader's strengths, development needs and potential.

The survey results come in handy when the results fall short of what the candidate expected. For instance, at The Ottawa Hospital, "both the executive and I had a very objective account of certain candidates and what their strengths and weaknesses were and what people thought of them," says CEO Jack Kitts. "That is invaluable. To be able to be on the same page and understand who you are and what the value people see in you for the organization, I think is priceless."

It does not mean that 360-degree survey results are always popular. But, Kitts remarks, "There were some feeble attempts to discredit it. But overall, candidates said, 'Yes, that is me.'" In other words, the survey accurately identified their strengths and weaknesses, providing a platform for improvement. "You are now planning skill and competency development around either enhancing their strengths or recognizing the need to work on weaknesses, and there is no argument what they are."

2. KNOWLEDGE AND EXPERIENCE INVENTORY

In the process of creating the leadership success profile, the knowledge and experience required by high-potential leaders to be successful in their next roles are identified. Knowledge and experience can be assessed by using a customized survey in which both the candidates and their immediate supervisors are queried about the candidates' expertise and accomplishments.

Figure 3.1 shows a portion of a Knowledge and Experience Inventory for a Global Knowledge client. The objective here is to get a clear view of

Position Title:	Vice-President, Facilities, Planning, Support Services

Knowledge (i.e., the degree of understanding that an executive must have about how the organization operates, such as functions, processes, systems and services)	1 No Knowledge	2 Adequate Knowledge	3 Expert Knowledge
• Organization's operations and procedures	❑	❑	❑
• Government relations practices	❑	❑	❑
• Government legislation	❑	❑	❑
• Government policies, procedures and protocols	❑	❑	❑
• Internal departments and functions	❑	❑	❑
• External alliances and strategic partners	❑	❑	❑
• Long-range planning process	❑	❑	❑
• Information systems	❑	❑	❑
• Performance management system	❑	❑	❑
• Leadership competencies	❑	❑	❑

Key experiences/Job challenges (i.e., the kinds of situations that an executive should have experienced, or at least had some exposure to)	1 No Experience	2 Adequate Experience	3 A Lot of Experience
• Lead the process and implementation for setting and achieving technical and nonclinical strategic goals.	❑	❑	❑
• Develop and implement a framework and direction with the senior management team for a timely response to current and future infrastructure and technology requirements and opportunities.	❑	❑	❑
• Implement innovation and continuous improvement practices.	❑	❑	❑
• Establish and sustain relationships with external service providers and partners in order to improve the quality of our services.	❑	❑	❑
• Set operational and capital priorities within the portfolio to ensure responsive and appropriate allocation of resources.	❑	❑	❑
• Identify opportunities for creating operational efficiencies, business development and other revenue enhancements.	❑	❑	❑

Figure 3.1: Sample Knowledge and Experience Inventory

what the leader does and doesn't know, and what and he or she has and has not experienced, in order to identify ways to accelerate that candidate's development through assignments or other methods that will close the gaps.

3. THE HOGAN PERSONALITY ASSESSMENT TOOLS

The assessment of personality factors is key for leadership positions and complementary to the competencies assessed with the Multi-Rater Survey. Global Knowledge has found that the Hogan Personality Assessment tools—the Hogan Potential Inventory and the Hogan Development Survey—work best in this area.

The Hogan Potential Inventory (HPI), which can be best described as a measure of normal personality used to predict job performance, allows organizations to fine-tune employee selection, leadership development, succession management and talent management processes. The HPI was the first inventory of "normal" personality based on the Big Five personality traits (see the description of the Big Five in "What the Experts Say," Chapter 1). The inventory provides a psychometric evaluation of personality characteristics that distinguish personalities and determine career success.

A companion tool to the HPI is the Hogan Development Survey (HDS). This identifies personality-based performance risks and derailers of interpersonal behavior. As mentioned in Chapter 1, these behaviors most often appear during times of stress and may impede work relationships, reduce productivity or limit overall career potential. The derailers are deeply ingrained in an individual's personality—the person may not even know he or she has them—and can negatively affect that individual's leadership style and actions. It's not all bad news, however. Once these negative behaviors are recognized, they can be overcome through personal development and coaching. The HDS is the only business-related inventory that measures these dysfunctional behavioral problems.

The HDS scales are interpreted in terms of risk: higher scores indicate greater potential for problems on the job. If these behaviors are recognized, a person can be coached to compensate for them.

Figures 3.2 and 3.3 show the results of the HDS given to Candidate A, a leader being assessed for potential superior leadership positions. The two-part profile reveals strengths and elements of risk. The candidate

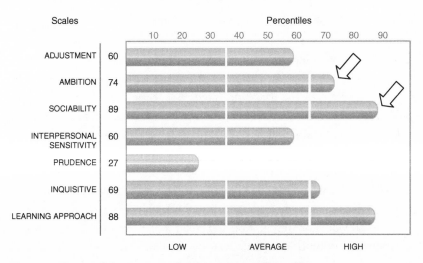

Figure 3.2: Candidate A: Leadership Potential Profile

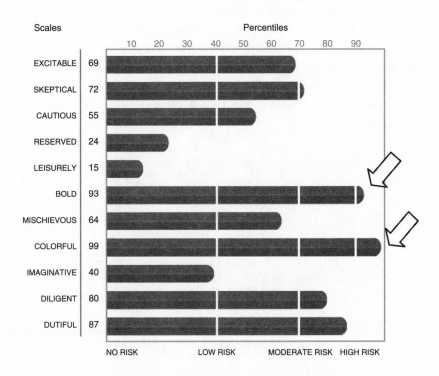

Figure 3.3: Candidate A: Leadership Challenge Profile

scores high on ambition and sociability—that is positive—and very high on bold (also called arrogance) and colorful (also called attention-seeking). The result is a leader who is competitive, eager to advance, talkative and socially confident, and who dislikes working alone. That is the bright side. But the derailers, or the dark side, indicate that the candidate is at risk of talking too much, often about herself, in order to be seen and admired. She wants to be successful and have the attention of others but too often will not listen to other people's points of view. This could lead to demotivation in the team and a higher risk of poor decision making.

This leader would benefit from talking less and listening more, and letting others contribute their ideas or take the lead in group discussions. She needs to provide more recognition and credit to her team for their ideas and contributions in both immediate team discussions and in senior leadership forums. She could improve team communication by striking a better balance between seeking/facilitating team members' input to the conversation and telling them what their input should be or speaking on their behalf.

Figures 3.4 and 3.5 reveal that Candidate B, also a current leader, has a much lower risk on all potential derailers and still scores high on Adjustment, Ambition, Sociability and Interpersonal Sensitivity. This person is performing very efficiently in good and rough times. He has a balanced profile, and the positive impact on his leadership is easily observable by his employees, peers and manager.

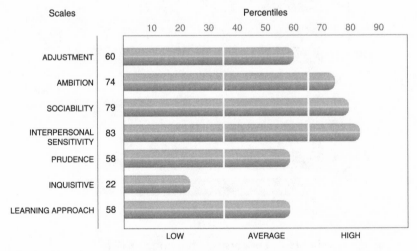

Figure 3.4: Candidate B: Leadership Potential Profile

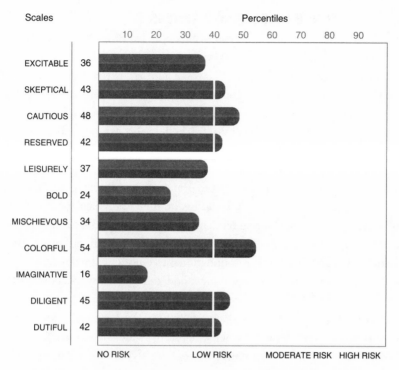

Figure 3.5: Candidate B: Leadership Challenge Profile

LEADERSHIP AND BUSINESS UNIT PERFORMANCE

Robert Hogan, researcher and founder of the Hogan Assessment
Systems, notes that an important meta-analysis of relevant research on
this topic yielded five important findings:

1. The personalities of managers directly influence employee satisfaction.
2. When employee satisfaction is high, positive business outcomes
   result.
3. When employee satisfaction is low, negative business outcomes
   result.
4. The link between leadership and unit performance is mediated by
   staff morale.
5. People don't quit organizations, they quit their boss.

THE IMPORTANCE OF SELF-AWARENESS

"What you think of yourself, even if accurate, is less important than how others see you," explains Ryan Ross, vice-president of Global Alliances at Hogan Assessments. "The 'you' that is worth a lot is the you that we know" through the Hogan assessment process and through other people's feedback.

Self-awareness is the level of consciousness and understanding of our own individual personality, value systems, beliefs and natural tendencies.

While organizations may rightly believe that diagnosing the development needs of high-potential leaders in their ranks is an end in itself, a side benefit of the process is that these proto-leaders gain self-awareness, a new level of consciousness and understanding of their individual personality, value systems, beliefs and natural tendencies. Daniel Goleman, an early propounder of the emotional intelligence concept, maintains that self-awareness (i.e., knowing one's emotions) is foundational to emotional intelligence. He describes it as being "aware of both our mood and our thoughts about that mood" (Goleman 2005).

Robert Hogan and Rodney Warrenfeltz (2003) ask a critical question: "What is it that one is aware of when one is self-aware? In a nutshell, there are two answers. On the one hand, one can be aware of one's *identity*— how one thinks about and evaluates oneself. On the other hand, one can be aware of one's *reputation*—how others think about and evaluate one's behavior." There is a self-view and a person's perceived performance as evaluated by others—an inner and outer perspective.

So what are the benefits of making future leaders self-aware? Primarily it enables them to focus, first, on the strengths they can leverage to maximize their performance and, second, on their critical development needs. Where are their blind spots? What are the areas they did not realize they needed to improve, the areas where their inner perspective, their identity, are different from their outer perspective or reputation? These gaps need to be identified so that you know what to do from a development standpoint or how to alter behaviors or work habits.

"It is interesting to note that the majority of leaders think they are better than average," says Ross. "We call it the better-than-average illusion. It is fairly frequent that the higher you go in the organization, the lower the self-awareness; the higher the leaders, the greater the delusion." Not only do leaders higher on the totem pole have fewer people senior to them and in a position to give them feedback and advice concerning their behavior and actions, but the people below them are less likely to challenge or engage them as they rise in the organization.

As powerful as self-awareness may be, it cannot overcome the derailers that are wired into some leaders' behavior. "I sat down recently with one of our senior leaders and told him that he needed to be a little bit less intense," says an executive at a Canadian bank. "He has tremendous upside, but he was viewed as listening not all that well and as being highly calculating in terms of his career." After receiving feedback, the leader was "listening better now and aware of some of the areas that he needed to work on. I will contrast that with another person who hasn't changed, and that will be a problem. He is constantly promoting himself. We continually say to him, 'Don't do that, they are not listening.' This is a very senior person we have, and we are now coming to a point where he might be comfortable in his role and he could be blocking people, and he doesn't get that." The negative behavior is obvious to everyone except, perhaps, to the individual who exhibits it. "When he is in meetings with peers, when he talks, his team disengages. That tells me something that I would not find out on a piece of paper in terms of how to deal with him. His peers have already tuned him out. But you can't fix everybody."

"You don't select yourself as a leader," argues Jack Kitts. "A leader without people who want to follow them is not a leader." Evaluating the strengths and development needs of a leader also cannot be done in a vacuum, he adds. "As well as understanding your strengths and weaknesses, you need to have an alignment with the vision and values of the organization. If you are not aligned, you can't take a leadership position."

Kitts has begun a talent management program for The Ottawa Hospital's physicians. "That is something that is completely new to health care, talent management for physicians. It used to be any warm body would do. We are now spending more time identifying leaders and asking them about their plans. If these physicians are to assume formal roles, we will sponsor them and support them actively."

WHAT YOU KNOW, WHAT OTHERS KNOW

Your golf pro will observe your swing before giving you advice. And so too in the world of leadership and professional development. Assessment tools make it possible to select the right development solution. The key is to enhance the candidates' self-awareness and guide them in leveraging their strengths and working on their development needs.

What do you do just before leaving the house, when you are all dressed up and on your way to an important event? You look at yourself in a full-length mirror, checking top to bottom, front to side and back. The mirror is your assessment tool to raise your awareness of how you look. The way to improve self-awareness in the workplace is to get feedback on your behaviors and work habits from various perspectives using approaches such as a 360-degree assessment, asking for direct feedback from your manager, and using assessment tools such as personality or style inventories, and self-reflection. The key word here is "feedback"; you must seek feedback from multiple perspectives to get a holistic view of who you are.

Feedback can be solicited on multiple factors, competencies and traits. You may ask for feedback on intrapersonal skills, such as self-confidence and attitude toward authority; interpersonal skills, such as your capacity for initiating, building and maintaining relationships with others; leadership skills, such as your capacity to build a strong team, as well as coach and motivate team members to achieve strong performances; and business or technical skills critical to your job role, such as business acumen and an understanding of the laws relevant to your field of operations.

The main reason to be very self-aware is to be able to focus: focus on strengths that you can leverage even more to maximize your performance, and focus on your critical development needs.

Improving self-awareness is analogous to preparing and enriching the soil before planting a garden: the whole purpose is to maximize the chances that everything will grow as effectively as it can. Improving self-awareness will help you grow and thrive in the workplace.

WHAT THE EXPERTS SAY
Personality and Leadership

American psychologist Robert Hogan is credited with demonstrating how personality factors influence organizational effectiveness, making him one of the most influential leaders in his field. Coeditor of the *Handbook of Personality Psychology*, he has devised a number of personality measures, including the Hogan Personality Inventory, the Hogan Development Survey, the Motives, Values and Preferences Inventory, and the Hogan Business Reasoning Survey. In a review of the empirical literature on personality, leadership and organizational effectiveness, Hogan and Kaiser (2005) account for the power of leadership to organize the collective effort and to convince team members to temporarily give up their individual pursuits to pursue a common goal, as well as for the predictive value of personality on leadership. They argue that in spite of the evidence that personality affects leadership, researchers have historically ignored personality. In a more recent article, Hogan and Benson (2009) build on their earlier work that leadership is both a function of personality and a fundamental determinant of organizational effectiveness. In other words, the authors confirm that who people are determines how they will lead and that it really does matter who is in charge.

In looking to how personality is defined and best understood in terms of its relationship to leadership, both studies (Hogan and Kaiser 2005; Hogan and Benson 2009) defend the focus away from the identity side of personality and toward its reputation side. Hogan and Benson (2009) theorize that the "best predictor of future behavior is past behavior" and that, since reputation is a "summary of past behavior," it is a stronger predictor of future leader performance than is how leaders view themselves. Hogan and Kaiser distinguish the two by arguing that personality identity concerns one's deeply held beliefs, whereas personality reputation is an index of one's success in life. From an assessment perspective, Hogan and Benson report on others' findings that reputation can be validly measured using the Five-Factor Model (FFM), also known as the Big Five, which in turn predicts performance outcomes.

Both studies expand on the reputation side of personality to distinguish between its "bright" and "dark" sides, and to explore how each side impacts leadership and performance outcomes. Hogan and Kaiser argue that our bright side reflects our social performance when we are at our best, whereas our dark side reflects the impression we make when we are at our worst. This has implications for hiring for leadership positions because it is the bright side that is highlighted in job interviews, while the dark side tends to be masked by well-developed social skills. Hogan and Benson report extroversion, conscientiousness and openness to experience as the strongest bright-side personality determinants of leader performance, and that the dark-side traits accounted for significant variance above and beyond the effects of bright-side traits when predicting leadership performance. They point to a widely popular competency model (see Hogan and Warrenfeltz 2003) that identifies four competencies—intrapersonal skills, interpersonal skills, technical skills and leadership skills—each easily measured using well-validated personality measures. This has practical implications for organizations in that, compared with technical skills, which can be gained through training and development, intrapersonal and interpersonal skills are considered more relevant to leader selection criteria. And, of course, leadership skills are relevant both to leader training and development and to selection criteria. The authors' Domain Model of Job Performance, Example Competencies and Personality Measures are clearly described and provide a clear and useful framework for leader assessment and development practices.

Hogan and Warrenfeltz see organizational effectiveness as a function of an organization's ability to outperform the competition, established through five core components: talented team members, talented managers, motivated team members, an effective strategy and a system that effectively monitors talent, morale and how well the strategy is working. Hogan and Bensen (2009) present their leadership value chain model to demonstrate clear and logical ways that affect organizational performance, moving from personality to leadership to leader behaviors (impacts morale), values (impacts culture) and decision making (impacts strategy and staffing). Of key significance is the authors' example of Toyota, considered by many economists as the best-run organization in the world, identifying nine themes that characterize its model: focus of long-lasting returns on investment; continuous, steady improvements in processes and products; research and development; organization-wide teamwork; customer service; service to every kind of customer; organic or steady step-by-step growth; quick and public identification of mistakes; and last and most important, quality of leadership.

Self-Knowledge and Managerial Development

Drawing on the empirical literature that has established a positive relationship between self-awareness and leadership in effective organizations, a recent article (Nesbit 2012) presents a framework of self-directed leadership development that the author argues holds advantages over formal managerial-development programs in enhancing self-awareness skills. Nesbit suggests that, compared with formal leadership development approaches, which tend to be episodic in nature, a self-directed approach that helps leaders take greater control of their development better addresses and supports the continuous dynamic environments facing organizations. He claims that if leaders become self-directed learners, they become more aware of their competency strengths and deficits and are better able to set goals, choose appropriate learning strategies and evaluate learning outcomes. Building on the support in the literature associated with experiential learning, emotion research and social cognitive theories of change, the author argues that effective self-development leads to development of other skills, including managing emotional reactions to feedback, carrying out self-reflection practice and enacting self-regulatory processes.

Nesbit admits to challenges in motivating leaders to engage in self-directed learning, specifying that leaders are typically less attentive to learning opportunities from their experiences than its performance implications, that self-directed learning from experiences requires considerable cognitive effort and that there exists a lack of guidance within the field of human resource development for individual leaders in their self-development efforts. He points to others' findings that leaders' attention and motivation to engage in self-directed learning depend on the personality, values and interests of individual leaders, as well as on the nature of organizations and their cultures. Nesbit argues that leader self-awareness is acquired through a self-initiated self-reflection process involving an introspective analysis of feedback information from a variety of sources, including feedback from their immediate managers, from other stakeholders, and from self-observation of their work-related experiences. He argues that self-awareness of development is typically concerned with negative evaluation of one's behavior and skills, and agrees with others' findings that the self-awareness gained is often not accurate, leading him to suggest that organizations offer training in self-reflection to deepen the quality of self-understanding that can arise from reflecting on performance feedback. Pointing to research that found that reflection is more effective in stimulating insights when it involves either talking or writing, Nesbit recommends that training for self-development of leaders incorporate the use of reflective journals and coaching.

Nesbit identifies the four stages of reflective analysis for personal development as:

1. Efforts to describe events, people and actions to be focused on
2. The questioning of why things happened as they did and why one acted the way one did
3. An evaluation of how one could have better handled the event or acted differently
4. A planning stage where the leader considers the "what now?" for their development

Nesbit also identifies three approaches to reflection training: reflecting alone, reflecting with one other person, and reflecting in a group. He reports on the findings of one study (Daudelin 1996) that found that the individual and dyad approaches were superior to that of a group in terms of the number of learning insights. As well, the learning by individuals and dyads related to personal-development insights tended to be intrapersonal, whereas group reflections tended to produce interpersonal learning.

Nesbit draws on social cognitive theory and other research findings to explain the relationship between self-development, emotional reactions to feedback and goal attainment. He concludes that negative performance feedback for a person with self-efficacy for goal attainment leads to a greater effort to reflect on and pursue goals, but when negative feedback is interpreted as questioning one's self-concept, cognitive processes become directed toward protection of the self-concept rather than goal attainment. This has implications for self-development programs in terms of introducing training that enhances emotional intelligence (EI) and emphasizes techniques that involve reframing emotionally sensitive feedback.

Based on the discrepancies in past studies that investigated the relationship between elements of EI, including self-awareness and transformational leadership, a recent study by Harms and Crede (2010) seeks to evaluate these claims. In a review of the literature, the authors acknowledge the popularity of the research linking EI to transformational leadership but found some skepticism of the link between EI and leadership outcomes. This study used a meta-analytic approach to find out whether and under what circumstances EI is related to transformational and transactional leadership behaviors. It is worth noting here that the research has conceived EI as either a trait or an ability, with implications for choice of assessment tools used by both researchers and organizations. The authors report that, to date, there remains no single universally accepted measure of EI; that most research into trait EI has used self-report measures such as the Emotional Quotient Inventory (Bar-On 1997) or the Swinburne University Emotional Intelligence Test (Palmer and Stough 2001); and that most research into ability EI has used measures that assess EI based on performance, such as the Mayer-Salovey-Caruso Emotional Intelligence Test.

Drawing on broad source data of studies published up to 2009, and after accurate coding for reliability estimates, sample size, source of EI and leadership ratings and inventories used to assess EI and leadership, 62 independent samples, representing data from 7,145 leaders, were analyzed. The finding was that there is a positive, moderate relationship between EI and the various dimensions of transformational leadership behaviors. Overall, trait-based measures of EI were more strongly related to transformational leadership than were ability-based measures of EI, with the Emotional Quotient Inventory determined to have the highest validity estimate. Of special significance and with implications for organizations' assessment practices, the study found that both trait- and ability-based measures showed similar and significant reductions in validity when multiple sources for raters were used. The study found that organizational rank showed little difference in validity of EI ratings when only participants who were ranked manager or above were considered.

Harms and Crede (2010) argue that the results of this study warrant continued investigation into the relationship between elements of emotional intelligence and transformational behavior, and suggest a number of theoretical implications for future research. The authors note that few studies have been conducted using each of the different measures of EI, and see this as an oversight that should be addressed in future studies. They also suggest that since transformational leadership measures are behavioral in nature, transformational leadership should be studied from the point of view of those who are meant to be affected by them, indicating the need for multiple ratings sources. Since only a few of the studies included in their meta-analysis were conducted outside the United States, Harms and Crede recommend extending research to cover different cultural contexts to establish universality and look for possible cultural moderators. Considering the growing interest in EI and leadership and the only moderate empirical research to support it, the authors suggest future research look to possible moderators of the relationship between the two. Based on this study, the authors warn against marketing EI assessment tools as management screening or training devices and instead recommend that they be used to encourage self-awareness and self-reflection in managers until better EI measures can be developed and validated.

In an experimental study that examined the EI scores of 186 executives belonging to one of two high-profile executive mentoring associations with that of the general population, Stein et al. (2009) sought to contribute to and improve on the findings on the relationship between emotional intelligence and both leadership and performance outcomes. Using the trait-based model of EI only, the study measures a cross-section of interrelated emotional and social competencies and skills that determine levels of self-awareness and self-expression, emotional management and regulation, change management and self-motivation, together and separately, using the Emotional Quotient Inventory. The authors report a summary of the findings of others that the instrument is reliable, consistent and stable, with an internal consistency reliability of overall emotional quotient of 0.76 (Bar-On 1997). The trait-based model of EI was chosen based on past research that shows strong links between EI and leadership, its application to organizational settings and its positive relationship to teamwork behavior and job performance. The Perception of Business Challenges Survey was used to measure current indicators of organizations' performances and challenges faced, including revenues and profits, the history of the CEOs' involvement in the organizations and the amount of difficulty they were experiencing in nine areas: hiring the right people, managing people, keeping good people, training people, raising capital, managing growth, marketing, innovating and dealing with changes in technology. Management effectiveness and successful leadership were evaluated and measured in terms of a series of specific questions related to company profitability and used to select for analysis only executives who met the criteria for the high-profit group.

The study found that, compared with the general population, executives demonstrated higher intrapersonal scores, reflecting greater self-regard, emotional self-awareness, assertiveness, independence and self-actualization, pointing to the leaders' overall capacity to remain self-directed, thereby enhancing their level of influence over others. It also found that executives scored significantly higher than the general population in terms of optimism and stress tolerance, suggesting that in order to empower an organization and face adversity, leaders need to maintain a positive and calm attitude. Of particular significance is the finding of a lower score on Social Responsibility for executives compared with the general population. The authors support these findings by suggesting that it is reasonable to expect that in order to make tough decisions (layoffs, restructuring, mergers), executives may at times need to lower their level of social consciousness.

In terms of the relationship between EI and perceptions of business challenges, EI was found to be positively related to the degree to which a challenge was perceived as easy with respect to managing growth, managing others, training employees and retaining employees. Significant relationships were found between EI and challenges that focused on interpersonal activities, as opposed to more task-oriented challenges. Correlations between intrapersonal and general mood and the business challenges of managing others, training employees and retaining employees suggest that top executives are aware of emotional information, both their own and that of the people they lead, and use the information to increase staff motivation and dedication. In terms of EI and profitability, the study found that Empathy and Self-Regard EI competencies contribute to organizational profitability, suggesting that effective leaders regularly demonstrate empathic behavior and respect and acceptance of others, which serve to strengthen working relationships and unify teams. The results of the study point to the use of the Emotional Quotient Inventory as a useful tool in the assessment and development of individuals who are in or who are being considered for executive positions. Looking to the strengths of the measures used in this and other studies, and the evolving demands of executive positions, the authors point to the importance of ongoing assessment and development of executives to avoid career derailment.

A recent study by Smollan and Parry (2011) contributes to and extends the existing literature on the relationship between emotional intelligence and leadership by focusing on the follower perceptions of the EI of change leaders. This study also fills the gaps in the literature related to qualitative investigations, and to how the context of organizational change increases the need for leaders to be seen by followers to be exhibiting emotional intelligence. The research question they sought to answer was how employees' perceptions of the EI of change leaders influence their own cognitive, affective and behavioral reactions to a change. The authors report on and support their research question with literature that suggests that when employees experience the emotions involved with change, they often find the support of others, like their managers, to be helpful. They argue that it is reasonable to expect—and that it is in the best interest of the organizations—that organizations select, train and develop for the leadership competencies and skills necessary to support and manage their own and their followers' emotional experiences associated with the challenges of change. The study builds both on the follower-centric approach to the study of leadership recommended by Meindl (1995) and to its application to leader EI (Dasborough and Ashkanasy 2005).

The study by Smollan and Parry (2011) emphasizes more than the other studies reviewed here the controversies over the concept of EI and organizational behavior, questioning whether EI is based on ability or personality or both, how it is measured and which measures are best, and whether EI offers anything useful beyond studies of cognitive intelligence or personality. The authors back up their thorough and objective views of past literature on EI and its relationship with organizational leadership with the assertion that a solid base of evidence is needed to support the methods, measures and analyses of their study given its qualitative nature, and use the controversies around EI mentioned above to criticize quantitative studies and thus defend their qualitative one. The literature review section of the study includes a comprehensive and unbiased view of the research related to EI and leadership, leader EI and follower emotional expression, EI and organizational change, and the model used to explain and account for follower perceptions of change leader EI. The model is adapted from the Mayer and Salovey (1997) model and three others derived from it and contextualized for organizational issues. As part of a series of studies on affective reactions to organizational change, Smollan and Parry interviewed twenty-four mostly white participants who worked in various industries, organizations and departments at various hierarchical levels, and who were involved in different types of change, such as restructuring, job redesign, relocations, mergers and acquisitions. The study found that followers reacted better to change when they perceived their leaders to be high in the EI abilities necessary for them to demonstrate an understanding of follow-ers' emotional responses and to express and regulate their own. Below is a summary of some of the specific interview findings:

- Participants appreciated when leaders understood how they felt about the change; this kind of support gave them strength in coping with the emotional demands of change processes.
- Acknowledgment by leaders of followers' feelings reinforced good relationships.
- Leaders who failed to regulate their emotions were considered by their followers to have acted inappropriately and led to negative consequences for followers' well-being and attitudes to the change.
- The willingness or reluctance of participants to share their emotions with their leaders during an organizational change partly reflected their beliefs about their leaders' history of emotional responsiveness and expression.

4

Prescribing Development Solutions

Learning without thought is labor lost; thought
without learning is perilous.

—Confucius

In the first few chapters, we have laid the groundwork necessary to start
the process of developing high-potential leaders. We have outlined how
to take the first step by creating a blueprint that contains the scope and
overall plan, followed by defining the success profile required for leadership
positions, identifying those high-potential individuals within your organization and, finally, diagnosing their specific development needs.

Now comes the big question: How do you develop these people you
have identified and measured? Or put another way, what is the plan to
grow people in various key competencies?

THE IMPORTANCE OF SHOWING UP

At Global Knowledge, we like to start with the simple 70-20-10 rule. It's
not a hard and unyielding formula like that of the percentage of nitrogen
to oxygen in the air we breathe, but generally it's a good way to look at how
people learn in the workplace.

Most of us learn by doing. So the majority of our skills in the workplace are learned over time simply by being exposed to different challenges.

(It's a bit like Woody Allen's famous quip that "Eighty percent of success is showing up.") Most of us acquired about 70 percent of our skill set by showing up and doing—learning by doing and by being exposed to situations ranging from everyday ones to extraordinary ones. The best part of this type of learning is that most of it occurs daily in our regular work.

Jack Kitts has lived the 70-20-10 rule in his years as CEO. He recalls: "I was appointed CEO in 2002, and SARS hit a year later. Up until then, my leadership style was all about consensus and collaboration. I had not had to make a decision that was unpopular or perhaps even contrary to the consensus of the senior team."

His most memorable learning as CEO came during the SARS crisis of 2003, when the Ontario government directed hospitals in the province to shut down operating rooms for elective surgery. Kitts, who prided himself on being a collaborative leader, was presented with his first major decision. "We were going to prevent 100 patients from coming in the next day for elective surgery, yet allow 10,000 employees and visitors to come in. So I said it doesn't make sense, it is a really tremendous hardship; it's a compromise on care, so we are not going to do it. The team was surprised."

Reaction was swift and negative. "The next day we were in the local media because we were the only hospital in Ontario that had not closed operating rooms for elective surgery. But the day after, the minister of health said it was actually a miscommunication, that it was only the Toronto hospitals that were to close their elective procedures. That was perhaps a turning point in my confidence as a CEO and a leader," he adds. "Not that I enjoyed the experience in any way, but it certainly reaffirmed my confidence in my ability to lead."

While 70 percent of what we know comes from daily experience, 20 percent is gained from others—from our peers, superiors or even people outside our immediate work circle. You can also throw feedback into that 20 percent bucket. That's the incidental information, both official and unofficial, that comes from those who interact with you at work. That feedback may be especially valuable if it focuses on your competencies or personality traits.

Kitts owes some of his success as an executive to knowledge gained under the 20 percent rule. "The mentorship and encouragement to get me into this came from my chief of staff, Dr. Chris Carruthers," he says.

"I would not have had the confidence or initiative to be here if he wasn't very much involved in identifying me, promoting me, mentoring me, supporting me. I feel very strongly now that people like me and other physician leaders really need to be proactive in selecting and then supporting physicians to be leaders."

Finally, the smallest percentage of tools in that organic tool kit you carry around in your skull each day, the 10 percent, comes from formal learning. This could be anything from what you learned in school to that learned while taking a part-time course, attending an industry conference, reading a book or participating in a webinar.

For Kitts, that formal learning took the form of an executive MBA. "I did the MBA because I was weak in finance and reading financial statements. But in the end, it was more organizational development, change management and strategic management that was vital to my success. You have to understand clearly that culture is everything, and you can't change culture by willing it or by forcing it."

In a similar vein, Brian Branson, a career financial executive who became CEO at Global Knowledge, saw the need for additional traditional training. "I went to a business school and took a negotiation course," he says. "I felt some formal training would benefit me in that particular area, and it clearly has." The key concept that for a business relationship to be really good it has to be a win-win was a revelation for him. "I am a very competitive person, I wanted to win, not at all costs, I didn't want to be unethical, but I wanted to win," he says. "Going through that course helped me understand that a lot of people believe that if they don't get their way, it is not a successful deal. I don't think that is right."

It may sound strange coming from an organization that makes its living by selling companies training programs, but believe me when I say that consulting firms such as ours account for only a small fraction of learning in the workplace. It's not so odd when you think about it, really. How much of the past year have you spent on formal learning in conferences or a course? It's likely a small percentage of your time.

And simply showing up is not enough. Well-designed practice is a critical factor in an effective training program. A significant body of research now suggests that as work becomes more complex and knowledge-based, practice exercises that are part of formal learning programs (whether classroom or e-learning) are not enough to meet the need for expertise in the modern workplace.

DELIBERATE PRACTICE MAKES PERFECT

Research conducted by Anders Ericsson at Florida State University and popularized in recent books such as Malcolm Gladwell's *Outliers* and Geoff Colvin's *Talent Is Overrated* indicates that the type of practice needed to develop true expertise is more intensive and deliberate than we thought, and that it must be embedded in the context of real work. Also, it must occur on a regular basis over a much longer period of time than we previously thought necessary.

The research suggests that expertise is hard won, the result of years of effortful, progressive practice on authentic tasks accompanied by relevant feedback and support, with self-reflection and correction. Ericsson and his colleagues have labeled this activity "deliberate practice." It entails considerable specific and sustained efforts to do something you can't do well—or at all. Six elements are necessary for carrying out deliberate practice:

1. It must be designed to improve performance. Opportunities for practice must have a goal and evaluation criteria. The goals must be job-/role-based and authentic. General experience is not sufficient, which is where deliberate practice varies from more laissez-faire approaches to informal learning. Years of everyday experience do not necessarily develop an expert. Years of deliberate practice do.
2. It must be based on authentic tasks. The practice must use real work and be performed in context. The goal is to compile an experience bank, not a vast list of completed formal training programs.
3. The practice must be challenging. The tasks selected for practice must be slightly outside the learner's comfort zone, but not so far outside that it produces panic and anxiety. Deliberate practice is hard work and stretches the individual beyond his or her current abilities. The experience must involve targeted effort, focus and concentration.
4. Immediate feedback on results must be conveyed. Accurate and diagnostic feedback must be continuously available both from people

(coaches) and from the business results produced by the activity. Delayed feedback is also important for actions and decisions with longer-term impact.

5. Allowance is required for reflection and adjustment. Self-regulatory and metacognitive skills are essential to the process. This includes self-observation, monitoring and awareness of knowledge and skill gaps. Feedback requires reflection and analysis to inform behavioral change. Experts make mindful choices of their practice activities.

6. Mastery takes 10,000 hours. For complex work, ten years seems to be the necessary investment in deliberate practice to achieve expertise. Malcolm Gladwell drew attention to the 10,000-hour rule in his book *Outliers*. It is, in fact, one of the most robust findings in this research and poses a real challenge for our event-based training culture. Of course, the less complex the work, the less time required to develop expertise.

If you take away just one message from this chapter, let it be this: You must broaden your definition of learning beyond the 10 percent of traditional training that most of us would consider as "learning" or "skills development." Whether it is your skills being developed or someone else's within the organization, the focus needs to be on complementing what can be acquired through formal learning. Tap into the 90 percent that is made up of workplace learning opportunities beyond a book or conference room.

LEARN WHILE YOU WORK, WORK WHILE YOU LEARN

What form would the less traditional "learn while you work, work while you learn" way of learning take? Individuals can be coached or mentored by another person in the organization. They could learn simply by observing a particular task or function being performed. As well, they could acquire a new set of skills by being exposed to them. An example is taking a marketing executive out of her usual role and putting her into a team that has been charged with drawing up part of the company's budget. Just by being part of that team, the executive improves her financial acumen and improves her planning and organizing skills.

While individuals are partly responsible for their own development—if you have been stuck in the same job, doing the same basic set of tasks for the past five years, you aren't growing and developing—some organizations are better than others when it comes to helping employees manage their career. Companies that are leaders in this regard are more open to job rotation, moving people around and challenging them to get out of their comfort zones. Perhaps the most famous corporate example is that of Toyota, where workers are rotated through various jobs in an effort to make them more well-rounded. This deliberate disruption of routine puts new sets of eyes on familiar tasks and problems, and leads to new and better solutions.

While Toyota has raised job rotation to an art form, there is a danger for organizations to have too much movement among employees. Among leaders or high-potential leaders, however, the advantages are obvious. Individuals acquire an understanding of how the entire company operates and, perhaps more critically, how departments or units other than their own operate and interact. Suddenly, the chasms between head office staff and the sales force in the field, or on the factory floor and in the accounting department, do not seem that wide. The intimate understanding that comes from hands-on exposure to different units cannot typically be accomplished through a yearly tour of the plant or a meeting with the sales team. It comes from working in the plant or in the stores or in operations for a period of weeks or months.

When that leader goes back to a head office position, he has a hard-earned and invaluable understanding of the realities and challenges of a particular part of the organization. It's hard to put a price on this type of knowledge. This idea has been brought to life in the popular reality show *Undercover Boss*, in which senior executives work undercover at relatively low-level jobs in their own companies. They typically come away with a better idea of what life is like in the trenches and have come up with ideas about how to improve the way the company is run.

A real-life example of an undercover boss occurred after Claude Mongeau assumed the top job as president and CEO of CN Rail. In his case, he literally rode the rails to expose himself to everyday situations confronted by line workers in order to gain experience and broaden his knowledge of the company's operations.

Most successful leaders have had plenty of movement during their careers before they had any need to go undercover. Their career paths may seem odd or random but, in most instances, steps were deliberately taken to expose them to the different experiences and skills necessary if they wanted to have a top leadership role in not just the organization they were in at the time but any organization.

Colleen Johnston, CFO of TD Bank, recognizes that her professional background will be a rarity in the future. "I have had a career where I have always been in Toronto and I have always been in finance, and I think I'm a dinosaur in that respect," she says. "I don't think the next CFO of this bank is going to have that kind of profile. We are a North American organization, and I think people realistically will have done different jobs on both sides of the border and have more business experience outside the finance department."

To that end, the bank is taking steps to broaden the experience of its leaders through the ranks. "A lot of it has been thinking outside the box regarding opportunities not just in finance but in broader areas of the bank, getting people exposure in different areas. For example, a number of my senior executives are involved in diversity initiatives. So they are stepping out of their initial comfort zones, taking on other leadership roles, taking on things outside the bank, getting exposure to senior leaders."

CHANGING THE LINEUP

Sylvia Chrominska, former group head of Global Human Resources and Communications at Scotiabank, is a big believer in the practice of shifting leaders to other areas of the organization to broaden their experience and accelerate their development. "The people who we have moved for development purposes have found that to be the best single learning that they have been exposed to. Taking them out of one particular business line and moving them to another business line with the appropriate amount of coaching from the line boss and someone who has been prepared to invest in them is rewarding."

(continued)

Scotiabank, and other organizations, will often face resistance from that leader's superior, she acknowledges, "because at the end of the day they are held responsible for the P&L of their business, and to move someone who may have been with them for three or five years and may have been a very high contributor, all of a sudden they have a void to fill and you are asking them to fill it with someone who is on a learning curve. So it tends to be challenging."

The bank has managed to overcome that all-too-natural resistance by stressing that it is a key to its future. "I think that we have been successful in embedding the importance of leadership and the fact that leadership is one of our top business priorities, and certainly we hold people accountable at the most senior levels for leadership development.

STAYING ON TRACK

Linking this theme of practice and development to themes in previous chapters, we have now reached the point where we are looking at high-potential leaders and asking, Can we now determine the areas in which a person is strong and weak (diagnosing development needs) by benchmarking that individual, and create the success profile? It doesn't mean that individuals must be formally moved out of their current positions to other roles in the organization, just that they acquire the desired skills and knowledge. Management may decide to include those individuals in a task force or identify a new project or committee where they can participate two or three times a month while still working in their current positions.

Many companies regularly have all-employee meetings or sales conventions where leaders have the opportunity to present a department success story, present a new product or facilitate a discussion or working session on a certain topic. Taking on one of these roles—facilitator, speaker or presenter—is another example of exposing a high-potential individual to an opportunity to learn by experience.

We learned in Chapter 3 that some high-potential leaders may carry very real flaws along with their desirable tool kit of strengths, skills, and motivations. We call them "derailers"—though coworkers may have more colorful labels for the traits and quirks that make up the individual.

INFORMAL LEARNING

We recently worked with a client to design an onboarding-program framework based on the 70-20-10 rule. Although, like all onboarding programs, it is designed for the new employees joining the organization, we took a modern approach whereby we maximized the various ways of learning. When preparing to get started on the program development activities, the client raised some important questions: What are the costs associated with implementing the informal components of the program? How do learning professionals influence or create activities that typically happen on their own? How do you convince stakeholders that the informal aspects of the program support their formal training investments?

We think there is an opportunity to make informal learning more tangible and focused in the workplace today. Whether you actively lead the learning function in your organization or develop strategies and processes that maximize the investments made in your people, there is a role for you in the process. Here are three ways you can influence informal learning in meaningful ways: communities of practice, action learning and informal learning assets.

Communities of Practice

Learning consultants can help teams plan, establish and maintain communities of practice (CoP). CoPs are an excellent way to help a team whose members have a common professional goal to generate, share and maintain knowledge. An effective CoP focuses on the process of knowledge creation and exchange, rather than on technology. Many of the best CoP tools now have Web 2.0–inspired collaborative features. They also focus on tasks and team accomplishments rather than on the social meandering that some social-networking technology can result in.

Action Learning

Another proven approach is action learning. This involves small teams working together on real workplace problems or tasks. Learning through doing, reflecting on the results and impact of those actions and making necessary adjustments is at the heart of the natural learning process. Action learning following formal learning events is also effective at transferring learning gained in the classroom to the work employees actually perform.

Another form of action learning is the development of a learning action plan. Such plans integrate learning and work by scheduling time for planned learning activities alongside regular work responsibilities. Learning activities have associated objectives and time frames. Employees reflect upon the outcomes of their learning and then make any adjustments to how they perform their work. These plans can be used either as a transfer activity with a formal learning program or as a component of employee development, onboarding or performance coaching strategies.

Informal Learning

Informal learning assets are digital and paper-based tools that evolve from formal classroom programs and organization knowledge. Think about the tools and models taught in your formal programs. In all likelihood, there is an opportunity to create templates or small "chunks" of information from this content and feed it to the organization through social media, the intranet or CoPs. These assets can be used as informal learning assets available on demand as refresher job aids after participants return to their jobs, as learning content for employees who did not attend the formal event or as tools reviewed with a learning coach for on-the-job learning.

These suggestions represent a few of the many ways you can facilitate and influence informal learning in your workplace. Look for opportunities to introduce a focused approach to informal learning in your organization or to enhance what you are already doing elsewhere in its learning services. By taking learning outside the classroom and bringing it into the workplace, you will have a much larger and dynamic field to play on.

MAKING INFORMAL LEARNING A LITTLE MORE FORMAL

Learning is most effective when integrated with real work. While experts in the field encourage this integration, they don't always offer practical strategies that busy learning professionals can use to make it happen. Here are ten strategies to bring learning to the job:

1. **Understand the job/role as a system.** If you're going to integrate learning with work, you had better understand the work. Watch people, talk to people, use appropriate analysis tools and think like the performer. Understand their world, their day-to-day pressures and the tools they use (or could use)—and how they use them. Understand the job inputs, processes and feedback mechanisms for job incumbents.

2. **Link learning to business process.** Once business processes have been identified (or made visible), use process phases to effectively embed relevant learning resources. All business processes contain knowledge leverage points—those points in the process where key information is needed for optimal performance.

3. **Build a performance support system.** Reduce the need for training (or eliminate it altogether) by providing information, decision tools, performance aids and learning on demand, using tools available at the moment they are needed. An excellent performance system becomes part of the task and complements human abilities (compensating for weaknesses and enhancing strengths).

4. **Build a community of practice.** CoPs are grounded in the communication and interaction between people as they solve shared problems. CoPs create knowledge as much as they transfer it—an essential feature in effective knowledge work—and they foster informal learning focused on specific problem domains.

5. **Use social media to facilitate informal learning.** Social media has been enormously popular in the public sphere but so far has met with resistance inside organizations. Organizations are still worried that social media is a little too, well, social. However, what we've learned somewhere between learning 1.0 and learning 2.0 is that learning is

(continued)

also, well, social—and that the informal networked organization is as important as the formal structure for accomplishing valuable work.

6. **Implement a continuous improvement framework.** Continuous improvement, or Kaizen, is essentially the scientific method built into jobs and workflow. W. Edwards Deming translated the method to the Plan-Do-Check-Act (PDCA) Cycle at the heart of the Toyota system and most quality approaches since the 1950s. The PDCA cycle is as much a natural learning cycle as it is a work improvement methodology. But it is the "check" step that is the real driver of learning. It requires a meaningful measurement and feedback system. Without it, improvement is nearly impossible.

7. **Use action learning.** Action learning is essentially the PDCA cycle applied to personal effectiveness—personal Kaizen, if you will. It involves teams or individuals learning from experience. Again, the emphasis is on observing results from action and making adjustments.

8. **Use organizational learning practices.** Organizational learning is broader than the label implies. It is usually focused on individual and team transformation through participating in systems thinking and tangible activities that change the way people conduct their work. It builds new capacities in individuals and teams that collectively begin to shape the culture and performance of an organization.

9. **Design jobs for natural learning.** Natural (or incidental) learning involves numerous factors but most powerful among them is the feedback we receive (or don't receive) on the results of our actions. We intuitively use that feedback to adjust our actions, decisions, methods, and so on, to try to get it right the next time. In other words, we use feedback to learn, to get better at what we do and accomplish.

10. **Bring the job to the learning.** Broadly speaking, the goal of training is to compress on-the-job experience to bring people to standard as quickly as possible. Somehow over the years that goal has been reduced to lots of telling and very little doing. The last strategy is an appeal to bring structured experience back to formal learning. I don't mean generic experience (like a management outdoor education or

(continued)

abstract team building exercises, for example) but experiences based on authentic performance tasks.

Source: Adapted from Tom Gram, senior director, Leadership and Business Solutions, Global Knowledge, *(Re)Organizing for Performance Effectiveness: 10 Strategies for Integrating Learning and Work*, http://performancexdesign.word press.com/2009/06/15/10-strategies-for-integrating-learning-and-work-part-1/.

WHAT THE EXPERTS SAY
Prescribing Development Solutions

Robert M. Fulmer is a specialist in strategic leadership development and an academic director at Duke Corporate Education; he is also the coauthor of *The Leadership Advantage*. Stephen Stumpf is a professor in business leadership at Villanova School of Business, and Jared Bleak is executive director at Duke Corporate Education and the other coauthor of *The Leadership Advantage*. In a recent article, Fulmer, Stumpf and Bleak (2009) point to the lack of highly effective leader development programs in organizations today and to how best-practice firms are managing succession planning and leadership training. Considering the recessionary business environment, in which effective leaders will need to be increasingly capable of innovating and improvising, and the fact that a whole generation of senior executives are near retirement, more than ever before, the authors argue, it is crucial that organizations adopt and align high-potential leadership development to their business strategies. Drawing on information from best-practice organizations, the authors point to the important role executives have in developing the next generation of leaders, and outline effective succession management practices and specific techniques for developing high-potential leaders.

They identify the strategies that are implemented by senior leaders in companies that have excellent leadership development programs, including:

- Hosting a high-profile talent management conference or leadership summit that specifically links strategy and talent development.

- Designing and operating a curriculum of education or action learning for transition points.
- Facilitating an internal coaching program where high-potential leaders practice on senior executives.
- Requesting that boards meet and assess high potentials.
- Designing and implementing a comprehensive plan for accelerating leader development and linking it to developing business needs.
- Aligning and linking talent development to business strategy.

They also describe start-up succession management practices for determining high-potential talent:

- Create a time frame for achieving planned development actions.
- Build in flexibility to change in response to changing strategic business plans.
- Share information with candidates involved in succession planning.
- Provide high-profile support by senior management.
- Involve line leaders in identifying and developing succession candidates.

Fulmer, Stumpf and Bleak emphasize that HR and line managers should be involved in the talent identification process in order to make sure that the assessments reflect performance needs and the organization's culture and vision. They report that companies with the highest shareholder return often link compensation to a leader's future potential.

They cite a number of techniques used by best-practice firms for developing high-potential leaders and note that such firms routinely provide high-potential managers with access and exposure to senior management. The "best firms" use more techniques and do them more consistently than less successful firms. They identify cost- and resource-efficient practices for starting up a high-potential program, including:

- Specialized leadership developmental tracks
- Developmental/stretch assignments
- Specialized learning opportunities
- Technology-enhanced learning

- Action learning
- Coaching/mentoring

They point to two specific organizations, PepsiCo and Caterpillar, whose high-potential talent development programs were collected and identified as part of a benchmarking project involving Duke Corporate Education and the New York–based Center for Creative Leadership. Strategies PepsiCo uses to develop and promote talent from within the organization include building bench strength; emphasizing cross-divisional talent movement for experience; and readiness development through experience, on-the-job training, and coaching, mentoring and formal training.

Caterpillar, whose leadership framework is integrated effectively into its core HR processes such as selection, development, performance management, succession management and career management, is also highlighted. It reports on its successful succession plan, which involves the opportunity for nominated high potentials to attend a Leadership Quest program at Caterpillar University. Once a year, managers at the middle level and above have the opportunity to participate in a talent assessment process that involves the employee's manager, management and officer team representatives, along with a member from the executive office. The assessment process involves the high potential's recommended moves over the next three years, the career experiences he or she needs and an assessment of his or her long-range potential.

Individual Leader Development

In her review of the research literature on leader development, McCauley (2008) identifies three primary focuses on development: individual leader development, developmental methods and organizational practices for leader development. Of these focus areas, development of the individual has received the most attention. Although she admits that most of the leader development research deals with individuals in manager roles, she offers the distinction between leader development and manager development, clarifying that whereas management is more about maintaining the stability of an organization (e.g., through planning, organizing, securing resources), leadership is more about the relational work of generating collective action (e.g., generating a vision, motivating people, shaping the culture).

McCauley points out that leadership development can be conceptualized in several ways, such as development of leader competencies, transformational change, development of social as well as human capital, development of leader expertise and development of leader self-concept or identity. She notes that different conceptualizations tend to draw on different theories of learning and development. She identifies leader competencies as the most frequent conceptualization and emphasizes that most organizations use a competency model that describes their assessments of the capabilities individuals need to lead effectively in their organizations. She reports that leader development that is conceptualized in terms of transformative change focuses on developing leaders with more complex ways of thinking and acting. The leadership expertise conceptualization of leadership development focuses on developing leaders from novice to intermediate to master leader. McCauley identifies three types of studies that look at how individuals develop the skills needed for effective leadership, those that:

1. Describe previous development experiences in leaders' careers
2. Look at development within the context of the leaders' current jobs
3. Examine how transition to new roles affects development

Based on the four major studies she examined, involving almost 500 executives from successful global companies and how previous experiences helped develop their leadership skills, McCauley pinpoints five major categories of development situations or areas: challenging assignments (learning by doing), other people (learning from others), hardships (learning from difficult situations or mistakes), coursework (formal learning) and personal life experiences (learning outside work), with participants reporting a wide range of lessons learned, such as learning to lead and manage others, run a business, deal with problematic relationships, deal with cultural issues and develop the qualities of a leader, as well as learning about self and career. McCauley refers to one study

(Bennis and Thomas 2002) involving in-depth interviews with forty-three leaders that found that each leader had experienced at least one transformational or crucial experience in becoming a leader.

From studies that examined the degree to which managers developed in their current jobs, McCauley identifies five challenges associated with developing as a manager:

1. Learning new ways of thinking and responding to problems in job transitions.
2. Learning to deal with the uncertainty and ambiguity associated with creating change.
3. Learning to deal with the added pressure associated with new jobs with higher levels of responsibility.
4. Learning to manage boundaries when working laterally across internal and external boundaries.
5. Learning to work with diversity.

From studies on the effects of work transitions on leaders' development, McCauley identifies an early study by Hill (1992) that found that new managers needed to address the following developmental tasks:

1. Learning what it meant to be a manager.
2. Developing interpersonal judgment.
3. Gaining self-knowledge.
4. Coping with stress and emotion.

Another study (Gabarro 1987) found that learning to be a manager took place in stages, involving taking hold, immersion, reshaping, consolidation and refinement—and that it took, on average, two and a half to three years for managers to pass through these stages.

McCauley identifies six types of leader development interventions: development (training) programs, multisource feedback, developmental assessment center programs (consisting of a series of leadership and management simulations), action learning, executive coaching and mentoring. She refers to two comprehensive meta-analysis studies that found that leader development programs vary widely but overall provide support for leadership programs. In terms of the criterion measures used, the study by Collins and Holton (2004) found the largest average effect sizes for knowledge/learning and the smallest average effect sizes for systems results (organizational results such as reduced costs, improved quality and quantity, and promotions). Although the study is fairly old, the second meta-analysis, by Burke and Day (1986), categorizes various studies by training content and found that human relations and self-awareness training produced higher than average effect sizes than did training on general management, problem solving/decision making, rater training and motivation/values. McCauley suggests that future studies examine possible moderators, including individual characteristics, such as conscientiousness, anxiety, age, cognitive ability and self-efficacy, as well as situational ones, such as sufficient resources, frequent feedback and opportunities to use the skills. Based on her review of multiple studies and research, McCauley notes that programs can be effectively categorized to distinguish them from each other in terms of methods and targeted outcomes and could include:

1. Conceptual understanding (heavy use of theory, models and case studies)
2. Skill building (learning skills through description, examples, discussion, practice and feedback)
3. Multimethod feedback (360-degree surveys, personality measures, experiential exercises and simulation)
4. Personal growth (psychological exercises to stimulate personal reflection)

McCauley notes that research on 360-degree feedback (assessments) found that these multisource ratings:

1. Are positively correlated with performance appraisals and objective performance measures
2. Show positive, although small, improvements in performance
3. Suggest that leaders with high self-esteem, openness to experience, learning goal orientation, self-efficacy and an internal locus of control have a more positive attitude toward multisource feedback than do those who lack these qualities

Research on developmental assessment centers indicate that because they generate a lot of data, they have the potential to be a good source of in-depth feedback for an individual. These research found that of individuals who participated in such a center's program, those who followed more of the developmental recommendations were more likely to advance than those who followed fewer recommendations.

Drawing on the results of a comprehensive meta-analysis of leadership development interventions (Avolio et al. 2009) that showed considerable variation in the impact of those interventions (from −177 percent to 200 percent returns), this meta-analysis sought to examine a leader's readiness to change as a moderator of the relationship between leadership interventions and the return of the development investment. Hannah and Avolio (2010) argue that before spending billions on leadership development programs, organizations would be wise to invest in how to get leaders and their organizations better ready to develop. Based on relevant literature on clinical, cognitive and social psychology, and on organizational behavior and leadership, as well as their theory building and empirical testing over a five-year period on the individual differences that serve to accelerate leader development, they propose that leader developmental readiness is a function of motivation and ability to develop.

Hannah and Avolio identify leader interests and goals, goal orientation and developmental efficacy as the avenues through which motivation to develop is promoted. If a leader lacks interest in exploring a new skill, a lower level of engagement in a new learning experience is expected. In terms of goal orientation, Avolio and colleagues suggest that, compared with individuals who have a performance goal orientation, those who have an incremental goal orientation see task feedback as developmental rather than performance, which in turn motivates them to seek out new experiences. Compared with individuals having low confidence, individuals who are confident in their ability to develop and use the knowledge, skills, abilities and attitudes (KSAAs) developed in future leadership contexts can be expected to be more motivated to engage in development programs.

They identify leader self-awareness and self-concept clarity and meta-cognitive ability as the avenues through which ability to develop is promoted. They suggest that while we would expect leaders with high levels of self-awareness to be more capable of incorporating new KSAAs into their knowledge and identity structures, it is through self-concept clarity that leaders are able to determine how new KSAAs become integrated with their self-concepts. Hannah and Avolio argue that the more cognitively complex the leaders are, the more capable they are of processing developmental information, including discriminating and seeing commonalities among the different information dimensions. The greater a leader's metacognitive ability, the greater his or her ability to make meaning of and develop new insights about the experience.

Initial empirical testing by Hannah and Avolio (2007) on the effects of learning goal orientation, metacognitive ability and self-concept clarity in predicting the acceleration of leader development found that these three developmental readiness constructs significantly moderated levels of development of transformational leadership, authentic leadership and self-efficacy, and predicted future leader performance. Their study has implications for organizations in that, except perhaps for goal orientation, the developmental readiness constructs are malleable and so can be expected to respond to development.

5

Ensuring and Reviewing Development

The secret of success is constancy to purpose.

—Benjamin Disraeli

So far we have discussed the qualities that make a great leader and suggested approaches to building a success profile suited to particular situations. We have recommended that management, ideally represented or assisted by an HR professional, takes a proactive role in identifying high-potential employees, assessing their strengths and weaknesses, and diagnosing the areas in which further development is required.

Now the rubber really hits the road. How do companies ensure that their leadership development plans, so carefully assembled and custom-tailored for their next generation of leaders, actually does what it is intended to do? Unfortunately, this is not a process that runs on autopilot. If it did, organizations likely wouldn't be facing the leadership crisis that they frequently find themselves in today.

So how do we ensure leadership development is happening and that appropriate monitoring and review measures are in place? In a rather straightforward way, thankfully. The path to success is achieved by establishing follow-up procedures that ensure development activities are executed and results captured. Rather than running on autopilot, distinct checkpoints are established that prompt us to measure the degree of success that has been achieved and to determine what still needs to be done.

It is relatively easy to recognize success. All along the process of preparing leadership succession, a flurry of measures and outcomes will occur, but the single most important one is this: the organization has a greater number of ready leaders for promotion to higher levels. Success or failure can be easily measured: if the process does not produce a cohort of future leaders at the end of its two-year or three-year time frame, the whole exercise was a failure.

The old way of planning for succession was to insert a bunch of names on an organization chart and hope that they would be ready through some magic sleight-of-hand to assume a more demanding position sometime in the future.

We advise companies to do more with less when it comes to identifying and developing high-potential leaders. In other words, don't make the leadership pool overly large by stuffing as many candidates in it as possible. Rather, make it the right size to produce the required number of future leaders in a given period—say, two years from now—and devote more resources to their development. Don't put too many candidates in the pool, but instead select carefully the number you need and do more with them. Do more coaching, provide more development opportunities and formal training.

How many people are designated for the leadership candidate pool really depends on the demographic of the organization. If the leadership team comprises mainly aging boomers looking forward to a not-so-far-away retirement, the pool will be bigger than it is for a company with plenty of young blood in its management ranks.

Just who gets into the pool tends to be a bit of a political game. For example, some managers, for reasons of their own, may want to place a few marginal candidates into the development process. Favoritism based on a personal relationship rather than objective assessment of individual qualities may be a factor in their choices.

Research from the Corporate Leadership Council found that only 29 percent of high performers across a number of international organizations surveyed were also high-potential candidates. Put simply, the fact that a person is a fantastic performer in his or her current position does not mean that that person necessarily has what it takes to be a great leader. The biggest risk companies face in turning all that leadership potential into leadership reality is the natural tendency toward inertia—both personal and organizational. Those high-potential leaders, their superiors and everyone else around them expected to help them with their development already have full-time jobs to do. People are busy, leadership development can be a fuzzy concept for some and the tendency is to put the whole program on the back burner. The real autopilot, in other words, is for people to just carry on as they have always done.

The motivation of high-potential individuals may have nothing to do with their progress. They may be eager to learn the leadership skills that could put them on the fast track up the ranks. It's really up to the organization to ensure that the development program proceeds and is monitored.

It is quite likely that those tagged as high-potential leaders are also the stars or workhorses of their departments. The development plan may call for them to work outside their area, perhaps to take part in a special project, say, one day a week. So for the development plan to actually be effective, it has to overcome the quite natural resistance of the potential leader's superior to lose the top performer for a period.

To overcome this kind of resistance, we recommend not only involving the high potential's manager but also going up another level and involving his or her manager's manager. Going two levels up reinforces the idea with the candidates' superiors and senior management that the high-potential pool is "company property" and not just a resource to be jealously guarded by the high potential's immediate leaders. Senior management needs to be responsible for nurturing this company resource and safeguarding it from the forces that retard its development—turf wars, petty jealousy and department protectionism.

There are plenty of other legitimate barriers that can crop up over the span of the development plan that can stall it or stop it dead, including employee turnover and workplace crises. For that reason, it is critical for organizations to formally track the high potential's progress by building in processes and actions to follow up.

Many organizations, particularly those in the public sector, underestimate the need for creating a robust talent management system. "I did not understand the logic or benefit of succession planning and coaching in the public sector, and particularly in the health sector," says Jack Kitts, of The Ottawa Hospital. "The reason for that is the CEO in the health sector never picks their successor. So it would be inadvisable for a CEO to take someone into [their] confidence and say, 'You are going to be the next CEO.'"

Similarly, when a vice-president position comes up, the board will not have a homogeneous point of view, except maybe for the nursing and medical perspectives. You can't really have a direct-line succession plan.

"It was not until I worked with Global Knowledge that I learned that it is really about managing and promoting your talent, which is a very different concept that caught my attention and made sense," Kitts adds. "No promises, no guarantees and no direct line. It's just basically taking various members of teams and managing their talent, and the first step of managing talent is learning what the talent is."

THE OTTAWA HOSPITAL'S TALENT MANAGEMENT SUCCESS

When it became apparent that several of its senior executives were nearing retirement age, the hospital's board of governors mandated that some form of succession planning be set in place. Typically, succession planning calls for the identification of a few promising candidates to be groomed for senior positions, and in certain situations this approach works well. In the case of The Ottawa Hospital, however, the CEO and HR department saw the need to fill the organization's senior pipeline and boost its overall leadership capacity. To that end, a broader executive talent development program that incorporated succession planning was adopted.

Prior to hiring Global Knowledge to design a talent management program, The Ottawa Hospital's HR department had begun to identify the competencies required for various leadership roles throughout the organization. It required some help and guidance to design a more comprehensive development program that targeted those competencies.

Global Knowledge worked with the HR department to design a talent management program intended to build individual leadership capacity in alignment with the hospital's long-term vision. The first step in the process was to create a talent management blueprint that described the program goals and outlined steps in its implementation. Many of those steps involved senior executive participation or feedback, a process that gave these key stakeholders a sense of ownership of the process.

(continued)

The executive leadership solution recognized that the higher an employee rises in an organization, the greater the impact of his or her personal characteristics, strengths and development needs. The hospital and its advisers worked together to create detailed success profiles for each executive position, covering the four key factors of success—competencies, knowledge, experience and personality.

Next came an intensive diagnostic phase that identified individual strengths and development requirements and singled out people with the potential to move up in the organization. The talent management team used a customized Multi-Rater Survey, the Knowledge and Experience Inventory and personal characteristics inventories. Results were sorted into individual profiles, which were then compared with the relevant success profile.

The presentation of the results of the assessment phase was used as a coaching opportunity in which a consultant coach met with each executive individually and offered guidance for improving in his or her particular role. The CEO and, when appropriate, the COO sat in on a portion of each executive's session. Their participation communicated the importance of the process and reinforced the top executives' own coaching roles regarding each executive's development.

The final step in the process saw the creation of individual development plans to maximize each executive's performance. Rather than simply prescribe a plan, the talent management team challenged each executive to create his or her own plan based on feedback received. That plan was reviewed by the Global Knowledge coach, the CEO and the COO, and finally presented to the board before it was put into action.

One important reason The Ottawa Hospital talent management intervention was a success is the regular follow-up done by the CEO, Jack Kitts, with each member of his executive leadership team and the board. The positive and regular follow-up became a reinforcement and a "learning tension" supportive of the leaders' development.

One of the most tangible results of the talent management initiative at the hospital was the analysis and documentation of talent assets at

(continued)

the executive level. Today, the hospital has a pipeline of leadership talent inside the organization, with a number of candidates being groomed for more positions with more responsibility. The board has a clear understanding of the strengths, weaknesses and opportunities in the hospital's senior ranks. Finally, by establishing the requirements for effective leadership, the HR team has a clear direction for future development efforts and hiring practices.

CREATE LEARNING TENSION

The motivation levels of high potentials when they enter the leadership development process will be specific to the individual, but they all should be told implicitly and explicitly that their positive progression is important to the organization. The best way to accomplish this is by what we like to describe as creating a learning tension. This is a positive pressure—the expectation of success—that the high potential (and his or her superior) should feel coming from management.

The process starts with fixing and defining accountability. Who is accountable for tracking the success of the high-potential candidate? Every organization will carry out this step a little bit differently, but the high potential, his or her superior and others who have to be identified will play a key role in the individual's development.

How can we create this learning tension that keeps the high potential and superior motivated? We recommend, for one thing, that our clients make sure that there are regular meetings at a senior level to review the progress of their development plan, facilitated by the HR department.

"There are three things you absolutely need to ensure it will happen," says Kitts. "First, an agreement between the CEO and board or between the CEO and subordinate that this is the plan. Second, any support for professional development has to be approved by the CEO or the board and has to be aligned with the talent management plan. Third, what I do with my executives, on an annual basis, is report on their development progress to the board and adjust the status on their abilities so that they could take on more responsibilities, a more important portfolio, or even could perform the duties of the CEO in a pinch." Letting leaders in an organization know that their progress is being monitored and reported in and of itself can be a spur to executives to follow their development program, Kitts noted. "I think it does create that little bit of tension that sort of motivates in the right way to get things done."

I generally recommend that companies establish a panel to review the high potentials' progress biannually. The duties of the panel should include:

- Ensuring that the development is happening.
- Removing barriers as necessary.
- Supporting or directing the assignment of the high potential to specific projects.
- Deciding when a high potential is ready to move into a position at the next level.

SUCCESS CRITERIA

Success management is not a "fire and forget" process. The progress of high-potential employees needs to be systematically monitored and adjusted over time. Perhaps just as importantly, high potentials should know that their progress is being watched by leaders higher in the organization. Keep an eye on the following criteria; they can maximize the success of your succession management efforts:

- The succession management process must be supported by the executive leadership team.
- The succession management process must have integrity and transparency, and show linkages to all the work that goes on in the organization.
- There must be effective communication regarding the succession management process and plans so that people understand what is being done. There must be time and resources committed to the process.
- The succession management plan must be integrated with other people practices and strategy.
- Employees must be committed to invest in their own development without the guarantee of promotion.

(continued)

- There must be integration with training that is already underway without duplication of efforts.
- There must be some flexibility in the application of the plan; it is not a case of one size fits all.
- The plan must focus on a small number of targeted roles initially, with expansion to additional roles planned for the future.

IMPLEMENTATION AND REVIEW

The organization, of course, has plenty invested in the process in terms of time, energy and often money, such as that spent on professional learning programs for the individual. Our experience at Global Knowledge confirms that a vibrant and meaningful succession program depends on clearly defined accountability—for the succession candidates, their immediate superiors, the succession management working group, and the senior executives in the client organization. We have identified five distinct steps that need to be taken to ensure and review development:

1. Establish accountability for the execution of development plans.
2. Develop and implement follow-up processes.
3. Define and implement the communication plan.
4. Develop a leadership dashboard and succession activities using lead and lag measures.
5. Plan and execute reviews of high potentials' development and incorporate lessons learned.

1. Establish Accountability for the Execution of Development Plans

I recommend that organizations always push accountability and knowledge of the high potential's development program one level (or more) above the high potential's superior. That individual or group is informed not only who the high potential's manager is but also what the high potential's needs are and what type of development plan has been created for him or her.

Going two levels above the high-potential candidate allows those higher in the ranks to support the candidate's development when called upon and, more critically, puts them in place to remove any barriers. At some companies it might be a talent management committee, succession management board or, for senior candidates, perhaps the CEO or board of directors.

By revealing the identity of the development candidates to more senior management, their sponsors also make them top of mind. This makes it more likely that when opportunities for sideways movement or advancement in the organization crop up—and when these opportunities fit their development program—the high potentials are considered for those positions.

As high-potential candidates begin to execute their plans, questions will arise about accountability for various aspects of the plan. It is unlikely that all questions can be anticipated. Table 5.1 lists typical issues. It is up to senior management to fill in the blanks—assigning responsibility—for each.

Table 5.1: Assigning Responsibility for Ensuring Success

Typical Issues	Typical Accountability Determine Who and What
Who makes decisions about deviations from the planned development activities?	
Who decides about the priorities between development activity versus daily operational requirements?	
Who pays for training or development activities?	
Who pays for replacement staff if an employee is given a development assignment in another department?	
Who determines whether the development actions have achieved their intended impact?	
Who decides whether open positions are offered to succession candidates before external candidates?	
Who decides whether succession candidates can be considered for roles not necessarily aligned with their core and functional expertise?	

2. Develop and Implement Follow-Up Processes

Developing follow-up procedures must be completed in the context of the previous decisions that are documented in the planning phase. This is where processes will be established to determine how follow-up will be made, by whom and how often. As mentioned, we strongly recommend the involvement of the high potentials (they own their development plans), their managers and the managers at the next level up. The following questions will help determine the process to put in place:

- What data is needed for follow-up?
- Where does the data reside?
- Who creates and/or gathers the data?
- How is the data acquired?
- How is the data reported?
- To whom is the data reported?
- How frequently is the data reported?
- What happens when data is not available?
- How are exceptions from planned progress communicated and addressed?
- How are lessons learned identified?
- How are lessons learned communicated?

3. Define and Implement the Communication Plan

A high-level communication strategy should be developed during the planning phase of any succession management initiative. At this step in the succession management process, the specific details of the communication plan must be established. The purpose of the communication is to keep participants in the succession process aware of the organization's requirements, their responsibilities, the actions being taken and the results being achieved so that the targeted success criteria can be met.

The communication plan must include answers to the following questions:

- What will be communicated?
- Who will create the communication?

- Who will distribute the communication?
- To whom will it be communicated?
- How frequently will communication take place?
- What are the required actions after communication?
- Who will address ongoing queries?

4. Develop a Leadership Dashboard and Succession Activities Using Lead and Lag Measures

It is critically important to measure the results of succession management initiatives. Succession management requires a considerable amount of time between establishing the organization's focus, determining how candidates will be identified and developed, and then assessing their progress.

Lead measures are indicators of progress toward the ultimate succession management goals. They allow the organization to confirm that the right steps, to the right degree, are being executed. Lead measures sustain motivation and interest about succession management, give confidence that progress is being made and indicate if changes or adjustments are required. Lag measures reflect the results achieved, allowing the organization to gauge its success by comparing the actual results with the originally targeted success criteria.

Examples of lead measures:

- The level of satisfaction indicated by the participants in the succession management process with the approach and the candidates' progress
- The number of development plans that have been established
- The number of development activities that have been realized

Examples of lag measures:

- The number (or percentage) of positions filled by high potentials
- The retention percentage of high potentials (this should be higher than the retention rate in the rest of the organization)
- The candidates' acquisition of knowledge and experience, and the development of competencies identified in the development plans
- The number of ready candidates in the pool

5. Plan and Execute Reviews of High Potentials' Development and Incorporate Lessons Learned

Even the best-laid and thought-out plans can feature elements that look great on paper but do not work so well in practice. In one real-life example, our firm got mixed results when asked to provide executive coaching to a client. The reason for the mixed results is this: the organization identified candidates who wanted coaching, but it also selected a second group of people who needed development but did not want coaching. It should not be hard to figure out which group is succeeding and which is lagging behind the plan.

The succession management committee not only needs to monitor candidates' progress but also must closely consider their assessment results to evaluate if and when to recommend them for promotion. While an individual may be in what has been designed as a two-year development plan, his or her development may in reality take longer. In such cases, the succession management committee may judge that the aspects of development that are missing or incomplete—for example, strategic thinking skills—can be acquired in the new role. Conversely, the skills that are lacking may be judged to be critical to the new role, and therefore the candidate is judged not ready and should remain in the program for further development.

SUCCESSION MANAGEMENT BEST PRACTICES

In order to generate the results expected, it is important to respect certain best practices. The ultimate measure of success of a succession management initiative is the number of leaders and professionals ready to fill open positions, ideally before the incumbent in a role leaves the organization for retirement or other reasons. Succession management is not simply a long list of names identified for certain roles, with few or no actions to grow them. Here are the best practices to observe:

- Focus on development, rather than simply replacement of key roles.
- Clearly define accountabilities and roles.
- Involve senior leadership.

(continued)

- Align succession initiatives to the organization's vision, business strategy and values.
- Synchronize the succession plan with annual business plans.
- Integrate the succession plan with other people practices, such as success profiling, selection and recruiting, onboarding, performance management, training and development.
- Make sure the plan is implemented consistently across the organization.
- Engage impacted line managers and targeted employees in the process.
- Establish an ongoing communication process at both the organizational and individual level.

WHAT THE EXPERTS SAY
Identification and Development of High Potentials

Although many organizations identify accelerating the development of high potentials as a key objective, most do not have a succession management system that effectively identifies, develops and measures the progress of high potentials to ensure optimal development of the leadership pipeline. Organizations that exhibit leadership development and succession management best practices fully utilize managerial personnel, including high potentials, in their talent management systems. These best-practice organizations have processes in place that stress the importance of senior executives, as well as leader development plans and training opportunities that ensure the organizations' credible commitment to the development of high potentials. Holding leaders and organizations accountable for results is the cornerstone of an effective succession management system. A study by Saslow (2004) found that 63 percent of European-based multinationals reported never measuring return on investment in learning and development, even though these same companies reported that the importance of learning and development was at its highest ever.

William Rothwell (2002), National Thought Leader for a best-practice study of succession planning, identifies questions that organizations should ask themselves when considering whether a succession planning and management program is really necessary for them. For instance: Do managers complain that there is nobody ready when a vacancy opens up? Is the organization spending increasing sums of cash on external searches? Is the company losing more and more of its star performers? Do employees complain that promotion decisions seem to be made based on favoritism? Rothwell identifies eleven best practices in succession planning and management:

1. Clarification by executives of the purpose and desired results expected from the program.
2. The use of competency models for determining what performance is required of high potentials in current roles.
3. Measurement of performance by integrating competency models with high potentials' measurable work results.
4. The creation of a competency model that describes characteristics of individuals needed in future leadership roles.
5. Assessment of potential by comparing high-potential individuals to future competency models, using 360-degree assessments in a regular, continuing and systematic way.
6. Establishment of individual development plans for high potentials to narrow the gap between their current competencies and performance and their assessed potential.
7. Follow-up talent review meetings to evaluate high potentials' developmental progress and to hold managers who are responsible for development accountable.
8. Documentation of work-related, company-specific competencies of high potentials.
9. Establishment of incentives for developing high potentials in line with organizational needs.
10. Senior management asks the question of whether there are qualified internal applicants who may be considered for a position when a key position becomes available.
11. Leadership from the front: CEO and other senior leaders become active participants, as "talent developers."

Barnett and Davis (2008), both leadership development and succession planning specialists, identify a five-step approach to succession planning that is based on best practices and applied role theory. The practical steps are:

1. Doing preliminary planning (e.g., rationale and criteria for evaluation of high potentials through the organization's competency model).
2. Preparing for succession planning and talent review (i.e., ensuring evaluation criteria reflect the organization's future leadership requirements, conducting aspiration conversations with high potentials to determine interest and willingness to be included in the process, communicating about the process to high potentials and to show commitment of senior management to the process, collecting ratings about high potentials based on evaluation criteria).
3. Holding talent review meetings (i.e., agreements on feedback and development recommendations for high potentials).
4. Providing feedback and facilitating individual developmental action to high potentials.
5. Measuring effectiveness of the plan (i.e., agreement on measures of effectiveness—e.g., increased number of internal promotions, reduced turnover).

The plan assumes interest and active involvement from senior management and that decisions about participants are data-based and made by group discussion and consensus. Each step involves accountability criteria, such as roles and responsibilities of senior management, line managers, HR and the high potentials themselves, and measurement and evaluation criteria. Barnett and Davis point out that accountability and data-driven evaluation criteria help ensure that the right individuals have been chosen for development, that there is buy-in by high potentials and that development is monitored in the right way, at the right time and by the right individuals. The authors report that best-practice organizations show that sound succession planning and management practices directly impact and strengthen leadership bench strength; provide leadership continuity, reduced turnover and increased retention of key personnel; and directly or indirectly improve business and financial results.

An organization's credible commitment to the development of high potentials drives the leadership succession plan and is critical to ensuring that high potentials maintain the same commitment to the organization and to development action plans that are aligned with the needs of future leadership positions. In a comprehensive high-potential management survey, the Corporate Leadership Council (2005) identifies the importance of these three classes of drivers:

1. Senior executive leadership
2. Developmental plans
3. Training

In terms of senior executive commitment, the survey found that a sincere commitment from the "top" drove employee commitment by up to 29 percent, and when senior leaders displayed openness to new ideas, employee potential increased by up to 31 percent (Corporate Leadership Council 2005). The survey found that when organizations successfully integrate senior leaders into developmental strategies, the development of high potentials and their intent to stay is accelerated. This survey's findings of the importance of the CEO and other senior managers in leadership development and succession management planning is hearkened by Rothwell (2002), who emphasized that the hands-on involvement of the CEO is critical to the credibility of the commitment and success of the program, noting that it is only the CEO who can ultimately hold other senior executives accountable for grooming talent, and reward or punish them for their results. Bleak and Fulmer (2009) found that, ultimately, it is the senior leaders who are accountable for developmental results. They report how best-practice firms tie leadership development to performance and rewards systems. In their report, they refer to a study (Hewitt Associates 2005) of how Top 20 companies grow great leaders that found that best-practice succession management companies successfully integrate competency measures into formulas for senior leaders' base pay (60 percent use leadership competencies to determine base pay, versus 30 percent who don't), annual incentives (60 percent vs. 31 percent) and long-term incentives (65 percent vs. 23 percent).

The Corporate Leadership Council (2005) survey found that executive commitment to the development of high potentials impacts employee potential by 30 percent; development plans and training program qualities were found to account for 27.8 percent and 13.8 percent respectively. The survey found that development plan characteristics helped convince employees of the organization's sincere commitment to their development and led to the following characteristic-specific driver impacts on potential: plan achievability (37.8 percent), individual customization of plan (30.5 percent), plan's demonstration of organization commitment to development (28.2 percent), plan's impact on achieving career goals (25.5 percent), manager dedication to the development plan (25.0 percent), organization dedication to developmental plan (19.6 percent) and, unremarkably, the presence of a developmental plan (<1 percent).

In terms of training program qualities, the survey found that the organization's sincere commitment to the development of high potentials led to the following quality-specific driver impacts on potential: enables current job performance (20.6 percent), enables future job performance (19.0 percent), builds internal networks (14.4 percent), enables understanding of organizational strategy (13.9 percent), enables understanding of the business (10.2 percent) and builds external networks (4.9 percent). Of particular interest are the findings that compared the overall maximum impact of developmental plans (37.8 percent) on three potential components: change in ability, change in aspiration and change in engagement. Compared with the impacts of change in ability (15.7 percent) and change in aspiration (22.5 percent), change in engagement is much higher (45.4 percent). In addition, the maximum impact of a developmental plan, achievable on specific types of engagement, yielded the following results: emotional commitment (68.4 percent), rational commitment (34.3 percent), discretionary effort (51.7 percent) and intent to stay (55.2 percent). The survey also found that "no plan was better than a bad plan," indicating that presenting an employee with an unachievable development plan can reduce his or her potential by as much as 19 percent. Overall, the survey found that administering unachievable and/or unsupported development plans leads to decreased engagement, diminished effort and higher retention risk.

While leveraging development programs to achieve their own objectives, executive-level leaders can also contribute to the development of the next generation of leaders. Bleak and Fulmer (2009) report that best-practice learning and development organizations point to the "lead and lag" evaluations of success, with people development as a leading indicator and financial results as a lagging indicator. The authors summarize the overarching strategic objectives noted in five best-practice organizations, in terms of evaluating their successes in developing a pipeline of leaders:

1. Developing people as a growing measure of executive success.
2. Seeing corporate success as the ultimate measure of success in leadership development.
3. Moving leadership development from events to process.

In terms of developing people as a strong indicator of executive success, Bleak and Fulmer (2009) highlight PepsiCo as an exemplar of an organization in which senior leaders teach lower-level executives and managers, and where in return for senior leaders sharing their personal perspectives, helping build participant confidence and skills and demonstrating support for their growth, they get greater teamwork from participants, while developing more productivity, loyalty, motivation and better alignment with the company's vision and strategic initiatives. In terms of corporate success as the ultimate measure of success in leadership development, the authors identify Caterpillar University as possessing the most rigorous process for measuring the return of its learning investment, including values ratings of key developmental initiatives based on net benefits and return of investment, such as leveraging focus groups, surveys and in-depth discussions with participants.

Further, Bleak and Fulmer (2009) point to Cisco as a model organization using a formal system to measure the outcomes of leadership development strategy, including, for example, the "price range for a one-week course," "customer satisfaction scores" and the "percentage of high-potential learners who stay with the company." The authors emphasize that best-practice organizations such as Cisco have learning and development plans that are process-based, where high potentials process through phases in their developmental programs that encompass preparation, program and application to the job. Best-practice development programs leverage key transition points in its leaders' careers, build on one another and provide systematic opportunities for checkpoint evaluations, to ensure that the development is progressing and is in alignment with future leadership position needs.

In a study of thirty CEOs and HR executives across fifteen best-practice organizations, Groves (2007) found that these organizations integrated leadership development and succession planning by leveraging managers as talent developers who follow and monitor the progress of high potentials to help ensure development plans are carried out, and modified when needed. Based on interview data, the author presents a model that encompasses the critical roles that managers play in developing each other and in identifying and developing other high-potential employees in the organization. These roles include:

1. Developing mentoring relationships (i.e., mentoring direct reports and high potentials from other work units, career planning, leadership competency development).
2. Identifying and codifying leadership talent through:
   a. Multiple methods to identify high-potential managers, such as committees, survey tools and a coding system.
   b. Assessing managerial bench strength.
3. Assigning developmental activities, including internal coursework and workshops taught by managers, action learning projects, stretch assignments, 360-degree assessments and executive coaching.
4. Enhancing high potentials' visibility by exposing leadership talent through organization-wide forums and leadership academies.
5. Engaging with senior executives and board members regarding succession decisions where a diverse pool of candidates, not just direct reports, is considered.

The model reinforces the role that CEO commitment to leadership development programs (i.e., active participation in teaching and facilitating action learning projects) and managerial performance appraisals and reward processes (i.e., identifying and developing high potentials, and succession planning progress and performance criteria) have on reinforcing an organizational culture of leadership development.

A survey of 199 leaders attending development programs at the Center for Creative Leadership (Campbell and Smith 2010) examined talent management through the eyes of high-potential managers and found that:

1. Formal identification as a high potential is important.
2. High potentials expect more development, support and investment than other employees.
3. High potentials feel good about their status.
4. High potentials are more committed and engaged when they have a clear career path.
5. High potentials help develop others.

Of particular interest to ensuring that investments in high potentials yield the intended return are the last two points on this list. The authors emphasize that commitment and engagement are two of the most important talent measures for organizations. They note that greater levels of commitment increase the likelihood that high potentials will remain with the organization, and their greater engagement increases the likelihood that they will be more satisfied and productive in their work. Interestingly but not surprisingly, the survey found that informally identified high potentials are more likely to be actively seeking other employment (33 percent) at the same time as they are being developed than are formally identified high potentials (14 percent). This means that the level of transparency and formality in identifying high-potential talent has a direct impact on retention.

In terms of what high potentials think organizations could do to increase their commitment and engagement, the survey produced the following results: developmental opportunities such as special assignments and training (11 percent), rewards and incentives (11 percent), nondevelopmental support such as increased work-life balance and other resources (11 percent), career pathing (27 percent), greater authority (16 percent) and increased feedback and communication (13 percent). In regards to developing other talent, the survey found that 86 percent of high potentials agreed that, in their current roles, they play an active role in helping identify and develop other high potentials. The authors note that, again, a formal process matters, with the survey finding that, compared with 99 percent of formally identified high potentials who are likely to actively identify and develop talent, only 78 percent of informally identified high potentials do the same. In summarizing the strategies high potentials see as important for organizations to consider to ensure success of the high-potential process, the survey found that organizations should:

1. Work to ensure transparency and formality of the high-potential identification process
2. Work to create a mutually beneficial relationship between the organization and the talent, including investment in leader development in exchange for their commitment in engagement
3. Leverage high potentials as developers of talent

By incorporating the perspectives of high potentials, organizations help ensure leadership development and help maximize their return in its investment.

PART II

Leadership in Action

6

Leaders as Coaches

Effective leaders coach their people and
actively seek coaching themselves.

—Robert Steven Kaplan

Part 1 outlined the best practices and latest research on succession management, leadership attributes and identifying future leaders. Part 2, Leadership in Action, covers the skills and competencies that determine whether leaders are high functioning and successful or are, sadly, just names on an organizational chart. One of the key skills of leaders of today (and most definitely of tomorrow) is that of coaching. Leaders not only need to get their team motivated and engaged, they also are required to ensure that as they move up in the organization their knowledge and skills are passed on to those who fill the leadership void they leave behind.

As a practice at the leader level, coaching is relatively new. Gaining a firm foothold in organizations in the 1970s and 1980s, it was adapted and developed, perhaps not surprisingly, from the sports world. Leaders recognized the success that coaches were having with athletes on the field, on the ice and on the hardwood, and went from there.

Coaching got its start with the practice of providing a coach to an executive leader and was considered initially as a remedial or prescriptive process. "John in marketing is not performing as well as he should; let's assign him a coach," was the sort of rationale that underlay early coaching.

A coach was seen less as a positive force for development than as a last hope for an executive whose career was stalled or who was on the road to termination. Coaching in the early days was a secretive business and carried a social and workplace stigma. Individuals were about as likely to admit to having a coach at work as they were to divulge that they were seeing a psychiatrist.

The amazing thing about coaching, therefore, is how the practice has emerged from the shadows. Today, the coaching profession boasts international associations, certifications and university degrees, and has shed the stigma from its creation as a remedial tool. As far as we at Global Knowledge are concerned, coaching is a well-established practice that can help those who manage others in the workplace to raise their game, build trust and mutual respect and open up new possibilities. Coaching now is seen as a leadership competency, a skill that leaders with the organization must demonstrate, not only a function assigned to an outside professional.

While coaching is becoming more formalized, it doesn't need to have a formal structure to be effective. "I don't distinguish between coaching and mentoring," says Jack Kitts, CEO of The Ottawa Hospital. "Basically, I see it as an opportunity for someone early in their development and aspiring to be a leader having access to a leader that they respect and admire. What I tell them is, 'I'm not teaching you. If you have a situation in your position and are a little bit unsure about it and want to run it by someone, that would be a mentoring opportunity.'"

The physician-turned-health-executive has found that downplaying the process of coaching removes the fear and anxiety for participants and works best when it's informal. "It makes it a two-way discussion on your experience and how you lead, what would you do and what have you done, with the understanding that there is no right or wrong answer."

So what exactly is coaching—and what isn't it? Coaching is:

- **A powerful conversation**. Coaching is a two-way communication in which the manager is there to help an employee become more successful in a given task or area, rather than a one-way discussion in which one party talks and the other listens.

- **Empowering.** Rather than just telling someone what to do, a coach in the workplace is driven by the determination to resolve a problem. Coaching is collaborative—and unlike the stereotype of the animated coach on the field, barking orders and encouragement or criticism at his players.
- **A mindset.** Coaching has evolved alongside the management style that went from strict command and control to a model that is more respectful and inclusive. Employees expect to be managed differently today, and coaching represents this more modern approach.
- **Creative.** Coaching is driven by the idea that if the parties get together and work on a problem, they will come up with more potential solutions than they would if the manager/coach simply imposed a solution.
- **Future-oriented.** Coaches ask what we can do today and tomorrow to improve an employee's capabilities.
- **Focused on improvement.** Coaching is capable of expanding people's capacity. Just as athletes, with proper coaching, should get better at their game over time, if a manager coaches employees regularly, they should become more autonomous or better at what they do.
- **A link between performance and development.** This is not an intellectual exercise: coaching isn't practiced in a vacuum; it is linked to the business by the ultimate goal of improving people's performance within the organization.

Coaching isn't:

- **Teaching.** Neither teaching nor training should be thought of as aspects of coaching. Take the example of coaching two salespeople to grow their business. Rather than teaching them theory or sales basics, a coach will have a collaborative discussion about various situations and strategies in order to come up with the right plan to grow the business. Coaching is a dialogue rather than a training session.
- **A pep talk.** There is nothing wrong with a pep talk, but coaching is not a one-time event intended to cheer up or motivate an employee. It is an inclusive, two-way process in which the assumption is that the employee has some of the answers that will lead to improved performance. He or she just needs the opportunity to bring them out through coaching.

- **Delegation.** There is nothing wrong with delegation. There is, however, a great difference between delegating a task and coaching an individual on how to be successful doing that task.
- **A performance review, progressive discipline or counseling.** Coaching brings with it a more positive outlook and dwells on future performance rather than past or current performance.

COACHING AND ACCOUNTABILITY

Coaching can be done for different reasons and at different moments. Sylvia Chrominska, former group head of Global Human Resources and Communications at Scotiabank, explains her point of view on the subject and describes the practices that have been put in place at the bank: "I would say that there is lots of confusion as to what is meant by coaching. There is coaching against your performance appraisal, coaching for results, and then there is coaching for developing leadership competencies. We strategically, a few years back, separated the development discussion from the performance appraisals discussion. Even though I have had a lot of pushback from the business line that this requires a lot more time on their part, I still think it was a smart decision."

"In the performance discussion," she continues, "what was happening is people were basically waiting for the bottom line: 'So how much are you going to pay me? What is my incentive, what is my rating?' I wanted to separate those and have the development discussion about how they can be a better leader, or how they can perform better. So I think with coaching a lot of people don't know what to say. I am always amazed that I get calls, even from senior people in the bank, saying, 'Well, I'm not sure this person needs some coaching; I am not really sure how to position that.' We identified that as something we needed to work on as an organization—as a core competency—and we have given courses and so forth, which I think has upped the profile of coaching, whether or not it has increased its effectiveness."

At the bank today, more leaders take part in regular coaching sessions and the development that goes hand in hand with it, says Chrominska. "People are doing what we asked them to do. Over several years we have asked people to take more accountability for their careers. With that has come an expectation that 'I want to sit down with you and have a conversation about what I need to do to advance in my career.' That is a good thing and has really, really changed in the banks."

EXECUTIVE, MANAGEMENT AND BUSINESS COACHING

One of the most succinct definitions of coaching that we have come across was written by the Madison Group's Jeff Matthews (2010). He writes: "Coaching is any conversation in which we support another in making progress towards a preferred future." Andrea D. Ellinger et al. (2011) offer a more encompassing definition that distances it from executive coaching:

> *"Coaching" is a helping and facilitative process that enables individuals, groups/teams and organisations to acquire new skills, to improve existing skills, competence and performance, and to enhance their personal effectiveness or personal development or personal growth. "Executive Coaching" is a process that primarily (but not exclusively) takes place within a one-to-one helping and facilitative relationship between a coach and an executive (or manager) that enables the executive (or manager) to achieve personal-, job- or organisational-related goals with an intention to improve organisational performance. "Business Coaching" is a collaborative process that helps businesses, owner/managers and employees achieve their personal and business related goals to ensure long term success.*

Put another way, the business coach, in most cases, is external to the organization, someone who is brought in by the organization to coach. In the case of managerial coaching, the manager has a vested interest in the outcome, improving the performance of the individuals who report to him or her. Simply put, the coach cannot win if the team does not win.

An obvious question you might have at this point is whether one type of coaching is better than the other. However, there is still very little research on the subject because coaching is a relatively new field of leadership development. The anecdotal evidence suggests that coaching is a powerful practice for development—and is behind the explosive growth of coaching generally. Figure 6.1 illustrates how coaching can be viewed along a spectrum of intensity.

Low Intensity _____ High Intensity

| Coaching in the moment | Performance management coaching | Developmental coaching | Career coaching | Mentoring |

Figure 6.1: Coaching Intensity

Coaching in the moment might be as simple as a discussion to solve a problem or issue, prompted by an employee coming into a manager's office with the problem. *Performance management coaching*, just as it sounds, is more performance-focused: "What can we do over the next six months to improve operations in the department?" *Developmental coaching* is often called "executive coaching." A certain range of competencies and behaviors is identified as either missing or in need of improvement, and the coach works with the leader to get to the level both expected and needed to perform effectively in the role. *Career coaching* can be seen from a career progression standpoint: "How can I grow to another, more progressive role in the organization?" *Mentoring* is more than coaching; it may involve the functional role of the coach, but mentoring has an important relationship aspect. Mentoring crosses job boundaries and is clearly future-oriented.

COACHING IN ACTION

Just as coaching can be a brief conversation or a formal, longer-term process, so too are there several types of coaching in action. It can be thought of as a short-, medium- or long-term commitment depending on the problem it is aimed at resolving, as follows:

- **Short-term coaching aimed at an immediate task.** For example, you initiate a coaching conversation with one of your employees in order to resolve a sensitive issue in a project he or she is leading.
- **Medium-term coaching aimed at an imminent task.** For example, you ask your manager if she'd be willing to coach you over the next few months on how to plan the upcoming marketing campaign, as it's the first time you've done this on your own.

- **Long-term career conversation.** For example, a colleague asks if he can spend an hour with you sometime in the next week to discuss his career development ideas. He trusts you, and coaching may offer the chance to consider additional ideas, test out his current thoughts and generate new options.

At the UK's Royal Mail, which is in the midst of the difficult process of shifting from the established mail delivery model to one that is based more on parcel and direct mail delivery, and from a public to private ownership model, coaching is being used to transform its rank and file. "We want to coach rather than just supervise workers," says John Duncan, Human Resources group director at Royal Mail. "We don't want them to be order takers, we want them to be innovators, to think about process and how work is organized, and improve upon it."

COACH OR REFEREE?

To be a successful business manager, you have to be both a coach and a referee. Like a referee, leaders are required to ensure that everyone respects the rules and regulations set out by their organization, government and industry. But being a referee is not enough. Referees do not help anyone to win—they are meant to be impartial. Their role is simply to ensure that the rules are being followed. Managers cannot worry only about whether their employees follow the rules. Although both coach and referee are important roles for managers, ideally they are more coach than referee.

THE COACHING PROCESS

At Global Knowledge, we encourage line managers to become better coaches for their direct reports, employees and colleagues. Coaching is a competency that we see gaining in popularity in modern organizations: increasingly, it is a competency that leaders are simply expected to possess. There are numerous reasons for this development, but one of them for sure is the complexity of work in the contemporary workplace. It is not uncommon now for a leader to have employees who possess knowledge or expertise in specific areas that exceeds their own. In these situations, the most effective way leaders can support their direct reports is not by telling them what to do but by coaching them to come up with the right solution or course of action. Employees expect to be more empowered today than ever, and their expectations, combined with the broad range of duties commonly assigned to leaders, are among the factors that are conducive to coaching. The years of "telling and dictating" are long gone; coaching is in!

The coaching model Global Knowledge uses to train coaches involves a four-step program. It calls for coaches to initiate, clarify, explore and act.

1. Initiate

Like a well-built house, a solid relationship needs a sturdy foundation. The building blocks of the relationship are trust and mutual respect. Creating an environment of trust and respect is not as easy as it may sound. It can almost feel like a first date, tentative and cautious, which isn't a bad way to look at the start of a successful coaching relationship. Both sides have to feel comfortable and be willing to take some time to ease into the process. For the coach, that means that timing is everything. It likely won't work when the other person is burdened with hectic month-end deadlines or is getting ready to go on vacation.

Presuming that you have identified a time when the other person is not snowed under with work or distracted, how do you approach him or her to get started? It may sound obvious—actually, most coaching is common sense when you get right down to it—but the would-be coach (or coaching subject) needs to approach the other person directly and bring up the topic, skill set or issue to be discussed, and determine if that person is willing to discuss it. That query coming from the coach could be something like: "I've been wondering how the new marketing project is going. Do you have time to talk about it right now, or do you want to set a time?"

From the subject's perspective, to open a coaching conversation, he or she might say something like: "You were district sales manager a couple years ago, and that position is open again. I'd like to apply for it but really wanted to know from you what's involved and whether I have what it takes."

With the topic broached, the person who brought up the coaching opportunity needs to "seal the deal" by gaining a commitment to proceed. This is when the person initiating the coaching lays out what is involved and tries to secure a verbal okay to go ahead. This step can be best carried out with questions that seek a definitive answer. For instance, a would-be coach might say, "So, you would like me to show you how you can try to reduce the turnover in your department?" or "This sounds pretty critical; can we pursue it in more detail?" Asking questions in such a way demonstrates to the other party that you take the problem or opportunity to be discussed seriously and prompts the other person to commit or consider committing to a coaching relationship.

2. Clarify

You have successfully broached the coaching topic and secured early commitment from the other person. Now is the time to ensure you have a firm grasp on just what has to be accomplished. That means not just listening to the other person's words but also trying to understand what emotions are behind them, by asking neutral questions and by being aware of your built-in biases and assumptions.

Listening—really listening, rather than simply waiting for your turn to talk—is the mark of a great communicator. It is also a critical skill for a world-class coach. A coach needs to intently listen to the person seeking coaching to get beyond the surface concern. Someone may ask for help or advice regarding a particular issue, but what he or she really needs is advice, understanding and assistance—coaching—on an underlying issue. So how do great coaches find those buried issues? By asking questions. Although it may seem counterintuitive that a good listener will ask more questions, it's actually not: you need to ask probing questions and listen intently to the responses in order to identify the source of a person's anxiety, problem or concern.

Three types of questions make up the tool kit of a great listener:

1. **Open-ended.** The open-ended question puts the onus on the other party to frame the information from the start. Examples of such questions are

"What do I need to know about the problem?" and "Can you outline the events that got us to this point?"

2. **Clarifying.** From there, clarifying or identifying questions allow the coach to explore the situation or find out how the person being coached understands it. These neutral questions typically explore a person's thinking or emotions—how deeply held their opinions and beliefs are. An example of a clarifying question is: "Do you mean that John isn't capable of handling the project, or is it the case that he just has too much on his plate right now?" Essentially, you are trying to get the other person to open up and tell you what is truly going on, rather than just what you might want to hear. Putting people on the defensive by asking aggressive questions or those aimed at apportioning blame and responsibility short-circuit the entire clarifying step by shutting down the flow of unfiltered information from the other person. "What do you think are the obstacles we need to overcome to resolve this situation?" is another example of a clarifying question.

3. **Confirming.** Finally, a confirming question can serve to ensure that you heard and understood what the other person said and believes, rather that filtering it through your assumptions to come up with a different view of the situation. An example of a confirming question is: "So it sounds like you are excited about the new position, but you are worried about how much more responsibility it entails, is that right?" Such a question sums up what you think you have heard from the other person and asks for confirmation that it's correct.

Active listeners—and active questioners—must remember that the person being coached needs to do most of the talking. Be patient: resist the urge to "jump to the end" and suggest a solution.

Check for built-in biases. We all carry with us a set of prejudices and assumptions. We all have our own particular set of beliefs about how things are supposed to go in the workplace. We need to identify these biases while coaching so that they don't obstruct what is being said, or block possible solutions or strategies. Coaches need to worry about two sets of biases: their own and those of the coaching subject. It would be great if both sides were aware of their biases, but at the end of the day it is the coach's job to identify them to ensure they are not limiting the coaching subject's progress. Examples of common unhelpful biases are: "If it works, don't fix it" and "It's the way we have always done it."

Like a workplace detective, the coach needs to uncover the other person's self-limiting biases in an effort to isolate them and let that person move beyond them. Rather than dismiss or challenge the biases directly, however, it's your job to get the other person thinking about them in the coaching process. Questions to examine biases might be: "You keep saying you will never get budget approval for the project. What are you basing that on?" and "What would be the best result for this situation?"

3. Explore
The exploration step rests on three key actions: reposition, identify alternatives and select alternatives.

- **Reposition.** At this point, the coach has heard the coaching subject's take on the problem, listened for built-in biases and prompted him or her to look at the issue in a new way. Repositioning is an attempt to get people past their built-in limits. When expressed, those limiting beliefs are often along the lines of: "You can't fight head office" or "It doesn't work, but that's the way we have always done it, so it's not going to change." The coach needs to show the person just how self-defeating such beliefs are. Surprisingly, questions rather than statements work best. An example of a repositioning question is: "That's one way to look at it; can you think of another way to tackle it?" It brings to mind a famous Winston Churchill quip: "The pessimist sees the difficulty in every opportunity. The optimist sees the opportunity in every difficulty."
- **Identify alternatives.** Up to now, we have been stressing how important it is to listen, but it is time to point out again that coaching is a two-way street and that good coaches need to not only jar people occasionally out of bad habits or viewpoints but also to help them come up with ways to get out of a dead-end situation. Some "out of left field" questions

often have the effect of prompting a person to start with a clean slate. Examples of left-field questions are: "If you were in charge, what would you do to resolve this?" and "What would an outside expert do if he or she were in your position?"

- **Select alternatives.** Now that you are near finding out what needs to happen to address the challenge or problem, it is time to think about any roadblocks or objections thrown up by the coaching subject. Chances are there are a few acceptable solutions to the problem, but as coach you should try to not impose a course of action to which the other person objects, but rather jointly select a path forward that the other person is comfortable with and will actually implement. The first option carries with it future conflict and likely failure. That does not mean following the path of least resistance. As a coach, you are helping to make a choice among alternatives, which means changing the way the person accomplishes or thinks about something in the workplace—not always an easy thing, even if it is the alternative the coaching subject has agreed with and helped select.

4. Act

By now you are probably saying to yourself, "Finally, about time we get down to doing something." The reality is that, as coach, you've been pretty active seeking, identifying and destroying dead-end biases and behaviors and setting the stage for meaningful change. So what happens in this final phase? Essentially, laying it all out and making everyone involved accountable for the final result by establishing next steps, establishing accountabilities and following up. This is the point where those involved summarize what has been done, come to agreement of who has to do what and determine the process to be carried out.

ESTABLISH NEXT STEPS

"Contracting" is coachspeak for getting agreement from those in a coaching situation about what steps have to be taken to create a mutually desired result. The contract—it doesn't have to be in writing—needs to cover what the coaching subject will do as he or she takes responsibility for improvement or change; what new behaviors or challenges are planned, such as going to a training session or seeking feedback from you the coach or from others; and, of course, outlining what you as coach has agreed to do to encourage and ensure the coaching subject's development.

ESTABLISH ACCOUNTABILITIES

Once the contract has been established, it is time to go over who has agreed to do what by when, as well as anything else that was agreed to or promised. It is also a time to review milestones and even a finish line, with answers to questions such as "How can we judge success?" and "How will you keep this going in the right direction?"

Finally, follow-up needs to be built into the coaching process to ensure that the person undergoing coaching has followed through with the next steps agreed to. If those next steps have not been taken, it does not necessarily mean the process has failed. Rather, the question needs to be asked whether something has disrupted the process or the goals were too ambitious. If, however, the coaching subject displays a lack of buy-in and resists taking accountability for required achievements, coaching at this point may move to performance management and setting out the consequences of not achieving what has been agreed upon.

As people increasingly adopt a coaching mindset and use the skill sets of the coaching process, a more collaborative, supportive, trusting and creative workplace will be created.

WHAT THE EXPERTS SAY

Leader Development

D.C. McCauley (2008) suggests that executive coaching is the fastest-growing leader development method. Based on a review of the studies, she identifies three key elements of executive coaching:

1. One-on-one counseling about work-related issues
2. Use of 360-degree assessments on strengths and weaknesses
3. A goal to improving the manager's functioning in his or her current position

McCauley reports that studies of the impact of coaching found that clients who used coaching were more focused in forming developmental goals and more successful in achieving their goals, and that their new behaviors were more closely related to their roles as managers and leaders. The author suggests that organizations would benefit from additional research topics on coaching, including:

- The relative effectiveness of different approaches to coaching (psychodynamic, behaviorist, cognitive therapy, person-centered) and of different kinds of relationships (internal coaches vs. external coaches, employed by executive vs. employed by organization)
- The patterns of coaching behaviors that are most helpful to clients
- The development of positive coaching-client relationships
- The organizational processes for choosing coaches, matching coaches with leaders, setting expectations, and so on

McCauley reports that research is lacking in the area of mentoring. She reports that there is sufficient evidence to suggest that mentoring improves leaders' cognitive, skill-based and affective learning, as well as organizational and technical knowledge; interpersonal, time management and self-management skills; and self-confidence. The author points to a recent study (Finkelstein and Poteet, 2007) that reviewed mentoring-program best-practice recommendations and raised certain questions that are worth addressing in mentorship research or practice:

- How much organizational support is minimally necessary for a program to be successful?
- What level of participation in the mentor-protégé matching process is most desirable? That is, to what degree should the mentor and the protégé be involved in selecting each other?
- What matching characteristics are more or less important?
- How does mentor-protégé similarity and dissimilarity impact the outcomes of the relationship?
- What kind of training do mentoring-program participants need?

McCauley reports that two methodologies, the systematic use of developmental assignments and the fostering of leader networks and communities, are being used in practice but that there is very little research available to assess the impact of these methods. The author summarizes several recommendations in terms of leadership development methodology research, including:

- Online delivery of program content to e-coaching, e-mentoring and virtual networks
- Impact of societal beliefs and norms in development methods
- More theory-driven research on developmental methodologies that elevate knowledge beyond "what works" to "why it works"
- Understanding ways in which organization context influences the impact of leader development interventions

On Coaching

Longenecker and Neubert (2005) engaged forty-five focus groups consisting of 225 middle managers from more than twenty U.S. organizations to explore the issue of managerial coaching and its implications for organizations and individual managers.

They found that the things that make for a great coaching relationship are pretty obvious, but that there are also key intangibles that make these relationships hard to patent or duplicate without great care, caring and commitment. Beyond the benefits of coaching, our research invited managers to answer the practical question of which practices are most important for coaching to be an effective performance-enhancing tool. There was an obvious passion and excitement among the managers in sharing their experiences about how to coach effectively. Most managers had a mix of positive and negative coaching experiences, including occasional horror stories involving coaching mistakes and what can happen without effective coaching. In addition, participants exhibited self-admonition, which suggests they believed they had room for improvement themselves in the coaching area. Finally, the focus groups generated extremely strong consensus on the practices discussed below.

Key Practice 1: Effective managerial coaches will clarify the results/performance outcomes that are truly needed or desired from junior managers

Today's managers are commonly caught up in myriad competing demands and pressures, many of which are presented in a crisis mode requiring immediate attention. In this environment, important individual and organizational outcomes/results can be obscured or lost in the management of daily short-term activities. Good managerial coaches assist managers in clarifying the results and outcomes that are needed to support both the organization and their own career success. Although most managers are very busy, the real question is: Busy doing what, and with what end in mind?

The first responsibility of a managerial coach is to help a junior manager clarify and define the results he or she is ultimately trying to achieve, and how these will add value to the organization.

Key Practice 2: Effective managerial coaches provide honest, ongoing, balanced performance feedback to junior managers

It is common for managers to receive occasional comments such as "Good going," "Nice work" and "Keep up the good job." While appreciated, these vague comments are of limited value in providing the kind of feedback managers can use to make adjustments or reinforce specific behaviors or activities. Managers in Longenecker and Neubert's study clearly indicated they want more from supervising managers—specific, ongoing feedback that includes detailed comments about current projects, performance metrics and management style, as well as about broader individual developmental issues. Adding feedback to performance goals can result in a dramatic increase in performance (Neubert 1998). Effective coaches should provide both specific and usable feedback for the continuous improvement of their subordinate managers. In other words, when a learner is performing on the job, he or she needs structured and timely feedback to accelerate the learning process (Caproni 2001).

Key Practice 3: Effective managerial coaches know how well subordinate managers are actually performing

Managers suggested they sometimes weren't coached because their superiors didn't always know the specific and current details of their performance. Often, managers are left to handle workplace issues with little input or direction from outside or superior sources. Sometimes, this is a very good approach, as it allows subordinate managers to have relative freedom and responsibility in handling their daily operations and can help them grow and develop. However, when it's taken to an extreme, managers can find themselves without a reliable, detailed source of performance information, short of their own limited interpretation or understanding. Managers seek accurate performance feedback that is based on their actual performance results, not on "educated guesses" or conjecture on the part of their superiors.

The practices of effective managerial coaches can reduce this problem through monitoring managerial performance on a regular basis and collecting not just detailed information on global performance metrics/outcomes but also information from peers, employees, customers and other sources. This allows the superior to coach the junior manager using accurate and timely information and to modify performance before it becomes ingrained behavior or more significant problems arise.

Key Practice 4: Effective managerial coaches understand the junior manager's strengths and weaknesses

Managers are hired based on their technical and management competencies, with the assumption that future development will likely be required. While managers were quick to point out they all had strengths they utilized to drive their performance, they also admitted having real concerns about weaknesses that might destroy or undermine their careers. Effective coaches work with junior managers to assess the strengths and weaknesses of skills, with the focus on long-term career development.

Good coaches help junior managers think in terms of matches between their knowledge, skills and values and their projected career paths within the organization, suggesting alternative career tracks when necessary.

Key Practice 5: Effective managerial coaches provide expert advice on how to improve performance

When junior managers are told their performance needs improvement, they are often left on their own to determine what they need to do to improve. In this sense, superiors are doing only half of the coaching job in that they are providing the junior manager with feedback that things need to change but stop short of providing guidance about *how* to change. That is, the missing piece in many managerial coaching relationships is specific advice. In today's complex organizational structures, managers frequently supervise people whose jobs they do not fully understand.

This suggests superiors need to draw upon resources outside themselves to help develop an improvement plan and provide the contacts and resources junior managers need. A senior manager who is truly interested in performance improvement will not only assist the junior manager in developing a detailed improvement plan but will also be committed to providing the necessary information and input from the most appropriate human resources, even if it entails going outside the organization to get it. Further, an effective coach will ensure that any coaching process is more than a one-time affair, and that it involves the coach witnessing attempts to practice new knowledge and skills, and providing immediate feedback and reinforcement.

Key Practice 6: Effective coaches develop a working relationship based on mutual benefit and trust

A senior manager should have every incentive to be an effective coach, as both subordinate and superior can benefit from increased high performance. When the junior manager does well, it should make the senior manager's job and life at work easier. Mistakes and performance shortcomings are opportunities to teach more effective behaviors to junior managers. This time investment in coaching will be rewarded in improved performance, which allows the superior to devote less time to monitoring and more time to the specific challenges he or she faces as a senior manager.

Managers emphasized that a climate of openness and trust is vital to a successful coaching relationship. Alternatively, a superior-subordinate relationship (Longenecker and Neubert 2005) characterized by fear will drive junior managers to hide mistakes and withhold information. This creates an anxious performance mindset that reinforces short-term performance and minimal compliance, rather than a mastery orientation that contributes to the development of expertise and encourages innovation (Janssen and Van Yperen 2004). A mutually beneficial relationship is based on openness and trust and encourages the learning and mastery that precedes performance excellence. Effective coaches recognize that their own performance is intertwined with the performance capability, or lack thereof, of their subordinates.

Key Practice 7: Effective managerial coaches understand the context, pressures and demands of the junior manager's job

As senior members of management, coaches should fully understand the organizational pressures and demands required of junior managers. Benefits are twofold. First, the senior manager can have a real sense of what the junior manager is up against on a daily basis, allowing the senior manager to understand the context, pressure and demands of the junior manager's job. A failure to understand the work context is likely to contribute to supervisors falling prey to the fundamental error of attributing performance problems to personal causes, instead of to causes in the work context.

Second, an accurate diagnosis of the context provides a coach with the appropriate prescriptions for personal development and interventions in the work context. Effective coaches need to understand the work context and to use this knowledge to help the subordinate focus efforts and energies in a strategic manner, given organizational constraints and challenges. Junior managers also need coaches who will bring their influence to bear upon improving or removing causes of poor performance in the work environment.

Key Practice 8: Effective managerial coaches support problem solving

There are times when even the most effective manager could use supervisory assistance to solve a problem, resolve a conflict or remove a performance barrier. These conflicts and challenges are often political, in need of senior-level power and maneuvering to resolve (Pfeffer 1992). Senior managers have an understanding of how things get done that is not written down and that junior managers have yet to experience. In many cases, the political challenges of the work environment are beyond the scope of the subordinates' expertise and control. These problems are resolved only when a senior manager takes action.

Key Practice 9: Effective managerial coaches help junior managers prioritize and manage conflicting goals

In some cases, a junior manager is tugged in opposing directions by different managers or differing sets of goals. Although the research is clear that specific and challenging goals increase effort and promote performance (Locke and Latham 1990), goals are not always aligned with organizational objectives. Thus, senior managers must help junior managers prioritize goals. In the absence of such help, junior managers can be immobilized by conflicting goals or too many to accomplish in a limited amount of time. Not only do coaches need to establish the priority of various goals, they also must explain the reasons for such priorities.

A common mistake for senior managers who employ goal setting is to assume that once goals and priorities are established, their task is finished. Instead, coaches need to make goals and priorities a frequent focal point of their conversations with junior managers. Junior managers, without continual reminders of priorities, can be drawn away by the tyranny of urgent demands and trivial concerns of fellow employees or their own subordinates. Without clear priorities, it doesn't take much for junior managers to run themselves ragged without contributing to the most significant goals and responsibilities of their position.

Key Practice 10: Effective managerial coaches create accountability for real performance improvement

An important tool in coaching is a mutually agreed-upon action plan. A participative approach to developing an action plan incorporates the expertise and ideas of both the senior and junior managers and fosters commitment to its implementation. An effective action plan contains specific, measurable, attainable and organizationally relevant goals, and a timetable for attainment. Goals that are measurable and linked to clear timelines provide accountability that otherwise is not inherent in goal setting.

Measurability also makes it possible to assess progress toward the goal. Effective coaches work with junior managers to monitor and assess progress before their performance is called into account. Intentional efforts to assess progress prior to performance evaluation also provide opportunities for the senior and junior managers to work collaboratively to adjust tactics to fit new circumstances, or adjust timelines or even goals. A mutually agreed-upon action plan is vital to effective and clear communication in the coaching process.

Motivate for Full Engagement

> If your actions inspire others to dream more, learn more,
> do more and become more, you are a leader.
>
> —John Quincy Adams

As a leader, how can you identify actions that motivate you and others, and enable everyone to fully engage in his or her work and achieve results? The sea change that is now occurring thanks to the aging, about-to-retire cohort of baby boomers will continue to shake the foundations of the workplace. While jobs-for-life disappeared decades ago, the idea of taking on a job simply to pay the bills will also increasingly look like an anachronism for the generations that are following the boomers.

Increasingly, people today are seeking roles in organizations from which they will obtain fulfillment and other rewards beyond the financial realm. It's not just common sense: reams of research have shown that highly motivated employees are the most fully engaged and productive people in any organization. Motivated employees are not only engaged, they are firmly connected with the organization, and buy in to the idea that their personal success and that of the organization are connected rather than independent.

An example of an organization that has put this concept into action is The Ottawa Hospital, which has worked to ensure that its "You're in Our Care" campaign is not simply an empty slogan. "We make sure that everybody at the hospital understands their value and what they need to do to bring our vision to reality," says CEO Jack Kitts. "If our employees don't think that they are valued in their role, then they are not engaged, and we are not going to get there."

The challenge for leaders, therefore, is to develop and encourage motivation in employees. It's not an easy thing to do considering the many drivers and drivers' ambitions that characterize the individuals within any organization. But the rewards can be so great that leaders cannot afford to pass up the opportunity to be great motivators.

So let's first of all take the mystery out of motivation.

The first and easiest way to tackle this question is to consider what motivates you. Think of a time in your work life when you were highly motivated. Or, perhaps, recall a time when you found yourself working alongside someone who was highly motivated. Chances are that you were (or your close coworker was) presented with a task or project that fit in a particular sweet spot, matching your skill set or ambition. It could have been something you already did well or enjoyed doing (it likely didn't involve filing!), that allowed you to hone skills or learn something new, that presented you with the freedoms to exercise your abilities or that gave you a chance to shine while benefiting your close coworkers or your department, or contributing to the organization's success.

You were given a stage, in other words, on which to perform at something you were good at, or likely to excel at and grow, and the stakes were important and measureable. It also brought with it the emotions we associate with motivation: excitement, enthusiasm, perhaps anticipation. You were charged up and eager to carry out the task. Contrast that with a project you dread, which would be characterized by procrastination or avoidance. Taken to the leadership role, a demotivated leader or negative leader will have a tremendous negative impact on the team or department.

The capacity to motivate is a key component in a successful leader's makeup. It drives how you function as a leader and how you demonstrate your leadership to those around you. Leaders need to reference their own motivation and what motivates others constantly. However, it is necessary to start with an understanding of what drives motivation.

Research, particularly in the field of psychology, has found that there are two well-known sources of motivation: extrinsic, or external, and intrinsic, or internal. It sounds obvious and commonsensical, and to an extent it is, but let's go through it.

In the case of *extrinsic* motivation, you do something because of the external rewards or benefits that come with it, or, conversely, you are motivated by the costs or consequences that come with not doing it. Extrinsic motivators are the types of rewards people most associate with the working world: a salary, bonuses, social benefits, awards, even praise from superiors and colleagues. They are concrete, most often measureable in some way and—bottom line—are the main reasons people get out of bed every morning and head off to work. We all need to eat and pay the mortgage and have a fulfilling career so, really, what else could there be to motivate us?

It turns out that extrinsic motivators are only part of the equation.

It is true that concrete rewards such as monetary compensation and benefits, as well as workplace recognition, need to be at a certain level to sustain motivation. If they are inadequate, logically, motivation will be too. One thinks of the old Russian joke: "They pretend to pay us, we pretend to work"!

An organization that focuses exclusively on extrinsic motivators risks creating unintended and negative consequences, such as establishing a workplace culture of entitlement and comfort, dampening creativity (why rock the boat with new ideas?) and reducing productivity over the long term. An example that often springs to mind is high-pressure, high-paying occupations in finance where the financial rewards may be considerable but the costs of "coloring outside the lines" are so great the people are inclined to do what they are told. They are not creative and, most likely, they aren't that happy to go into the office each day. In such cases, extrinsic motivators, rather than driving preferred behaviors, end up inhibiting them.

An *intrinsic* motivator comes from inside the individual. People who are intrinsically motivated carry out a task (or hobby) because they want to. The benefits in the form of enjoyment, learning and satisfaction from a job well done come from actually carrying out the task. What is unique about intrinsic motivation is that people have it in unlimited supply (unlike, say, money) and it is not dependent on outside factors such as an organization's rules and policies or on interactions with others. It is there to be tapped and harnessed within every person in the workplace.

As with much of the theory and research in the leadership field, the thinking on motivation is changing. In the "old days," motivation was pretty simple. Rewards were offered for good or approved performance, whereas punishment was meted out for work that was subpar. This was essentially the carrot-and-stick approach to motivation.

More recently, companies and leaders have come to recognize that the relied-upon extrinsic motivators are not good enough to move an individual's motivation needle over the long term. Organizations increasingly rely on intrinsic motivators because the old reward system simply fails to achieve the desired results. A good example can be found in automotive manufacturing, perhaps the clearest example of a business where extrinsic motivators once were relied on to attract and motivate workers. Stretching back to the pioneering days of Henry Ford, when workers were paid an unheard of wage of five dollars a day, financial rewards were seen as critical to keep people in boring assembly-line jobs, carrying out the same task hundreds or thousands of times a day. Automakers are still around today, and the jobs workers do are not much different. What has changed is that a considerable effort now is made to shake up the routine by having workers rotate into new or different tasks, or assume more challenging problem-solving and product-quality responsibilities. Leaders in the auto-manufacturing business realized that rich monetary (extrinsic) rewards were not enough. Smart leaders need to tap into intrinsic motivators.

At Global Knowledge, we focus on four key drivers of motivation: autonomy, mastery, purpose and self-expression. The first three, autonomy, mastery and purpose, were identified by author and researcher Daniel Pink in his bestselling 2009 book *Drive: The Surprising Truth about What Motivates Us*. Self-expression, the fourth driver, is an inner motivation that our research tells us is also critical. Let's take a closer look:

- **Autonomy.** It is a natural impulse of individuals to seek autonomy in the workplace. That is not to say that people want to work alone or do everything by themselves, but rather that they desire the ability to set their own direction or have some say in what they do and how they do it.

- **Mastery.** This refers to a person's inner drive to continually get better at something that matters to him or her. In the process of acquiring mastery, individuals seek to align the level and type of work they do with their abilities and interests. Daniel Pink (2009) writes of the three laws of mastery: "First, you have to believe in your own potential and capability to develop, grow and improve. Second, striving for mastery requires grit and determination to overcome obstacles, and the persistence to keep going when things get difficult. Third, mastery can never be fully achieved. The process of pursuing mastery is what motivates us, rather than its achievement."

- **Purpose.** Everyone wants the work he or she does to make a difference. More concretely, individuals increasingly want to work in companies or organizations that they view as attempting to make the world a better place—an organization they are proud to tell friends and family that they work for. That's why those annual lists of "most admired" workplaces are so avidly followed by job seekers and why organizations try so hard to get listed on them.

- **Self-expression.** It may sound odd, but people increasingly want to feel that they can be themselves at work, rather than having to wear a mask or alternative identity from Monday to Friday. Self-expression is made possible when individuals have the environment and ability to express their personalities, feelings and ideas in their work. This is much more than just putting up pictures of friends and family or favorite comic strips on cubicle walls. It is the ability of people to show their true selves and do what they do best instead of conforming and submerging their personalities to fit in with the organization's expectations and ideals. Because work today has become such a large part of an individual's makeup, people are less likely to be willing to give up their individuality and true character for a paycheck. Perhaps not surprisingly, people feel most motivated when they can reveal their true selves and utilize their unique skills and gifts at work.

The better the fit or match between the individual's personality, and likes and dislikes, and the job content and work environment, the better the possibility for self-expression. For example, a person may love the job but hate the company, not get along with close colleagues or clash with the overall organizational culture.

Beyond these factors, other potential motivation drivers are the organization, the employee him- or herself, the immediate manager, colleagues and clients.

- **The organization.** Let's start with the organization. Is the company offering systems to encourage learning and development, a positive and supportive work environment, the workplace trappings and unique characteristics (often hard for individuals to discern but that make them say, "This is a good/bad place to work")? Increasingly, companies are seeking to reach out to their communities and charitable organizations to support worthwhile projects big and small, or to give their employees paid time off to do charitable work for deserving causes and charities of their choosing. Part of that is a desire on the part of management to be good corporate citizens, but it is also a recognition that they need to foster an environment that employees are proud to work in.

THE CARING ORGANIZATION

Four Seasons Hotels founder Isadore "Issy" Sharp was the first prominent Canadian businessman to support Terry Fox during the darkest days of his 1980 run across Canada to raise money for cancer research. The hotelier helped start the annual Terry Fox Run and challenged fellow business leaders to raise money and support the cause, as well as motivated and engaged his Four Seasons employees through the company's support. Sharp's early recognition and support of Terry Fox and his efforts spearheading the annual run following Fox's death has proved to be a source of pride, engagement and motivation for employees of Four Seasons Hotels.

- **The employee.** The employee is also a potential factor. The organization may decide to put an individual in a particular position, but is it a good fit? Often when people jump from job to job and organization to organization, it is a case of the employees saying yes to a new position without asking themselves the obvious question: "Am I the right person for this job or company?" or "Is this the sort of position I will excel in or be happy in?"

- **The immediate manager.** It sounds obvious, but if the manager is not engaged or motivated, this attitude will quickly trickle down to his or her subordinates. Children often imitate the behaviors, good and bad, of their parents, without the parents consciously realizing that they are passing their attitudes, prejudices, and motivators and demotivators on to their kids. The same sort of unconscious mimicry occurs in organizations where we often, when conducting diagnostic study, see similar behavior from the top on down to the lower ranks.
- **Colleagues.** In today's workplace, there are few jobs that do not involve collaboration with colleagues. Teams, special projects and meetings are a reality of today's workplace. Just as an individual's direct superior (and other management) has an impact on that person's motivation and engagement, so too do peers and others who work alongside him or her.
- **Clients.** While it is true that most employees in an organization will not deal directly with customers, many have internal customers in the form of other departments that they regularly deal with and provide services to. For example, Finance and Accounting do not deal with customers but interact with individuals in virtually every other department within the organization. All these relationships impact the day-to-day experience at work. When people are in the right job, we often hear them say, "The clients are the best part of my work." This is where they get pleasure and rewards from their work.

MOTIVATION LESSONS FOR LEADERS

Whether you lead a department, a small team or even a special project, you as leader represent and reflect the organization. In this role, you need to inspire confidence that the organization can reach its objectives.

A leader also needs to demonstrate respect and recognition for subordinates. This is a point we stress again and again at Global Knowledge when we conduct leadership training: it's a day-to-day activity. Are daily communications with employees respectful? As a leader do you maintain subordinates' self-esteem? When it comes to recognition, it is often said that talk is cheap. Well, so is verbal recognition. The difference is that an occasional approving or admiring comment works. Most of the time it costs nothing to say, "Well done" or "Thanks for staying late." Some leaders might say it's all just part of the job—they believe that extra effort does not need to be overtly noticed or explicitly praised. But there is nothing lost when an employee is given encouragement, and potentially much will be gained.

As well as providing recognition, great leaders provide feedback to employees about what they can improve or do better or modify. Very often in surveys, employees complain that they do not receive feedback, either in formal reviews or in more casual discussions with their superiors. Compare that situation to the not-so-much-like-work worlds of professional sports, dance or arts, where performance can be measured by scores, awards and the most immediate feedback, applause.

In an effort to ensure that employees are motivated, a good leader will also ensure that job roles meet the expectations and skills of the employee. So if the leader hires an individual or moves him or her to a new position, the manager needs to ensure that it is a role with job content that will motivate that person.

An individual can also be the right fit, in the right job and in the right organization, but grow stale and under-challenged simply through having done the job too long. Forward-thinking leaders look for opportunities to take those highly skilled but not particularly challenged employees out of this work cocoon by engaging them in special projects or teams to engage and motivate them.

Workplace personality assessment expert Robert Hogan has long argued that employee engagement needs to be carefully tracked and measured by employers, calling it "the best predictor of organizational outcomes such as turnover, productivity and customer satisfaction."

The key to becoming an effective, even great, motivational leader is pretty much the same as what your mother told you when you were young: treat others the way that you would want to be treated. Leaders who treat their employees with respect and honesty, and provide recognition, feedback and attention to their needs will reap the rewards: an engaged workforce. As critical as the role of the leader is on employee motivation, we can't ignore the organizational level and the match between job content in relation to the personal employee preference.

UNLEASHING THE POWER OF GEN-X LEADERS

Much of the attention among employers has focused, perhaps deservedly, on the impact of the eventual retirement of the baby boomer generation from the workforce, but that departure cannot happen soon enough for Generation X. The follow-on generation to the boomers, born between 1964 and 1979 in Canada (the years differ slightly in other developed countries), often consider themselves blocked from key leadership roles by their older colleagues. At the same time, Millennials or Gen Ys, born between 1981 and 1994 and the children of the boomers, are large in numbers and typically new entrants to the workforce, or have returned to school because of limited job opportunities.

Marguerite Thompson-O'Neal (2012) has written about this generational conflict in the workforce, focusing primarily on how to motivate Gen-Xers, sandwiched as they are between two dynamic generations. She concludes that employers must embrace an intergenerational succession management framework to motivate Generation X and Y employees. (See Table 7.1.) Gen-Xers typically desire access to positions that allow for career progression, welcome change and competition and value achievement more than their boomer colleagues. Millennials generally want careers that are flexible and foster independence and creativity, while fulfilling their need for freedom. (See Table 7.2.)

With a particular focus on the motivations of Generation X, Thompson-O'Neal recommends five actions organizations take to engage Gen-X leaders:

1. Leverage and celebrate their individualism and strong interest in making a contribution to the organization and society.
2. Promote them relatively early in their career and let them design a job that gives them work-life balance.
3. Help them make peace with boomer colleagues. Discuss openly the perception of unfairness, and encourage them to look at what can be done, instead of dwelling on the downside of the situation.
4. Overcome their lukewarm interest in managing the work of others. Leading employees is not for all Gen-Xers, but certainly some will respond positively to encouragement and coaching on how Gen-Xers can lead others differently and more effectively than their boomer colleagues.

Table 7.1: Personal Values, Work Values and Definition of Career Success by Generation

Generation	Personal Values	Work Values	Definition of Career Success
Baby boomers (born 1946–63)	Value lifelong learning. Tend to use economic power and influence to initiate change.	Job security most impor- tant. Tend to view work as central to life. Driven and willing to go the extra mile.	Career advancement
Gen-Xers (born 1964–79)	Value time for family and leisure and to participate in community activities and education. High learning orientation.	Job security most important. Also value meaningful work, enjoy- ment of job and a sense of accomplishment. Continually evolving and growing. Some are adaptable and globally mobile. Seen as influenc- ers who are concerned with having an impact on their organizations.	Career security
Millennials or Gen-Ys (born 1980–94)	Tend to reject politics and "rite of passage" to participate in decision mak- ing. Skeptical of long-term com- mitments; prefer collective action, team work.	Value transparency, rela- tionships, authenticity, job security (surprisingly yes), sustainability and 24/7 work availability, with technology to sup- port it. Value on-the-job learning, such as mentor relationships with expe- rienced colleagues. Enjoy working in teams.	Career experiences

Table 7.2: Leadership Preferences by Generation

Generation	Preferred Leadership Actions
Baby boomers (born 1946–63)	Job security; opportunities for free agency; status recognition. Baby boomers desire promotion into positions, offices and situations that mark their status in the organization and society.
Gen-Xers (born 1964–79)	Quick promotion. They desire access to positions that allow for career progression with increased responsibility and respect from other professionals, as well as "adequate" compensation to enable a comfortable lifestyle. Recognition of education and experience. Opportunities on the job to build career security and include special assignments, control over schedules and up-to-date technology. Flexibility in work-at-home options.
Millennials or Gen-Ys (born 1980–94)	Flexible and supportive leadership. They value transparency, relationships and authenticity. They desire 24/7 work options with technology to support it; expect flexibility in work-at-home options. Arrange networked learning and on-the-job learning, especially mentoring from an experienced colleague. Reward merit rather than participation.

5. Tell the organization how important Gen-Xers are to its future. Soon they will be the successors of the boomers; organizations' leaders need to recognize the inevitability of this development and share the issues it entails openly.

WHAT THE EXPERTS SAY
Motivate for Full Engagement
Dent and Holton (2009) reported on results of a survey conducted at Ashridge Business School in the UK related to what employees say about motivators and demotivators at work. In addition, the authors introduced

a relational model of motivation they argue supports twenty-first-century working. Survey respondents identified intrinsic motivators rather than extrinsic ones as the most important, with the most important motivators being the need for work to be challenging, interesting and valued by the organization. They report that the survey identifies the following themes about what managers say is important for motivation:

1. Celebration of success, praise and recognition from their line managers
2. Autonomy and freedom in carrying out work and making decisions about how to deliver the task
3. Being trusted to "get the job done" without being micromanaged
4. Communication from managers of a shared vision and objectives

The survey identifies a number of demotivators, including:

1. Not being valued or given feedback
2. Micromanagement, faint praise and intellectual property theft
3. Organizational tolerance of poor performance

Dent and Holton reported that the survey recognizes five key entities important for motivational success:

1. The organization
2. The individual
3. The boss
4. Colleagues
5. Clients

The findings identify the organization as providing the structures and processes necessary for employee motivation (performance management, reward systems, training and interesting work), supported by a clear vision, effective decision making and communication and a respectful organizational culture. In terms of the individual, the survey found that organizations would be advised to encourage individuals to take responsibility for their own development and motivation, and also provide them opportunities to share their thoughts and ideas with colleagues and bosses. The survey identifies the importance of the boss as a role model and as engaging each of the team members in a conversation about their individual motivators. A positive working relationship between and among colleagues was recognized as another key motivator in terms of getting good feedback and energy from one another. The survey found that eliciting feedback from clients and sharing this information with staff provided opportunities for motivation. The authors summarize their review of the findings by identifying the following as keys to successful motivation:

1. Formal processes that involve communication of effective employee engagement practices
2. Clear support, commitment and involvement from top-level management
3. Creative reward systems
4. Learning and development opportunities
5. Coaching and support for new managers, especially for those who take over demotivated teams
6. Measurements of motivation and engagement levels, as indicated by staff turnover, response rates to opinion surveys, and so on

Does Money Motivate?

Money—perhaps surprisingly—is not regarded as an effective motivator. It is commonly understood that a lack of fairness in distributing financial rewards can undermine a commitment to work, but adequate financial rewards alone are not sufficient to generate motivation, hence the necessity to look at intrinsic motivators. The impact of money on motivation has always been controversial, and the subject has generated intense debate, most of it informed by personal and managerial experience rather than objective research. Jean Archambault (2013) is exceptional in this respect. In his doctoral thesis in finance on the impact of personal investment and emotional commitment on the success of small to medium enterprises, Archambault obtained data by analyzing 239 investment files of a highly recognized venture capital firm in Canada. Some of his conclusions follow:

1. Risk modeling does not allow us to accurately predict the future success of organizations.

2. Modeling the dependence is a key element when it comes to measuring the risks.

3. In attempting to model the risk by seeking correlations between variables and underlying performance, we have found that out of sixteen qualitative elements most venture capital firms consider when analyzing a given transaction, eleven are highly correlated to the performance of that file, another two are correlated per se and three are not linearly correlated.

4. This predictive value of highly correlated files are concentrated in the management family of the very qualitative data (including market, product/service, financial structure and profitability).

5. Out of this "very qualitative" data, the number one correlation is between the commitment and the financial involvement of the management team.

6. The results are confirming mathematically that the financial involvement and the emotional involvement is a source of motivation and commitment for the leaders.

7. The reason for this correlation? Knowing that in most small and medium enterprises in Canada, the pension fund of the leaders is embedded in the company they manage, it is intuitively conceivable that their motivation is highly related to the success of the company they manage.

8. It is now mathematically proven that this relationship is real and linearly correlated to the return when analyzing a potential investment by a venture capital firm.

Leadership and Employee Engagement

As the founder and executive director of the Kenexa Research Institute, W.J. Wiley is internationally known for his research linking employee survey results to measures of customer satisfaction and business performance. Wiley (2010) reports on the analysis of a 2010 annual, 115-item survey by 29,338 workers across more than twenty countries (controlling for industry, job type and gender) of their overall opinions of their companies, in particular their engagement levels and what drives engagement. The author defines employment engagement as "the extent to which employees are motivated to contribute to organizational success, and are willing to demonstrate commitment, loyalty, and willingness to go beyond basic requirements to accomplish tasks and organizational goals." He argues that a motivated workforce is critical in both good and bad times, noting that even when times are good and organizations are not faced with challenging economic conditions, high levels of engagement need to be maintained in order to retain the best talent. Wiley identifies several leadership behaviors that support employee engagement:

1. Inspiring confidence in the future of the organization and, in turn, minimizing employee perceptions of uncertainty.
2. Demonstrating respect and recognition for employees through praise for a job well done, valuing of their opinions and encouraging their input into decisions.
3. Aligning individuals in positions that they are interested in and excited about, which affords them the opportunities to really develop their competencies and be proud of what is being accomplished.

Based on the assumption that effective employee engagement is grounded in senior leadership effectiveness, the survey measures the perceptions of employees as to the effectiveness of their senior leaders. Globally, 55 percent of employees found their senior leaders to be effective. Among country comparisons, the survey shows India (72 percent), China (71 percent) and Switzerland (63 percent) having the highest ratings, while Japan has the lowest (35 percent) and the U.S. rating is just above the global rating (56 percent). Wiley concludes by pointing out several worker-perceived effective leader traits that he argues drive high levels of employee engagement. They include:

- The capacity to be innovative and demonstrate a sense of urgency
- Recognition of quality service as a vital component of customer satisfaction, retention, and financial growth
- Communication of a clear picture of the direction in which the company is headed, reducing uncertainty and helping employees find meaning in the work they do
- Adoption of a multistakeholder approach that ensures a common understanding of a shared goal

- The ability to inspire confidence by defining clear expectations and holding managers accountable for their actions

Wiley notes that employees who understand where they are expected to focus their time are more likely to achieve desired results and that creating a culture of accountability involves both rewarding employees for their contributions and taking action when employees fall short of expectations.

Wallace and Trinka (2009) review current research on what drives employee engagement and, in turn, its effect on productivity. The authors argue that the leadership of the immediate manager is more important than any other organizational variable in driving employee engagement and organizational performance. Wallace and Trinka report on some startling statistics related to employee engagement and financial cost of disengagement. Their research indicates that about 20 percent of the U.S. workforce may be actively disengaged and that the Gallup organization estimates the cost of disengaged workers at more than $300 billion a year in lost productivity. The authors report on their own research (2007) on leadership competencies of top-performing managers and engagement of their work teams that found specific and significant increases in the following areas:

- 39 percent more employee retention
- 37.2 percent increased employee satisfaction
- 29.4 percent additional organizational commitment
- 13.8 percent greater discretionary effort by the employee

The authors argue that there is no secret or magic solution to what leader competencies drive the highest levels of employee engagement, indicating that it comes down to a few vital competencies, including:

1. Coaching performance
2. Developing careers
3. Communicating the meaning in an employee's work

In terms of coaching, Wallace and Trinka (2009) report on research data produced by the international consulting firm BlessingWhite that indicates that only one of every two employees believes they get coaching, and of those that do get coaching, 87 percent appreciate the attention and believe their performance improved from it. This same research points out that top-performing leaders in the private sector spend close to 20 percent of their time coaching. The authors cite other recent research that found that whereas the ratio of positive comments (approval, suggestions, praise, appreciation, compliments) to negative comments (disapproval, pointing out faults, criticism) is about one to three in low-performing organizations, with leaders of high-performing teams it's five to one. Wallace and Trinka argue that, coached effectively, managers can be taught how to provide authentic appreciation for employee contributions in about thirty minutes. In terms of developing careers, the authors emphasize that managers who consistently develop and use a career learning plan for each employee gain greater employee engagement and commitment. They note, however, that in order to make these investment "engagers," the manager must show authentic interest in the plan and the employee's interest and not just have a "check the box" conversation once a year. In terms of communication, the authors suggest that managers who are able to create a "vivid line of sight" from an employee's work to critical organizational outcomes create greater engagement. They argue that this communication helps connect the dots for employees, where work takes on greater meaning as employees get a clearer understanding of how their job responsibilities fit into the larger organizational picture. Wallace and Trinka suggest that when top management points to organizational accomplishments and links them to the leadership efforts of their divisional management team, it teaches the next level of managers how to do so with their employees.

Leadership, Motivation and Employee Retention

Basford, Offermann and Wirtz's (2012) is the first empirical study to investigate the relationship between two levels of leadership support—immediate supervisors and senior management—on follower motivation and intent to stay. Past studies on the effectiveness of leadership support on motivation have focused on one leadership source rather than those across multiple levels, with most studies concentrated on the impact of immediate supervisors. Basford, Offermann and Wirtz also examined the possible role that employee job status plays in the relationship between the two levels of leadership support and intent to stay. The study used an experimental cross-sectional design, with employee self-report survey data collected from 69,568 employees across 677 locations of a large U.S. service-sector organization. The sample population consisted of an almost equal number of male and female employees, ranging in age from sixteen to seventy-eight, from a variety of ethnic backgrounds. The study found a strong positive correlation between employees' perceptions of immediate supervisor support and senior management support, suggesting that supportive managers may be more likely to hire supervisors who they believe share their values. The authors suggest that, alternately, immediate supervisors may model the behavior of their managers. Comparing the impact of the two levels of leadership support, the study found the relationship between senior leader support and motivation/intent to stay to be significantly stronger than the relationship between immediate supervisor support and motivation/intent to stay. This same trend emerged for employees in both higher and lower status positions: employees in the higher status positions were found to have stronger relationships between each level of leadership support and intent to stay than employees in the lower status group. The findings of this study have value and practical implications. The study suggests that organizations would be in better positions to promote employee motivation and retention if they developed strategies to ensure that senior leaders demonstrate employee support and communicate this support from the top down. The authors suggest that creating a supportive upper-level leadership culture may be easier than ensuring that every immediate supervisor demonstrates the support, considering there are fewer senior managers than immediate supervisors to be targeted. A top-down approach may help build leadership support at all levels of the organization by setting expectations for immediate supervisors.

Leadership and Motivation

Xu and Thomas's (2011) recent empirical study addresses the gaps in the literature by extending both theoretical and empirical research, as well as the practical implications of the possible direct effects of leadership on follower motivation. The authors note that past studies have been limited to indirect or moderating effects of leadership, citing research that has shown that, for example, transformational leadership is positively associated with follower commitment, job satisfaction and work motivation. Xu and Thomas (2011) trace the concept of employee engagement back to Kahn (1990) and support his definition: the "harnessing" of organization members' selves in their work roles, where in engagement, people employ and express themselves physically, cognitively and emotionally during role performances. Individuals who are engaged in their work have an energetic, enjoyable and effective connection with their work (Kahn 1990; Macey and Schneider 2008, cited in Xu and Thomas 2011). Xu and Thomas add commercial incentives as reasons for pursuing engagement, pointing to increased return on assets, higher earning per employee, higher performance, greater sales growth and lower absenteeism. The authors also emphasize that greater employee engagement is associated with decreased costs, including reduced turnover and fewer quality errors. Xu and Thomas (2011) point to Kahn's (1990) three psychological antecedents of employee engagement—meaningfulness, availability and safety—as the foundation upon which interventions can be introduced to increase employee levels of engagement. Psychological meaningfulness is associated with work characteristics, such as challenge and autonomy; psychological availability is dependent upon employees having enough psychological and physical resources to invest in their role performance; and psychological safety originates from organizational social systems that provide for supportive colleague interactions. The authors point to psychological safety as the antecedent that offers the most potential for leadership to influence employee engagement.

The study involved a survey of 236 employees from a large New Zealand–based insurance company who rated their immediate managers using 360-degree assessments. It found that holding a leadership position positively correlated with employee engagement but that tenure has no relationship with engagement. The study did, however, find variation in the relative importance of leadership factors in predicting engagement. While the study found positive associations between both relationship (i.e., supports team and displays integrity) and task-oriented leader behaviors, as reported by followers, the relationship-oriented construct of "supports team" was the strongest predictor of employee engagement.

This has implications for organizations in that direct reports may be more likely to react positively and with higher levels of engagement to leaders who take a genuine interest in team members' personal development and celebrate team successes. Xu and Thomas (2011) emphasize that leaders who are less able to develop their relational skills may be able to increase follower engagement through task-oriented behaviors, such as delivering performance through good decision making and effective task management, and by displaying integrity by being open and honest in communications.

8

Communicate, Communicate, Communicate

Every time you have to speak, you are
auditioning for leadership.

—James Humes

Ask any retail expert what the three most critical characteristics of a successful retail business are, and invariably they will respond, "Location, location, location!" Location is so fundamental to bricks-and-mortar retail that even if an organization has excellent products, services and people, it cannot be successful if it is in the wrong place. Location is to retail what communication is to interaction between people. Communication is undeniably the fundamental success factor of any type of working relationship.

Several times in this book already we have posed the question, what makes a great leader? When we look back through history, many great leaders come to mind: Winston Churchill, who held together a battered and outnumbered British population in the dark early days of World War II, when the country stood alone against Nazi Germany. "We shall never surrender" stands out among the many inspiring speeches he made during that time. Or Ronald Reagan, who took over as U.S. president after the country seemingly had lost its way following Vietnam, the Watergate scandal and the 1979 energy crisis. Or Margaret Thatcher, who turned around a foundering country and was said to have been an inspiration to Reagan. What did these leaders have in common? They were all effective communicators.

So great was Reagan's ability to inspire the country that an admiring press corps bestowed on him the title "The Great Communicator." Reagan was a former Hollywood actor who preferred simple messages and solutions to complex ones. He may not have been the most cerebral president that the United States ever had, but he got his message across. Everyone knew what he wanted to do and how he wanted to do it. That was even more emphatically the case for Thatcher, who wanted to break the unions' hold on the British economy, and for Churchill, whose goals were the survival of the British people and the defeat of the Nazis.

As a leader, you should not undervalue your role as communicator. Your team members and the rest of the organization take their cues from you. Whether you give positive reinforcement or helpful criticism, what you communicate has an impact.

Communication creates, shapes and sustains the environment in which you and your employees work. Just as Churchill and other leaders of his caliber proved, the way that you communicate can demonstrate your positive traits (such as steadfastness, optimism and determination), create buy-in and build employee engagement. It can demonstrate your trustworthiness as you "walk the talk," doing what you say you are going to do, and it can also reflect your honesty and authenticity.

For Alan Booth, an associate partner at professional services market leader Deloitte, leaders who are effective communicators need to have a bit of Churchill in them: "The message has to be given with candor, brevity and color."

THE MORE THINGS CHANGE . . .

In a national survey conducted by Global Knowledge's research group, communication was rated as the most important competency contributing to a leader's success. This discovery wasn't surprising. Studies and reports with similar results have been published every decade since the 1960s. Communication has long been touted as the most important factor in leadership effectiveness. But what, if anything, has changed? Is the way that people communicate today different from the way they communicated in the 1960s? The answer is what the French would call *une réponse de Normand: oui et non*—yes and no.

What has changed, quite simply, is the amount of communication, the pace at which it is exchanged and the variety of media used. Just think about your typical day. You read through—and respond to—a vast (and seemingly never-shrinking) pile of e-mail, discover interesting articles from the many RSS feeds you subscribe to and catch up on your Twitter account and Facebook page for both personal and business purposes. While you are doing that, you receive a few text messages on your mobile phone, and an e-mail updating you on your LinkedIn contacts.

Amid all the tapping, sending and downloading, it is likely that you haven't been engaged in the oldest and most powerful communication system there is, the one that predates our ancestors' paintings on cave walls: speaking. Yes, the computer revolution has been a boon to business, but we are still verbal animals at the end of the day. There are great orators, but few leaders today have been singled out as great electronic communicators.

E-mail is in some ways the bane of efficient communication in the workplace. It is so easy to bang out a few sentences, hit Reply or Forward or Reply All and send your nonverbal communication to one person, or thousands of people, in your organization. On the surface that's one of the great things about e-mail—it is so efficient.

What e-mail—and tweets, and Facebook posts, and even blog posts for that matter—are terrible at is conveying the subtleties and underlying emotions that are part and parcel of verbal communication. The British people had no difficulty understanding and being inspired by the resolute determination of Churchill's radio broadcasts. His message may not have been as rousing if it had been delivered in the form of short e-mails.

Let's get back to today's world. So once you've done your duty to the gods of electronic communication by reading, responding, blogging and tweeting, you now have to prepare for a virtual meeting (a meeting where participants are not face to face in the same room but are communicating via phone or a web-based system that allows for sound and visual exchange), where you will introduce to your colleagues a new system that your company is implementing. You expect some resistance because most people are comfortable with the current system. You suspect that they may be somewhat confrontational. Dealing with emotion or negative feedback is much more challenging in a virtual session, where you lose most nonverbal cues (e.g., gestures, shrugs, smiles and frowns). Hence the advantage of using tools like video conferencing or even simply a webcam to add the nonverbal to the communication.

This is the new element of communication, and it brings with it a multitude of inherent challenges. The fundamental model of communication is still the same: there is a sender and a receiver of information, and multiple filters in between that can alter the way the message is sent, communicated, received and interpreted. This process takes on a whole new reality when these new methods of communication, such as webinars and instant messaging, are the preferred media of modern businesses. As Stéphane Moriou, an industrial psychologist in France, said: "The amount of e-mail communications is becoming textual harassment."

We have developed numerous habits and behaviors in relation to these new communication devices and methods, including nearly constant connectivity, a new (and constantly evolving) vocabulary and microcoordination (i.e., last-minute decision making). It was fascinating to see the incredible intensity of people's reactions to Research In Motion's four-day system outage in 2011, back when the company set the unchallenged standard for business communication. BlackBerry users realized that they were so dependent on their mobile devices that losing them for four days caused them to react emotionally—as if a friend had abandoned them.

KEYS TO EFFECTIVE COMMUNICATION

Deloitte's Alan Booth studies and thinks a great deal about communication. He believes that effective communicators employ candor (giving the truth of what is happening, not a sugar-coated version), brevity (speak too long and you lose your audience) and color (your words need to be said or written in an interesting way). He considers great communications an essential element of building relationships and influencing others.

Booth stresses that leaders should be careful not to spin or oversell their message too hard to achieve buy-in from those in their organization. An insightful practice for the Deloitte executive is to look at online news articles. Typically, those articles with the most opinion or spin provoke a flurry of (often negative) commentary and reaction from their readers.

Ultimately, communication needs to be effective, no matter what medium is used. In fact, only a small amount of meaning is conveyed through oral communication alone. Speaking and listening are not just about hearing and processing words. There are also paraverbal and nonverbal cues that contribute to how a spoken message is understood.

Various studies show slightly differing numbers, but the consensus is that only 10 percent of communication is actually verbal (the words), while 40 percent is paraverbal and 50 percent is entirely nonverbal. The takeaway here is that it is not only what you say that counts, it is, more importantly, how you say it. So if approximately 50 percent of the meaning of the message is affected by nonverbal cues, what does that mean when we can't talk face to face—when we have to use e-mail, blogs, Twitter and even conference calls or webinars? Attention needs to be paid to apply good communication practices to the new shortened and speedy interactions of today's world.

The oft-quoted percentage breakdown of how we communicate comes, for the most part, from the research of Professor Albert Mehrabian, who pioneered our current understanding of communication, making a huge contribution to our early understanding of body language and nonverbal communication. Mehrabian found that in the communication of a message pertaining to feelings and attitudes:

- 7 percent of the message is contained in the words that are spoken.
- 38 percent of the message is paralinguistic (the way the words are said).
- 55 percent of the message is contained in the facial expression.

KUBA: Know, Understand, Believe, Act

Fortunately, there is an effective way to craft your message, face to face or in writing; at Global Knowledge we refer to it as "KUBA." KUBA—standing for know, understand, believe, act—is a four-step process that everyone can use to make his or her communication more effective and influential. It is also the process that people go through to learn new things and to change their behavior or that of others. When you are considering engaging in formal or somewhat formal communication, you should take a moment and think through the KUBA process and the intention of your communication. Do this from the receiver's perspective as well as from your own.

So, how do you KUBA your communication?

The first step, *know*, requires that you convey the core of your message to your audience as clearly and specifically as possible. People must know what it is you are asking them to understand. The key question underlying this first step is: What are the facts?

From there, your audience must *understand* the details of the topic you are discussing. It is one thing to provide the facts; it's another for the receivers of your communication to understand what you are sharing. It is important for you to do two things: provide them with a rational and solid context, and ask questions to confirm their understanding. Why? is the key question here. "Why do we need to do this?" or "Why have we decided that?" are examples of questions in which the "why" will bring the rational to the communication.

The third step is to have your audience *believe* in the value of what you are asking them to do, and to believe that they can accomplish it. Even if what you are communicating is not a request for action, you want the other people to believe in what you are communicating. This is the buy-in phase of communication. The key question here is: What are the benefits either for the person receiving your communication or other stakeholders?

Step four is to encourage your audience to *act*. It may not always be the case, but in many circumstances the communication will lead to an action. Only when people know, understand and believe will they be committed to act. The key question for this step is: What are the next steps or actions? The mistake leaders most often make is to communicate the facts and then expect everybody to get to the act phase immediately. It may work occasionally, but way too frequently we see active or passive resistance or even just plain confusion instead of action. The *understand* and *believe* stages are crucial yet often missed.

Once again, it may sound counterintuitive, but to be a good communicator, you have to ask plenty of questions. We like to say in training sessions that there is a reason humans evolved with two ears and just one mouth! We are meant to listen more than talk. The psychologist Carl Rogers, father of active listening, said, "Attentive listening means giving one's total and undivided attention to the other person and tells the other that we are interested and concerned. Listening is a difficult work that we will not undertake unless we have deep respect and care for the other" (Rogers 1980). Alan Booth likes to say that, as a leader, a good rule of thumb is to ask two questions for every statement you make. The types of questions that a leader as communicator-in-chief should be asking fall into the same three categories we listed in Chapter 6:

1. Open-ended
2. Clarifying
3. Confirming

Asking good questions is critical in communication. Too often when leaders want to convince or negotiate with others they fall into the trap of becoming verbose, using a barrage of words to make their point.

In some of our leadership and communication training programs, participants do an exercise in which we ask them to think of the best vacation trip they have ever taken and then give them one minute to persuade the person sitting beside them to take the same trip. Most of the participants take the whole minute to explain how great their holiday was and how much they loved, say, the beautiful white-sand beach and the chance to lie around doing nothing. Occasionally, however, a participant starts by asking, "What kind of vacation do you like?" You can guess what happens next. The other person might reply, "I like going to museums and learning about the history of the place I'm visiting. I don't like doing nothing." In this instance, a simple open-ended question results in information that greatly affects how the case for a beach vacation is made. The persuader now can choose arguments that are aligned with the other's preferences rather than his or her own.

At Global Knowledge, we coach leaders to be clear on the intent and content of the information they are communicating. Often, leaders, especially those new to a leadership position, focus on the words and substance of what they want to say. What they should be focusing on is what they want others to understand. After you have communicated with others, it is critical to ask them what they understood from your message. Simply asking "Is this clear?" is too general. It is necessary to confirm comprehension.

Your silence also sends a message. Take, for example, a manager who resists communicating a quarterly report because the numbers presented in it are poor. People will note the lack of communication and receive the message regardless. Your silence potentially leads others to misinterpret your message.

GETTING PERSONAL

A successful communicator has a firm grasp of what motivates and inspires others. At Global Knowledge, we encourage leaders to ask themselves, "What are the personal needs of my team members?" Everyone has numerous personal needs that must be satisfied if that person is going to reach his or her true potential. As a leader, understanding your personal needs and the needs of others is a key part of effective communication. By understanding your own personal needs, you will have a better grasp of:

- Why you communicate (talk and listen) the way that you do
- How others may perceive you
- How you perceive the actions and reactions of those around you
- How to alter your communication (whether verbal or written) to be more effective and to fit with the personal needs of your audience

Colleen Johnston, CFO of TD Bank, warns that when leaders fail to understand their own needs, they risk making themselves unapproachable. They may present themselves as individuals who are not open to receiving feedback or news—good or bad—and are in danger of putting themselves behind a kind of virtual wall. Johnston says, "As leaders, the situation you cannot have is to be stuck in the ivory tower and people are only feeding you limited information about what is going on in the organization." She continues, "You have got to be seen as someone who is approachable, who is real, down to earth, etc. If you create an environment where people always feel like, 'Hey, I'm being judged harshly if something goes wrong, I better solve it or suppress it,' that is when organizations get in trouble."

One of TD's seven leadership values asks leaders to live transparently. This value is about "being transparent around what is going well and what is not going well. Being real, being authentic about what the challenges are," Johnston says. "If someone comes to me with a problem and I say, 'Oh my God, how am I going to tell my boss?' then what you are going to do is discourage people from surfacing problems."

At Global Knowledge, we divide people's core personal needs into six categories:

1. Structure (the need for logic, order, processes and systems)
2. Success (the need for results, profit and quality)
3. Control (the need for authority over environment, decisions and people)
4. Caution (the need to minimize risk)
5. Attention (the need for recognition by others)
6. Acceptance (the need to be part of a team and liked by others)

We urge our clients to consider how they, as leaders, adapt the way they communicate based on what they know about the personal needs of their audience. In order to motivate people and understand how they will behave in a given situation, it is essential to understand their needs.

Keep in mind that people's needs are fluid and may change given the problem or situation. Therefore, resist the urge to typecast people based on a single core need.

STYLES OF COMMUNICATION

Michael Hackman, a professor of communications at the University of Colorado Colorado Springs, emphasizes that the primary job of any leader is communication, and that the greater the leadership responsibility, the more the job is a communication job. He maintains that leadership communication is, for the most part, a set of learned behaviors that are developed through knowledge and practice (Hackman 2006).

Essentially, this leader/communicator has the task of securing buy-in for a future that others may not see, a future the leader sees and wants others to follow. This is achieved in part by:

1. Sending many messages to your audience using many styles, rather than one message in one style.
2. Appreciating diverse points of view and promoting two-way communication.
3. Encouraging talk between organization members to promote learning.

Hackman refers to the Myers-Briggs Type Indicator assessment tool, which is based on Carl Jung's theory of psychological types, to describe different communication styles and how they help with understanding and improving teams and leadership. He insists that, to a large extent, the good connection one makes instantly with someone is based on shared or complementary communication styles. He suggests that we can expect to struggle when communicating with individuals whose styles differ from our own.

Hackman refers to the four basic communication styles or types, which were originally outlined by Jung: sensor, intuitor, feeler and thinker. Hackman notes that by using a pattern of dichotomies—sensor versus intuitor, feeler versus thinker—Jung forces a choice between psychological opposites.

The first two styles, sensor and intuitor, pertain to how we prefer to take in information, either by experiencing the present (sensing) or by imagining future possibilities (intuition). For example, the sensor will adopt a communication style that focuses on present-day reality, action and getting things done in a timely manner. The intuitor will be more future-driven, focused on ideas, innovation and big-picture thinking. He or she will be more of a problem solver than an implementer.

The second two styles, feeler and thinker, pertain to how we tend to make decisions, either by using logic-driven analysis (thinking) or by means of a more personal process (feeling). For example, the feeler can be expected to adopt a communication style that focuses on human interaction, by understanding and analyzing emotions of self and others and displays of support and loyalty. The thinker's communication focuses on identifying and solving problems.

Hackman argues that the more a leader/communicator is in tune with the communication style of team players, the better chance he or she has of establishing a cohesive team with predictable positive outcomes. He notes that although a consistent style provides predictability, to be effective the leader/communicator must develop flexible strategies for dealing with communication styles that differ depending on the person and the situation. To develop flexible strategies, take the following steps:

1. Work to identify the primary style of your team members and consider the impact of your communication style on their behavior.
2. Focus more on the message substance than its style.

3. Adapt to the style preferences of others based on the situation.

4. Look carefully at communication style preferences when assembling teams.

Organizations, like people, each have their unique set of experiences that make up their history. Some of these experiences are good, some mundane and some so shameful that they are never spoken of except in hushed tones.

As a leader, knowing and understanding the history of your organization—how certain facts and events or episodes are perceived, and the feelings they generate among your team members—can help you tailor messages to suit particular situations. If you are speaking at a celebratory event, perhaps marking a historic milestone or major achievement, and you want to generate or reinforce positive feelings, you would select recent, positive facts and events to share.

Conversely, if there are negative emotions or events from the organization's past that people need to deal with, then acknowledge rather than dance around them. Getting these issues out in the open allows you and others to deal with them. It also demonstrates that you, as a leader, are not afraid to address uncomfortable subjects and emotions.

You can use past facts and events, and the emotions they generate, to help frame meaningful questions when following up on your team members' project assignments and personal-development programs. This allows you to explore the emotions that an assignment or other task generates in the employee and gives you deeper insights into his or her perspective.

Confronting an organization's past can also help a leader plan the best way to communicate with employees. It allows the leader to gain a greater understanding of a team's personal history with the organization, predict team members' responses and prepare to deal with their concerns. Bringing up past facts and events can also prompt more authentic emotions and feedback from employees, which gives a leader a better understanding of their standpoint.

THE POWER OF STORYTELLING

From the earliest cave dwellers to modern corporate executives, people have always told stories to illustrate and convey their ideas and make their points. Stories use the magic of narrative to transform complex information into a message that is entertaining and memorable. Stories are powerful because they speak to both reason and emotion. A good story is easy to remember, and the listener will want to tell it to others. It is a powerful way to organize and think about information. A good story lets you share your expertise and experience with others.

The power of a story depends, in part, on its simplicity. A powerful story gets to the point quickly and effectively. If a story is too long, the audience is lost. If it is too complex, the audience is confused. Powerful stories are also visual. Listeners should be able to see the players, put themselves in the scene and feel the tension that makes up the story's plot.

The Four Ps of a Powerful Story

To ensure that your story has impact and purpose, consider these four elements:

- **Purpose.** Know why you are telling your story. This will help you focus on the essentials without bringing in unnecessary details and ensure that your narrative has a logical flow so that the message does not have to be explained—everyone will get it the first time.
- **People.** Talk about real characters. Describe the people so your audience can imagine them. Paint a picture in words. Use actual conversations.
- **Plot.** Give your story a beginning, a middle and an end. There needs to be tension for a story to work. Keep it simple—it's not a novel.
- **Place.** Situate your story in a location that your audience can visualize. Give them enough visual cues so that they can put themselves in the story.

WHAT THE EXPERTS SAY
Communication and Corporate Culture

The ability to speak is not the same as the ability to communicate. Most people in supervisory roles have the ability to speak, but they are not necessarily competent communicators. Communication is a two-way process that involves speaking and listening, as well as checking for understanding. Effective leadership communication is rooted in the values and culture of an organization, as well as in the character of its leader.

John Baldoni (2004), a leadership communication consultant who has worked with Fortune 500 companies, argues that the underlying purpose of leadership communication is to bring people together for a common cause. He says that leadership messages are designed to engage the listener, gain his or her commitment and ultimately create a bond of trust so that the speaker and listener can work together more efficiently. According to Baldoni, leadership messages do one or more of the following:

1. Affirm the organization's vision and mission.
2. Drive transformational change.
3. Issue a call to action.
4. Reinforce the organization's capability.
5. Create an environment where motivation can flourish.

Baldoni suggests that a leader skilled at communication regularly, in good times and in bad, reinforces what the organization stands for, where it is going and how it will accomplish its goals. A leader works to stay on message; repeats that message; and speaks and listens often to employees, customers and other stakeholders. Communication not only reinforces an organization's vision, it also affirms the individual's role, be it through teaching or quiet one-on-one conversations.

Baldoni presents four key goals of effective leadership communication (the four Is):

1. **Informing.** Informing team members what the issues are, and explaining how they relate to the team, provides members with the information they need to do their jobs.
2. **Involving.** When leaders involve employees by listening to them and valuing their input, employees will be more likely to buy in to the leader's message.
3. **Igniting.** A message delivered with conviction and genuine enthusiasm helps a leader to ignite his or her team's imagination. Members think about things they can do to make life better for themselves and for their organization.
4. **Inviting.** Inviting people to actively and more fully participate in an organization helps the organization achieve inspired results.

Baldoni acknowledges that there is no single way to communicate. What matters most, he says, is making the commitment to communicate—with consistency, constancy and frequency. Words alone say very little, but words backed by the leader's character, conviction and example have the power to communicate and to inspire.

Without effective communication, a manager is not a successful leader. Barrett (2006) reports on an early Harvard Business School study that looks at what it takes to achieve success and be promoted in an organization. The study found that the individual who gets ahead in business is the one who communicates and involves others in getting things done.

Barrett describes an interesting model of leadership communication that is made up of three rings:

1. Core
2. Managerial
3. Corporate

Rather than a hierarchy, the model is depicted as a spiral, with the core communication ability represented in the center. Barrett argues that all effective communication depends on the core skills at the center of the spiral, which consist of individuals' abilities to strategize, write and speak. Core communication involves the development of communication strategies that are congruent with the audience in every situation, writing and speaking in language expected of business leaders, and the confident and persuasive creation and delivery of oral presentations. Once the core skills are mastered, individuals expand their skills to those needed to lead and manage groups—emotional intelligence; cultural literacy; listening; managing teams; and meeting, coaching and mentoring.

Spiraling outward, people develop corporate communication skills, which include those related to employee relations, change communication, media relations, crisis communication, and image and reputation management. At the corporate level of communication, audiences become larger and more diverse. They are the leaders of change programs; they are in charge of vision development; and they are the public faces and voices of the organization. To speak to these audiences, leaders need to be able to develop more complex communication strategies.

Barrett (2006) focuses much of her attention on the connection between leadership communication and the leader's ability to project a positive image. This positive image, or "ethos," is an appeal based on the perceived character of the message sender. For example, it is based on the audience's perception of how trustworthy, believable and/or knowledge-able the sender is. The author acknowledges that positive ethos might be equated with charisma, since both characteristics are associated with the ability to "persuade others and move an audience." She distinguishes between the two by emphasizing that charisma suggests a power over others, based more on emotion than on reason. She identifies credibility as essential to creating a positive ethos. In order to build a positive ethos, leaders need to know how others perceive them.

The author cites research (Conger 1998) that looked into managers' ability to judge how they are perceived. This study found that most managers considerably overestimate their credibility. Barrett says that leaders can use emotional intelligence to effectively gauge how others perceive them. Through self-exploration and honest feedback from others, leaders are able to develop the self-awareness necessary to accurately judge themselves, as well as to interpret signals that others send through body language, actions and words.

The author notes that, ideally, ethos and ethics align with each other. However, it is possible for someone to project a positive ethos with little ethical foundation behind that projection. In the end, Barrett points us to leadership research indicating that if people are going to follow someone willingly, they will look for assurances that the person behaves ethically and is trustworthy.

Effective leaders must not only be successful in interacting with individuals whose communication styles differ from their own, they must also develop trusting relationships through transactional and transformational behavior. Trust is communication-based, and built on accurate and open information. Frank J. Flauto (1999) conducted a study in which 151 employees across nine organizations rated their leaders' leadership behavior and communication competence. He found these positive correlations:

- High-quality leader-member exchanges and perceived leaders' communicative competence

- Transactional leadership behaviors and perceived leaders' communicative competence
- Transformation leadership behaviors and perceived leaders' communicative competence

The study notes that, at the lower levels of leader communication competence, high-quality leader-member relationships do not exist. Flauto determined that transactional leadership requires a level of communication competence that allows the leader to negotiate the leader-member contract and to monitor the transactions.

A review of the literature on leader communication points to communication style, strategy and transformational leadership behaviors as the key components making it possible to bring people together to drive individual and organizational success. In one article on innovation as a strategic communication type, Zerfass and Huck (2007) emphasize the increasing role that communication should play in promoting innovation management. Considering the competitive and global nature of today's business world, it is obvious to all involved that the only way to sustain a competitive edge is through innovation. Zerfass and Huck point to studies showing that companies' attempts to implement innovations are largely ineffective (Friedmann and Maurer 2003) unless they are accompanied by a robust and strategic communication plan.

In contrast to communication efforts that support daily business, strategic communication prepares organizations for the uncertain future that most businesses face today. Innovation management can best be understood as an integrated and cooperative process that must be strategically planned and controlled, and well supported by communication. Zerfass and Huck (2007) remind us that companies no longer "create ideas in guarded research labs under the veil of secrecy" until they are ready for market. Instead, in the age of open innovation, internal and external stakeholders systematically get involved in the innovation process. This is an example of the importance of communication in leadership.

The authors point to the results of a survey conducted in Germany in 2004 and based on feedback from 460 public relations experts and journalists on innovation communication. The study concludes that innovations are hard to communicate, and that companies do not provide enough information about innovations. Interestingly but not surprisingly, the same survey shows that 90 percent of the public relations professionals interviewed think that employees are an important target for innovation communication (Mast, Huck and Zerfass 2006). The authors emphasize that although employees are an important source of new ideas when innovations are initiated, they are the first ones affected when ongoing innovations change the working environment or lead to a loss of employment. This makes it vital that organizations prepare for the challenges, benefits and pitfalls of leadership communication and innovation from within the organization first.

Zerfass and Huck recognize social theory's strong link between innovation and communication—that innovation arises only when social practices change. Communication is an integral support feature of the innovation process. It is important that communication supports each phase of this process, from the generation of ideas to marketing the product and building relationships with employees, research and development partners, customers, competitors, politicians, journalists and other relevant stakeholders. The authors refer to past studies (Mast, Huck and Zerfass 2005, 2006) that list the main barriers for communicating and translating an innovation, including:

1. The innovation's benefits in terms of profits may not be obvious because of its novelty. This leads people to consider the undertaking as rather abstract.
2. The potential change an innovation could mean for everyone, which often leads to instinctive resistance.
3. The lack of frames of reference that new ideas can be integrated into precisely because they are new ideas.

Zerfass and Huck suggest that, to overcome these obstacles, leaders discuss innovations with their audience by telling stories and giving examples of concrete applications for customers, research partners and others. Leaders should also use simple examples, graphs and pictures to set a frame of reference for an innovation within an existing cognitive structure. Of course, foremost on the list of ways to overcome an audience's reluctance to buy in to a new idea is the credibility and authenticity of the communicator.

Delegate Deliberately and Provide Feedback

I feel really grateful to the people who encouraged me and helped me develop. Nobody can succeed on their own.

—Sheryl Sandberg

The ability to delegate effectively is critical to a leader's success. On a regular basis, a leader must decide which tasks should be undertaken personally and which should be delegated. It is a necessary part of the leader's role as he or she works with, and through, others to get work done. Hold on too tight, and risk being isolated and overwhelmed. Delegate too much, and risk losing control and accountability.

Hand in hand with the process of delegation, a leader must provide effective feedback that is both positive and constructive ("constructive," that is, in the sense of addressing the need for improvement). This chapter discusses these two very critical leadership skills to assist leaders to understand the important considerations involved with delegating deliberately, and ensuring that meaningful feedback is provided to those to whom tasks have been delegated.

DELEGATE DELIBERATELY

At Global Knowledge, we train leaders on how to delegate effectively through a program titled Delegate Deliberately. As the name implies, the process needs to be conducted thoughtfully and systematically. The payoffs that come from delegation are not only a reduction in the daily, weekly or monthly tasks that leaders are expected to carry out (giving them more time to lead and manage), but benefits for the team such as personal and professional growth and development that come with added/delegated responsibilities. Deciding what to delegate and then actually delegating work is not easy for many leaders. Common challenges include:

- The team is already stretched and has limited resources available.
- The work to be delegated requires experience or expertise that is not readily available.
- Leaders considering delegating tasks focus too much on getting the work done at the expense of leading others.

It should not be surprising that faced with such hurdles many leaders simply decide to carry out the work themselves. As we explain in Chapter 12, this is a mistake commonly made by newly promoted leaders. Carrying out an assigned task that really should be delegated might be a "comfort blanket" for the new leader, or the leader may be uncomfortable with the idea of delegating the task to an appropriate team member. Doing it yourself often is a short-term fix for a long-term issue. Leaders who do the work that can be and should be delegated are really just widening the gap between dependency and empowerment.

THE DELEGATION MODEL

A leader needs to be aware of and account for the ability and motivation of individual team members when it comes to delegation. Every person is different, each armed with a different and unique set of skills and drive (or ambition). How a leader delegates to individual team members therefore needs to be customized to a certain degree.

The Delegation Model outlines the three delegation styles, each of which can be matched to the appropriate style of individuals and specific tasks, and helps determine when each style should be used to maximize the performance of others. (See Table 9.1.)

Ability (Demonstrated through Skills, Knowledge, Expertise, Experience)		
Low (A1)	Moderate (A2)	High (A3)
Is this the first time the person has ever done this task or a similar task? Does the person have little or no experience?	Has the person had some experience with this task or a similar task, but not yet become proficient?	Has the person done this task, or a similar task, many times in the past? Has the person previously completed the task independently and to standard?

Motivation (Demonstrated through Attitude, Willingness, Commitment, Confidence)		
Low (M1)	Moderate (M2)	High (M3)
Does the person have a negative attitude toward the task? Does the person demonstrate a lack of self-direction to carry out the task? Does the person question the purpose of the task, or whether it is part of their job, or whether they have time to do it? Does the person indicate they will not be able to successfully do the task, or learn how to do it?	Does the person show some interest and some self-direction in carrying out the task? Does the person express caution about whether they will be able to do the task? Does the person demonstrate some understanding of the importance of the task to the business unit team or to their role?	Is the person enthusiastic about, and interested in, the task? Has the person requested, or volunteered, for the task? Does the person show confidence and self-direction in their capability to do the task? Does the person demonstrate a commitment to continuous learning (mastery) in the execution of the task?

©2010 Global Knowledge Training LLC. All rights reserved.

Table 9.1: Delegation Model: Assessing Staff Capabilities

The starting point for a leader who has to delegate work is to assess an individual team member's ability and motivation. Ability can be defined as the skills, knowledge, experience and expertise required to complete an assigned task (or project). Motivation, similarly, can be defined as the willingness, attitude, confidence and commitment required to complete the task.

The ability of the individual, combined with his or her motivation and determination, will impact the outcome. To reduce the complexity of our model, we have broken both characteristics into three levels: low, moderate and high. Where the individual falls on the ability-motivation matrix determines which delegation style the leader should use. We have found that three distinct approaches provide the best range of options for a delegating leader: teaching, sharing and transferring.

- **Teaching style.** If a team member is new to the task or deemed low in ability, the teaching style of delegation may be the best approach. Teaching requires giving detailed instructions and guidelines on how to perform a task. It stems from an awareness that the team member doesn't come to the task with a great deal of experience and requires plenty of direction and guidance. Similarly, if a team member is low in motivation, use a teaching style. Ask detailed questions to determine why the team member's motivation is low. Provide detailed guidance on the purpose of the task, explain why it is important and detail the support that will be provided to the team member.
- **Sharing style.** If a team member is somewhat experienced but not proficient in the task, or deemed of moderate ability, the sharing style of delegation is recommended. Sharing means co-owning responsibility. As a leader, you understand that the team member has some of the knowledge and skill required to complete the task successfully. You encourage the team member to share ideas and solutions, and you also offer your own. The sharing style is recommended too for a team member with a moderate level of motivation. Leaders should build a plan of action by asking questions, listening to answers and providing input.
- **Transferring style.** If a team member is experienced and proficient, or high in ability, the transferring style of delegation is most appropriate. Transferring means turning over most of the task ownership from leader

to team member. You know that the team member is fully capable of completing the task, so you adjust the amount of guidance accordingly. Similarly, for a team member who is highly motivated, use a transferring style. Acknowledge the team member's self-direction and high level of motivation, and encourage self-expression throughout the task.

Referring back to the lessons of KUBA from Chapter 8, the styles can be ranked from high KUBA for teaching to low KUBA for transferring, with sharing falling somewhere in between. In other words, when skills and/or motivation is low, more time is required to ensure that team members *know, understand* and *believe* in the delegated task before they *act* on it.

A delegating leader may need to explain to a team member how the assigned task links or aligns with a larger project or process taking place in the organization. Explaining how the task impacts other parts of the organization and linking the task with the overall objective underlines the task's importance and may also increase the individual's motivation.

PERSONALITY AND ITS IMPACT ON DELEGATION

Robert Hogan's research on leadership personality traits (see Chapter 2) is applicable to delegation and feedback. Leaders who display the characteristics of highly cautious and risk-averse but who are also highly ambitious do not make great delegators. They tend to delegate reluctantly, worry about the risk of delegating and try to retain as much control as possible. Similarly, those leaders who display the derailer behavior described as diligent or perfectionist tend to be highly controlling and micromanaging. These leaders do not delegate enough and, even when they do assign a task to a team member, tend to pester and be overly controlling.

Another leadership derailer as described by Hogan that may work against effective delegation is what he dubs "colorful" leaders—though they are perhaps more accurately described as attention seekers. Leaders who display that derailer may be unwilling to delegate high-profile or high-publicity tasks such as presentations or outside interviews. In order to grow the people on their team, attention-seeking leaders need to delegate high-visibility tasks or accept that their team will lack development in this area.

DELEGATION AS A DEVELOPMENT TOOL

If you recall the 70-20-10 rule we outlined earlier in Chapter 4, most individuals' learning and experience (70 percent) comes from doing or, to put it a little more eloquently, by carrying out tasks often enough to gain proficiency. Viewed in this light, delegation can be used not just to lighten the workload of a leader but also to develop an individual and his or her team. For example, a vice-president may wish to delegate to a director in order to grow the director's skills and responsibilities. The leader, therefore, needs to look at his or her tasks and determine which can be delegated so that the team member is forced to gain new knowledge/abilities required to carry out the assigned task.

Typically, such strategic delegation provides individuals with knowledge of an aspect of the business they had not been exposed to previously, and perhaps even an unfamiliar part of the organization, and such a task usually results in high motivation for a new challenge on the part of these employees. The payoff for the leader is to meet both the individuals' motivation requirements and career ambitions. The process also encourages team members, provides a clear sign that they are valued by the organization and tells them they are viewed as long-term development candidates for increasingly responsible roles.

Bear in mind that delegation is not a "fire and forget" process. Follow-up is critical to successful delegation, especially for individuals who are unfamiliar with a task (low ability), or less than enthusiastic about the assigned task (low motivation). Leaders should agree with the team member on timelines, feedback channels, targets for status updates and, ultimately, deadlines for tasks. It should be stressed that leaders do not lose accountability for the task if they delegate part or even all of it. Responsibility for the task is delegated, but accountability in the end stops at the leader's desk.

FEEDBACK

For a leader, providing feedback to the individuals you are responsible for in the organization goes beyond delegation. Providing feedback is also part of your responsibility in your role as communicator as well as coach. Above all, leaders should understand what feedback is not. It is not criticism, or more precisely, it is not simply criticism. It is not all negative, but rather communication of the positive and the not-so-positive. Both are important.

"I think that is the hardest thing I have had to learn, and I struggle with that," says Brian Branson, CEO at Global Knowledge. "I think I have improved in the last year in order to sit down and give people feedback for improvement. I used to avoid it [giving negative feedback] more and let it drag out more. That is not good. So now I try to be more frequent with that feedback.

"There are tools, on a senior level, [such as] doing 360-degree feedback, to make sure perceptions are not far off. Being exposed to and leveraging those tools is going to be valuable" in giving feedback, he says, but emphasizes that it must be positive and constructive.

It is human nature to zero in on things when they go wrong and even harp on mistakes or missteps. Conversely, when a job is done well, our natural tendency is to say little or nothing about it. That is just poor leadership behavior. Yet we all do it, whether it's going over our child's report card, training the family pet or even cheering for our favorite team. To err on the side of negativity is human. The tendency must be recognized and guarded against.

When a project or task is carried out well, leaders need to recognize and reinforce it. Say that it was done well and explain in what way it was done well so that such a task will be carried out well in the future also. That is, positive feedback is not simply a matter of recognition—stating that a task was done properly; the leader needs to reinforce it by giving specifics about what was done well. As a bonus, giving positive feedback not only enhances productivity, it feels good—both for the giver and the receiver.

In our consulting practice, we often see leaders avoiding giving feedback that could help a team member's development. They may have difficulty sharing their thoughts. They may feel that providing positive feedback makes them appear too soft. They may feel uncomfortable giving negative feedback, or they may be concerned about the reaction of the individual to what may be perceived as criticism. Too often in such cases, these leaders neglect entirely to provide constructive feedback, or the information is passed on ineffectively.

"Providing feedback is one of the most important things we do," says Christopher Hodgson, group head of Global Wealth Management at Scotiabank. "It has to be done and given in the right spirit, however. For example, if you have a management meeting and somebody brings up something that is offside, I am not going to take them to task in front of a group of people. What I will do is point out how they might think about that differently, but also I will meet them individually, one on one, and say, 'By the way, you raised this in the meeting, I didn't want to say it in front of your colleagues, but your intervention was offside and it impacted the meeting negatively.' And I am talking about very senior-level people. I think that it is very important to give candid feedback. If someone isn't getting something done or you are hearing different information from different areas, you have got to get tangible info. It can't be ad hoc, it can't be hearsay, but then you have to deliver it."

Constructive, or what some might term "negative feedback," can be softened somewhat with a touch of finesse. The objective is to suggest positive measures to correct actions or behavior that are counterproductive. "What I have [learned] over time," Hodgson continues, "is delivering constructive feedback, but then finishing the conversation with a positive aspect—such as, 'This is what I am hearing, perhaps you should have done it this way,' and finishing it off with, 'Well, you know you are very strong in these areas.'"

"Giving feedback is critical," he adds. "Not everyone is comfortable giving it. Some of our developing leaders struggle with it because they don't want to be viewed as either disagreeing or delivering hard news. But if you want to move along, that is a lot of the job, giving constructive feedback."

Guidelines for Giving—and Receiving—Feedback

- **Be timely.** Providing feedback for something that happened weeks or months ago is not effective. Similarly, providing for the first time a list of criticisms or negative feedback during an individual's annual performance review is a flashing red signal that feedback is not being provided in a timely manner. (And chances are the individual has not improved in those areas being criticized because he or she was not aware of them until that once-a-year review). On the other side of the desk, the responsibility of the feedback recipient is to act on the feedback soon after it has been imparted, to demonstrate a commitment to improve.

- **Be specific.** This applies to both positive and constructive feedback. Single out what was done well so the individual can repeat it, and describe what was done incorrectly so that it can be improved upon. Coaches provide specific and constructive feedback to professional athletes and other performers so that they can better hone their technique. Leaders would do well to visualize themselves in the role of a coach striving to improve the performance of a team member. The feedback recipient should similarly seek and ask for balanced and specific feedback that includes examples, and ask follow-up questions as needed for clarity.
- **Be consistent.** Leaders need to connect the feedback to the outcome, measurement and time frame they established when they assigned the task. It cannot be just once a year or when the leader feels stressed. The recipient needs to agree on next steps to put the feedback into action and follow through on this commitment.
- **Be clear.** Describe the impact of the behavior or performance for which feedback is being given in terms of how it made people feel and the consequences of it. The recipient should confirm his or her understanding of the message.
- **Be direct.** Stay focused on the message.
- **Be sincere.** Ensure that your body language, words and tone demonstrate your sincerity.
- **Be open.** Actively listen to the other person's view. Collaborate on an action plan if required and provide support.
- **Be comfortable.** Be sure the environment is comfortable and conducive to the type of feedback you are providing. Ensure privacy if it is required.
- **Maintain self-esteem.** Always focus on maintaining the other person's self-esteem.
- **Be grateful.** Show your appreciation for the other person's time and attention.
- **Be genuine.** Provide true and honest feedback: don't exaggerate if it is positive, and don't sugarcoat the facts or performance if it is negative.

Why should leaders provide feedback? By giving effective (actionable) feedback, a leader can help team members build on their strengths, address their development needs, improve their performance, take on more challenging work and feel more motivated.

THE FOUR-STEP FEEDBACK LOOP

Leaders can think of providing feedback as a sequence of four steps:

1. **Observation.** Identifies the specific behavior or performance on which you want to provide feedback.
2. **Impact.** Identifies the impact/value/result of the behavior.
3. **Request.** Asks/states that the team member continues (positive) or changes (constructive) this behavior.
4. **Agreement.** In conversation with the team member, the leader confirms and reinforces the continuance of, or discusses how to change, the behavior. The leader should make an agreement with the individual to go forward in a positive direction or to find ways to do better in the future.

These steps outline a practical and simple approach for leaders who are not accustomed to or comfortable with providing feedback to other team members to follow. Leaders need to remember that the process of giving constructive feedback is not about the individual per se, but about what the leader observed about how the task was carried out.

Feedback Fighters: Ten Archetypes

Jacqueline Boileau, a senior learning consultant with Global Knowledge based in Montreal, delivers feedback for a living. Doling out the good and bad on a regular basis to North American leaders taking leadership training, communications skills and performance management courses has made her an expert on how people react to feedback. Over her career, she has identified ten archetypes of those who are unable or unwilling to accept constructive feedback. Chances are, with a touch of honesty and humor, you'll recognize at least a bit of yourself here, or you may have met some of these "characters." In Boileau's words:

1. **The finger pointer.** The finger pointer says, "You're saying that to me? I'll tell you who you should really be looking at because that person is way worse." He will divert as a way to escape the feedback.

2. **The rebel.** "How dare you say that to me! With all the effort I've put out! If this is the way I'm going to be treated, I'm out!"

3. **The negotiator.** "Yes, but look at all I've done." He tries to balance the negative feedback with whatever good he has accomplished.

4. **The debater.** He argues about what he did or said, and in his opinion, it was the right thing to do. He willfully fails to see or recognize the feedback giver's position.

5. **The penitent.** He admits his mistakes, has remorse, feels very sorry. He apologizes. He wants to avoid judgment, and he respects authority. Instead of promising to try to improve, he promises that from now on he will be perfect. He is more afraid of getting the feedback than improving.

6. **The fighter.** He threatens you, thinks of revenge and is highly insulted. Threatening is bad enough, but if he is thinking of hijacking or deliberately messing up the work, that can be disastrous. The end goal is to intimidate you, through a physical reaction or words.

7. **The yes man.** "'Yeah, yeah, yeah.' He says exactly what you want to hear and has been buying time for years. But sincerity is not present and nothing will ever change."

8. **The boomerang.** It is not his fault, he had no choice, he was caught in a corner. He feels very comfortable about what happened because he is not at fault. The provider is getting the feedback right back at him.

9. **The justice officer.** He switches the roles, explaining to you what you have been doing wrong, giving negative feedback back to the provider.

10. **The user of the pseudo rationale.** He acknowledges to you without emotion, very rationally, that indeed the event in question happened, and explains the reason, but if you really pay attention, he's saying, "That was an exception." Therefore, your feedback doesn't stick. It's a false rationale and—bottom line—when the conversation is finished, he won't change a thing because it happened only once.

WHAT THE EXPERTS SAY
On Delegation

Although the value placed on fostering employee initiatives through delegating is becoming increasingly apparent in recent literature, there is little research on how organizations and managers can make delegations credible. "Credibility of delegations" refers to how managers make employees believe that they won't renege on agreements to delegate discretion to them. Foss and Foss (2005) argue that if organizations want to sustain the advantages that flow out of delegation (increased effort, creativity, competence and skill, initiatives), they need to develop and maintain the credibility of delegations. The authors point to employee motivation as the key factor upon which these advantages depend. They review the costs and benefits of delegation of discretion, describe the negative impact that management interventions to reduce delegated discretion have on employee motivation, and suggest how organizations can introduce structural designs to increase delegation credibility. The authors identify the following arguments and factors in support of delegation:

1. Centralized decision making, especially when an organization is going through rapid and unpredictable change, comes at a high cost.
2. Communication within the hierarchy similarly comes at a high cost.
3. Failure to delegate leads to managerial overload.
4. Delegation, on the other hand, leads to more effective use of knowledge by letting those who possess relevant information make the decisions.
5. Certain activities (e.g., creativity) are best undertaken by employees who are intrinsically motivated.

The authors cite a study (Osterloh and Frey 2000) that found that delegations raise the perceived self-determination of employees and strengthen intrinsic motivation, leading to an increase in creativity in the pursuit of goals. Foss and Foss (2005) point to the costs associated with reduced coordination of interdependencies within the organization. They note that any increase in the delegation of discretion may result in coordination problems related to getting access to knowledge and information held by different members, carrying out work activities that are physically interconnected, the overuse of common pool resources, and actions that are not in sync with the actions of other employees.

Organizational behavior literature suggests that when managers intervene and reduce the discretion that is delegated to an employee, employee extrinsic and intrinsic motivation is harmed. Foss and Foss point out that

these negative consequences can be expected to follow from managerial intervention because employees see the discretion as a contractual
obligation and, as such, it becomes part of their perceived entitlements.
The authors point out that credibility issues arise because even though
employees perceive these promises as contractual in nature, management's
promises concerning delegation to employees usually cannot be enforced
by a third party. They note that even if employees recognize the intervention is being undertaken for the sake of the organization, motivation may
still be harmed. Managerial interventions are unavoidable given the highly
competitive nature of organizations today, with organizations struggling
to meet their bottom lines. However, Foss and Foss caution organizations
to consider carefully the potential short- and long-term cost of any given
managerial intervention in terms of lost employee motivation. They see
motivation as the tricky and unpredictable part of the intervention. But,
from the perspective of the importance of making delegations credible, the
authors recommend that unless the need for an intervention is absolutely
clear-cut and critical to the organization's success, organizations should
strive to keep interventions at levels that keep harm to employee motivation at a minimum.

Foss and Foss argue that since coordination failures are the primary
incentives for managers to intervene in discretion delegated at lower
levels of organizations, organizations should be designed in ways that
allow delegated discretion to become the coordination mechanism for
handling interdependencies. The authors point out that the coordination mechanisms will differ depending on the kinds of interdependencies
they support, including whether they are pooled, sequential or reciprocal
in nature. Pooled interdependencies occur when each task can be carried
out separately, with no need for interaction between tasks as long as each
task is performed adequately. In the case of sequential interdependencies,
one activity needs to be finished before another takes place, or a decision
in one unit has to precede decisions made in another unit. Reciprocal
interdependencies are characterized by the fact that individuals or groups
working on two or more tasks need to adjust their efforts simultaneously
and/or in similar directions.

Foss and Foss identify additional organizational design variables that
can complement the organization structure and coordination mechanisms

and help make delegation of discretion credible. The variables identified and described are:

1. Formal decision procedures
2. Performance pay
3. Informational distance

Formal decision procedures include creating the formal liaisons and procedures that allow employees to influence the planning and control process and take part in the decision-making process. The authors note that organizations that have processes rather than functional structures are more likely to have formal decision procedures: "Performance pay to employees helps to make delegations credible because it encourages employees to search more intensely for the kind of projects that will yield high value for the organization, rather than look for projects that yield only intrinsic benefits to themselves." Delegation of discretion is more likely to be credible in organizations that have created a large informational distance in the hierarchy. Reporting systems can be designed to create an informational distance between managers and the employees to whom discretion has been delegated. Foss and Foss explain that if managers understand that because of informational distance they are not in a position to rationally decide whether to intervene, they will refrain from intervening.

Although global software teams provide a variety of organizational benefits, including lower cost human capital, access to otherwise unavailable expertise, flexible work arrangements and cross-function interaction, there are challenges related to how team leaders should delegate authority and responsibility to the team. In a recent study of the impact of leader delegation behaviors on global team performance of Fortune 100 IT service companies across four countries, Zhang et al. (2012) drew these conclusions:

- Delegation to distant competent team members helps motivate remote teams to work harder, in part due to the recognition and trust from upper management.
- Delegation allows remote subteam members to have flexibility to structure their work and accommodate local team contextual factors,

but requires resources to assess the capabilities of employees assigned delegation responsibilities, followed up by ongoing coaching and mentoring.
- Organizations need to create policies, processes and systems to compensate for the short-term productivity loss associated with delegation.

The authors point out that managers need guidance on the aspects or activities they should delegate. This study fills in the gaps in the literature by developing and delineating four major delegation categories of management functions that can be delegated:

- Planning
- People
- Process
- Control

Planning-related activities could involve scheduling the team's work, setting the team's long-term goals, setting the team's short-term objectives and setting the team budget. Delegation activities related to people might involve selecting team members, removing members from the team and determining team members' training needs. Process-related activities could involve assigning work to team members, selecting the tools they will use in their work, determining the team's operating procedures and work instructions, and determining communication and coordination protocols and practices. Finally, delegation activities related to control could involve determining quality-assurance procedures, evaluating the progress of the team's work, evaluating team product quality and determining corrective actions when performance objectives are not met.

The authors point out that the question of when to delegate in global software teams can be a tricky one. They refer to studies suggesting that most delegation occurs for two main reasons: either to reduce management's workload or to develop novices. Zhang and colleagues emphasize that these two reasons may be contrary to the typical goal of global software teams, which is to get a job done as quickly as possible. Delegation can cause short-term productivity loss as the employee assigned the delegation learns his or her responsibilities. Also, close monitoring, coaching and feedback are not realistic in teams that are constantly short of time to get a product out. Zhang et al. identify one real, yet less tangible, benefit to delegation in software teams: the noted improvement in virtual team members' motivation. The authors report that the autonomy of virtual team members in determining work objectives and methods improved the intrinsic motivation of the team. In summary, the survey results yielded the following insights:

1. Competence has the strongest influence over control-related delegation, meaning that if a team is competent, the project management will trust it to self-evaluate its work quality and progress.
2. Autonomy in work processes such as tools, methodology and communication patterns will increase the team members' satisfaction with the project leadership and motivate them to work harder.

The interview findings yielded these insights:

1. Project management judges whether a team is competent enough to take over decision-making responsibilities, even though it is often difficult to accurately judge the competence levels of remote teams.
2. Subteams compete for higher status in the organization, for recognition from the headquarters and for more challenging assignments.

Some interviewees responded that they did not want to be delegated more decision-making responsibility, citing the following:

- They didn't have time, given their busy life and work schedules.
- They didn't want the added pressure.
- They were comfortable with what the managers decided to do.
- They would like to get involved but were afraid of making wrong decisions.

The authors point out that these negative perceptions are confirmed in research findings about the power-driven and directive style of Chinese leadership, serving as a reminder that in this cultural environment, delegation is viewed with caution by both the leaders and the followers.

On Feedback

In general, managers don't like giving critical feedback and employees like getting it even less. More important than the disdain for critical feedback is that it seldom yields the desired results. Cannon and Witherspoon (2005) describe how cognitive and emotional dynamics complicate the process, making it far more painful and definitely far less constructive than it ought to be. The authors introduce a new label for a different kind of feedback—"actionable" feedback, which they indicate produces "learning and tangible, appropriate results." The authors provide possible explanations for why critical feedback tends to disturb its recipients to such a degree:

- Research shows that people tend not to view themselves accurately, therefore critical feedback is likely to appear inaccurate, and receivers are likely to disagree with it.
- In general, people have a self-serving bias, which means that we tend to see ourselves as responsible for successes and blame failures on others or external forces.
- Seeing yourself as more capable than you are enhances performance more than accurate self-perceptions, so people resist criticism because it could undermine their self-esteem and self-efficacy.
- Research shows that the feeling of being attacked tends to create stress, and a common reaction to stress is to get emotional and defensive.

Cannon and Witherspoon provide simple reasons performance feedback is often flawed and seldom useful. They note that the feedback may:

- Attack the person rather than address the person's behavior
- Make vague or abstract assertions
- Fail to use illustrations to make feedback more understandable
- Give an ill-defined range of application
- Provide unclear impact and implications for action

Vague assertions are difficult to interpret correctly and may encourage defensiveness, and unless provided with specifics related to problematic behavior, the recipient won't get a clear picture of what needs to be changed. Without clarity on why behavior is considered problematic, the recipient won't know what should be done to fix it.

The authors propose a number of cognitive and emotional dynamics that may impact feedback givers, including:

- Inference-making limitations
- Attributional biases: "Attribution refers to the way in which people explain their own behavior and that of others. An attribution bias occurs when someone systematically over- or underuses the available information when explaining behavior" (Turner and Hewstone 2009)
- Overconfidence
- Third-party perspective differences
- The emotional response, which can impact feedback formulation and delivery

Inference-making limitations account for the feedback giver unintentional neglecting how the receiver is feeling and responding. This is often because, constantly flooded with information from all five senses, we select bits of information to focus on. In terms of attributional biases, managers may experience "false-consensus bias," meaning that they overestimate the likelihood that others will see things the same way they do. Feedback givers tend to forget that their conclusions about other people are not just made up of "cold, hard facts" and that they may be missing something as a result of incomplete data, misinterpretation or relying on a faulty assumption, which may result in poor-quality feedback. Feedback givers tend not to see the flaws in their feedback because they are personally involved in the situation. If a more neutral observer was employed to view the situation more objectively, better quality and more accurate feedback may be produced. The feedback giver's emotions can influence formulation and delivery of feedback. Managers may be affected by their working relationship and history with the receiver. Cannon and Witherspoon emphasize that feedback is most helpful when managers understand the potential feedback flaws and how their emotions can impact the feedback they give. The authors stress that feedback is most helpful when it is given with the intent of development, when managers make clear to the recipients that there will be support built in to their developmental plans to address feedback information.

Recently, various theoretical models on learning, development and performance management in organizations has highlighted the importance of a construct called "orientation feedback." Dahling, Chau and O'Malley (2012) address the gaps in the literature by developing and testing a model of feedback orientation and performance, and provide a comprehensive review of the literature on the topic. Feedback orientation is defined as "a person's overall receptivity to feedback" and has been proposed to directly shape the way that employees seek, receive, interpret and use feedback information and indirectly shape the performance outcomes that managers hope to bring about when they provide feedback. The authors describe the key components of feedback orientation identified in the literature:

- A positive view of feedback and lack of apprehension toward it
- A cognitive tendency to process feedback mindfully
- An awareness of others' view of oneself
- A belief that feedback is valuable
- A sense of accountability to act on feedback

They report on research that suggests that employees with a high feedback orientation should be better able to:

- Control their emotional reactions to feedback
- Process feedback more meaningfully
- Successfully apply feedback to set goals and improve performance

The authors' model is based on feedback orientation, emotional intelligence and goal orientation research. The authors propose positive and direct correlations between feedback orientation and emotional intelligence and between feedback orientation and feedback environment perceptions. To this end, the study seeks to identify the mechanism through which employees with higher feedback orientation attain better performance ratings and higher quality relationships with their supervisors. They support their propositions with research on emotional intelligence that indicates that people with high emotional intelligence are:

- Aware of their own emotions and expressions
- Able to appraise and understand others' emotions
- Capable of controlling and regulating their own emotions
- Able to use emotions to facilitate performance

The authors point to the important connection and common quality between emotional intelligence and feedback orientation of accurately understanding the self and using this self-relevant information to achieve goals. They identify the feedback environment as being characterized by six aspects of the organizational context:

1. Perceived credibility of the feedback source
2. Quality of feedback that is available
3. Tact with which feedback is delivered
4. Extent to which favorable feedback can be received
5. Accessibility of feedback
6. Extent to which feedback-seeking behavior is supported and encouraged

The authors conclude that:

- There is support for the proposition that feedback orientation is related to environmental perceptions and individual differences.
- Emotional quotient and perceptions of supervisor feedback environment have a positive, moderating relationship with feedback orientation.
- Feedback orientation has a strong, direct effect on feedback-seeking behavior and indirect effects on supervisor ratings of performance.
- Managers who work to improve feedback orientation are more likely to benefit from having employees actively inquire when faced with uncertain situations and from improved employee performance and relationships.

In this chapter we addressed the what and how, and the ins and outs of delegation and feedback—two critical leadership skills that themselves are not new. What is new, or at least significantly different, is the context in which they are applied and the science we now have on them. Delegation has often been seen as the tactical thing a manager needs to do—delegating a task. It is still true that delegating tasks properly is necessary, and remains a challenge for many leaders. But the high added value of delegation is the development opportunities it can provide to employees and leaders. Connecting the concept of the 70-20-10 rule with delegation is a must.

Providing feedback is also fundamental but often misused. It can be brief or comprehensive, positive or for improvement, individual or in a small group, yet its impact is rarely negligible. Receiving feedback is a key component of engagement, learning and feeling valued. What leaders do not want all that for their employees? Growing employees and leaders to meet organizational business needs is not an option; providing feedback is a critical tool in the leader's toolbox.

10

Influential Leadership

Because everything we say and do is the length and
shadow of our own souls, our influence is determined
by the quality of our being.

—Dale E. Turner

The reality of organizations today, because of their matrix structure, size
or complexity, will place leaders (and non-leaders) in situations where they
are not only required to lead and manage their teams or colleagues but
also called upon to influence others in order to realize their objectives. Put
another way, modern business has placed many leaders and other professionals in a position with huge responsibility and accountability but without
the power to compel others to do the work. Those people might be peers.
They might be found in other departments or on other teams. They might
even be key individuals outside the organization.

That problem, in a nutshell, is what this chapter is all about. What
are the increasingly critical skills and techniques leaders can use to get
individuals—who are not under their authority—to do the work that needs
to be done? As a bonus, the techniques and strategies outlined here can be
applied by leaders for use with their own team.

For Alan Booth at Deloitte, great leaders all have influential skills in
their tool kit. "Influential skills are a critical part of leadership. You cannot rely on brute force. The streets are littered with leaders who only use
authority as leadership."

At Global Knowledge, we have developed four themes or skill sets that are required in order to be an effective, influential leader. These themes might be loosely described as:

1. Developing awareness.
2. Establishing credibility.
3. Identifying key stakeholders.
4. Building collaborative networks.

These themes or skills can be effectively employed when you have formal authority and, more critically, when you do not.

DEVELOPING AWARENESS

"What is important to be effective in influencing others?" asks Alan Booth. "Self-awareness and awareness of others. You have to know what they do well; you have to know how to relate to others. Managing yourself is part of managing others. You had better know who you are if you want to manage the relationship effectively."

An authoritative, top-down management structure is, at best, a dim memory in most organizations. Today, it can be said that the heart of successful leadership is influence, not authority. If you want to be an effective and influential leader, it is most important to study and learn about your best leadership tool: you. The first step in becoming an influential leader is to "know thyself": know who you are, and understand why you think, feel and behave the way you do. Self-aware leaders have discovered their behavioral strengths and know-how and can leverage these strengths in their leadership role. They take the time to reflect upon the impact that their interactions have on others, and they ask for feedback on their leadership style. Key questions influential leaders ask themselves are: "What do I value? What motivates me? What are my business goals, and how do those goals align or how are they disconnected from the business needs of others?" Notice that there is more to this than simply asking yourself about your strengths, weaknesses and leadership style. You need to arrive at a better understanding and awareness of your needs, goals and motives.

The most efficient and productive way to become more aware is to challenge your position and begin the process of unlearning by listening and observing what other colleagues share with you. Put another way, you can have full awareness of others only by really knowing yourself first. Among the types of assessment tools you will find useful are the various personal-style assessment tools (like the Myers-Briggs and Global Knowledge's Personality Needs Assessment), and personality inventories (such as the Hogan Personality Assessment, defined earlier in this book). The Multi-Rater Survey, or 360-degree assessment, will also be of use. With self-awareness comes the knowledge of what influence process works best for you. To be an influential leader, a significant part of your attention must be focused on other people—the golden rule is "listen and observe." Your success in influencing others is measured by your ability to tune into what other people consider to be important and how they make decisions—it's the old adage, "Put yourself in the other person's shoes." A smart, influential leader will ask questions in order to better understand what motivates others and what makes them tick, and will adjust his or her position based on these needs, a response known as "interpersonal adaptability."

Think about those memorable and effective salespeople with whom you have dealt in your work or personal life. They rarely tell you what you need. Instead, they take the time to listen, while asking plenty of insightful questions, and only after they have a good idea of your needs and wants do they start trying to sell you on their products and services. Great salespeople try to figure out what makes you tick, what your hot buttons might be and what big fears or concerns you have.

If you spend any time around such salespeople, you might also be surprised to learn that they don't talk and listen to everyone in exactly the same way. They're a bit rougher and earthier with some, more refined with others. That's because they've learned to function in the other person's comfort zone through interpersonal adaptability. They are able to change their style, behavior, presentation and even superficial aspects of their personality to suit the person they're with.

An effective, influential leader is doing pretty much the same thing a successful salesperson does almost unconsciously—listening attentively to that other person, figuring out what he or she needs and wants, and utilizing that information to influence them. And just like that salesperson, you may be in a position where you have no real authority over the individual to get him or her to do what you want.

If at this point you are saying to yourself that this all sounds familiar, you're right. Elements of the skill set necessary to be a self-aware and powerful influencer are discussed in Chapter 8. In particular, the concept of KUBA (know, understand, believe, act) can be applied by the influence-seeking leader. The principles are the same, but the KUBA focus is shifted to help you understand the impact of other people's messages on you. KUBA therefore serves as a lens to see and understand others and how your needs as an influencer have an impact on how you interact with others and how others interact with you.

So becoming a good influential leader starts with being a good follower—or at least being a good listener.

ESTABLISHING CREDIBILITY

It is fairly evident that without credibility, an influence strategy may not work. It's a cornerstone of your influencing efforts. We like to position the key components of credibility as the credibility equation:

Reliability + Capability + Integrity = Credibility.

Reliability is about your actions, meeting your commitments and doing what you say you will do. Can others count on you? Although perhaps not always the most reliable source, Wikipedia offers an interesting definition of reliability: "The ability of a person or system to perform and maintain its functions in routine circumstances, as well as hostile or unexpected circumstances." BusinessDictionary.com provides this definition of the reliability of equipment: "The ability of an apparatus, machine, or system to consistently perform its intended or required function or mission, on demand and without degradation or failure." I hope not to insult anybody, but I think we could apply this definition as well to the notion of reliability of people. A leader needs to be consistent in behavior and mood in various circumstances.

Capability is about competence, expertise and performance. It's about being good at your job. It is hard to be credible as a leader if you do not know what you are talking about. It does not mean you need to be an expert in every aspect of the work: it is common in today's complex organizations for leaders to have direct reports who are much more knowledgeable in some areas than they are. In cases where the leader's expertise is minimal, curiosity and a desire to learn and stay current will go a long way toward rectifying the imbalance. The desire to grow and learn can also be demonstrated when you ask for feedback or demand coaching to get better.

Integrity is about possessing and adhering to values, principles and professional standards. It's about doing the right thing every time and leading by example. As basic as it may sound, you should always be honest and fair in your professional interactions. Demonstrating integrity is about sharing recognition, not accepting—or worse—taking the credit for work done by others.

Building leadership credibility means doing what you as a leader say you will do. Leadership credibility can arise only when leaders develop strong relationships with others. Personal credibility is different from leadership credibility. Personal credibility is associated more with honesty, and while honesty in leaders is important, it is not sufficient. Leadership credibility is associated with integrity, which in contrast to honesty is values-based. Having a sense of integrity means possessing a set of core values that guide what you do, combined with the ability to project core values through your actions. Even when under pressure, the leader with integrity speaks and acts in ways that are consistent with what the organization stands for. This all contributes to generating buy-in, gaining commitment and influencing colleagues, subordinates and even those outside the organization.

"Integrity is coming up more frequently in success profiles as to what we expect from our leaders," says Stéphane Moriou, president of MoreHuman Partners in Paris. Besides integrity, organizations are calling on leaders to play a major role in filling the talent pipeline. "We see more organizations saying they want their leaders to develop others, develop their team. A lot of organizations are losing their employees, so you want to develop those that stay but also the younger generation who want to learn. It's an important factor in the engagement. 'Do I have an opportunity to learn here?' is what younger employees ask."

If a leader is deemed not to be credible, there is a firm limit on his or her ability to create and use influence. Most people will gladly take a leap of faith for a leader whom they perceive as credible and trustworthy. Credibility is built through actions. It is acquired by leaders who are known for thinking beyond their own immediate interests and for working toward a larger, mutually beneficial goal. "To be persuasive, we must be believable; to be believable, we must be credible; to be credible, we must be truthful," said broadcast journalist Edward R. Murrow.

Credible leaders are honest, forward-looking, competent and inspiring. If leaders expect others to get on board and join them in their business pursuits, they need to have a down-to-earth view of where they are going and how they plan to get there. While credible leaders do not necessarily have to possess all the expertise inherent in the project they lead (in other words, to be technically brilliant in their field), they do need to be competent enough to guide the team members. In other words, they need to have a track record for getting things done. Leaders can be seen as more credible if they are seen as enthusiastic, energetic and positive about the future. After all, if a leader shows no passion for a cause, why should anyone else?

IDENTIFYING KEY STAKEHOLDERS

Today's flat structures, matrix organizations and cross-functional teams have replaced traditional organizational hierarchies. Complex problems and the need for innovative solutions require the involvement of many people with diverse expertise and perspectives. Top-down command and control has given way to leadership roles that are distributed at every level of the organization. Informal leaders are increasingly asked to oversee a dynamic corporate structure, characterized by partnerships, alliances and virtual teams. In such an environment, an influential leader's ability to engage others is essential to the success of an organization, and comprises a constellation of leader capabilities, from persuasion to negotiation and consultation. Influential leaders are deliberate in their actions—they ask for and encourage input from others on issues that will affect them. Then they develop shared solutions to the problems that have been identified.

A successful leader working in a flat or nontraditional structure starts by asking, "Who do I need to influence in order to achieve my business objectives?" It may be one person, a group or a number of varied audiences inside and outside an organization. The influencing may also need to be conducted virtually, either verbally or in video conferences, with individuals who work remotely or at other locations. The value of the people you know, your network, is tremendously important when you want to influence across an organization. Dan Pontefract, head of learning and collaboration at Telus, sums it up nicely in the title of his blog post: "My network is my net worth."

As industrial psychologist Stéphane Moriou explains: "In business, your performance is primarily a perceived performance. Your reputation is so much more than your intentions. However, in complex environments and matrix organizations, it is not always easy to know who actually will help you build—or destroy—your reputation. And it is even more difficult to identify those who will influence indirectly. Recognizing its stakeholders—and considering a way to interact with them—is revealed as one of the core leadership competencies of the twenty-first century."

Influential leaders can also be thought of as "thought partners." They are effective at persuasion, and can use conversations, meetings and other forms of dialogue to learn more about their audience's opinions, concerns and perspectives. They are skilled at building coalitions and determining whose buy-in is critical to their success. Influential leaders are transparent with their audience, and they are able to put forth a compelling story to communicate the business case for their goal or project. They engage others and help connect their common objectives and mutual wins. In essence, influential leaders are good negotiators and strive to create win-win solutions for everyone involved. Influential leaders don't see leading as a contest in which one party wins and the other loses—an approach that likely will work only once—but rather as an ongoing relationship that will go on for much longer than the current task or project. A good question an influential leader might ask is, "Why would they work with me?" or perhaps even more critically, "Why would they work with me again in the future?" If you as a leader can't answer at least one of these questions, you are not leading with influence.

One strategic tool for influencers facing a complicated audience is the influence map. It can be real (an organization chart or rough drawing) or something envisioned, but it should include the names of those individuals who need to be influenced for the leader to achieve his or her goals. It is useful to assign weight or decision-making power to the individuals cited on the map. Quite often it is not the person who is highest on the organization chart whose views are decisive, but rather those who have particular expertise, skills or experience.

BUILDING COLLABORATIVE NETWORKS

When people hear the word "networking," their first thought is of attending external events in order to mingle, establishing contacts through social media platforms such as LinkedIn and Twitter or exchanging business cards in the course of a business encounter. Developing a network outside your own organization with people of influence is certainly a common approach for successful leaders. Unfortunately, leaders don't consider sufficiently the importance of internal networking with those inside their organizations.

Today, more than ever, it is imperative that leaders build a strong network of professional partnerships within an organization, and develop a keen understanding that their network is their business.

The question remains, "How can you influence others over whom you have no authority?" The short answer is that to have influence, you need resources that other people want, so that you can trade for what you want. Influential leaders know that being well connected and well respected are key to gaining information and resources, which means being visible and accessible to others who need your help. Rather than approaching business solely based on a "what's in it for me" attitude, they strive to understand what they have to offer to others. They also understand that it's much easier to sell their ideas when they have allies who will support them. By cultivating a strong and diverse network within their organizations, influential leaders create value for those around them, and in turn themselves, by connecting others and becoming a powerful resource.

Consider the law of reciprocity as a way to approach relationships. The term "reciprocity" in social psychology refers to the rule by which a positive action elicits a similarly positive reaction in response, as opposed to purely self-interested behavior. *Merriam-Webster* online dictionary defines reciprocity as "the quality or state of being reciprocal: mutual dependence, action, or influence." As a social construct, reciprocity means that in response to friendly actions, people are frequently much nicer and much more cooperative than predicted by the self-interest model. Conversely, hostile actions frequently lead to a response that is equally or even more nasty, and even sometimes brutal.

Ernst Fehr and Simon Gächter (2000) provide an interesting economical perspective on the notion of reciprocity in their article "Fairness and Retaliation: The Economics of Reciprocity:" "Reciprocity has powerful implications for many economic domains . . . Indeed, the power to enhance collective actions and to enforce social norms is probably one of the most important consequences of reciprocity." To look at it another way, relationships are like financial assets: it will be hard for you as an influential leader to keep making withdrawals (i.e., getting what you want from other individuals) if you are not also making deposits (i.e., offering back expertise to your colleagues). For an influential leader, those deposits might take the form of trust, support or advice. Are you creating value for the other persons in the relationship? What is it you can give them in return for what you require? You likely have a pretty good idea of what it is that they can provide you in terms of skills or expertise, but what is it that you can provide them today or down the road to ensure you are not creating a one-sided and short-term relationship?

If you have not laid the groundwork for being an influential leader, it will likely be harder to get others to "sign on" and support you in your project the first time around. In that sense, an influential leader's job should not start when he or she is first presented with a critical task, but well before it. Building up relationship "assets" can be formal (helping colleagues with tasks that they are working on or directing) or informal (suggesting books or websites on subjects that your coworkers are interested in professionally or personally).

Dan Pontefract (2010) illustrates the notion perfectly in his blog post "My network is my net worth: A personal story":

At my current place of employment, a colleague that I didn't really know reached out directly and asked if I wouldn't mind chatting with his wife to discuss career change opportunities in the learning space. My motto in life has always been a slice of "pay it forward" coupled with a dash of "quid pro quo" mashed with "the glass is half full" topped by "yes, I've got time." So, after saying yes to the request of my unknown colleague, he had this to say:

In the past few weeks I've actually done a lot of reading of your previous posts. I have spent most of my career managing some of the technology (or leading the people managing the technology) behind enterprise collaboration, from LAN in the early days, to IP-Telephony and then Unified Communications. But until coming across your blog, and those of your peer group, I never really explored the world of how the enterprise was actually making use of that technology—to me, it was just a bunch of features we were providing. So it's been an eye-opening and fascinating experience, to say the least. Learning 2.0 in action, I suppose!

Now I blog, microblog and submit all sorts of other learning content via videos, webinars, live chats, speaking engagements, etc. at my place of work . . . but this chap was viewing my external writing and it's here that helped him make an unbelievable connection.

WHAT THE EXPERTS SAY
The Self-Aware Leader

The heart of successful leadership today is influence, not authority. There is a shift occurring in the way we view leadership, from the old top-down command-and-control model to embracing leadership as a multifaceted dynamic force that exists at all levels of an organization. Flatter management structures, project management, outsourcing and virtual teams all mean that individuals have to get things done through a greater number of people, both inside and outside the organization. New skills are becoming important, and this partnership approach requires that individuals achieve their goals by using a variety of methods. Whether you are a leader, a project manager or a member of a cross-functional business team, influencing people and fostering cooperative working relationships is essential to your success.

We saw earlier in this chapter that self-awareness and awareness of others are critical to your ability to influence others. Self-awareness can be defined as the ability of individuals to understand who they are and recognize the impact and influence they have on others (Taylor 2010). Where does self-awareness come from? To a large extent, self-awareness comes from your experiences, environment, relationships, belief systems and values. In the context of leadership identity, self-awareness involves recognizing your character traits, strengths, weaknesses, core attributes and motivations. The value of being a more self-aware leader is that it enables you to make positive changes toward personal growth, and in turn have a positive impact on others (Heady 2008). Hence, the greater understanding you have of yourself, the more successful you will be at understanding and influencing others effectively. To be a successful influential leader, a significant part of your attention must be focused on other people—again, the golden rule is "listen and observe." Your success in influencing others is measured by your ability to tune into what other people consider to be important and how they make decisions. Do people believe that you want to hear their ideas and will value them? Influential leaders are excellent listeners. They are receptive and genuinely interested in the views and feedback of others (Barbuto and Wheeler 2006).

Credibility is the key to influence. An influential leader cannot promote a new position if people are wondering if they can trust the person's intentions. In the workplace, credibility grows out of two sources: expertise and relationships. Influential leaders have a history of sound judgment and have proven themselves knowledgeable and well informed (Conger 1998). Furthermore, they have consistently demonstrated that they can be trusted to listen and to work in the best interests of others—they "walk the talk," and their actions are consistent with their words. Reputation is a direct reflection of people's credibility, and it precedes them in any interaction or negotiation they have (Covey 2009). When a leader's credibility and reputation are high, it enables them to establish trust quickly. Credibility is built through actions, such as thinking beyond oneself and working toward a larger, mutually beneficial goal. Influential leaders work with others to create a positive working environment, including setting performance expectations, establishing accountability practices and sharing decision making. They are role models of accountability, making the conscious decision to live up to their responsibilities. They regularly evaluate their performance and learning and are transparent in their communication with others (Frisina Group 2012).

Influential leaders realize that in order to achieve their desired outcomes, it is imperative that they identify and communicate effectively with key stakeholders. They are skilled at asking questions, uncovering and exploring stakeholders' needs, and connecting their influence objective to each stakeholder's leadership and behavior style. In doing so, they are deliberate in their actions: they ask for and encourage input from others on issues that will affect them, and they develop shared solutions to problems (Johnson 2003). Influential leaders are effective persuaders who use conversations, meetings and other forms of dialogue to collect information and learn more about their audience's opinions, concerns and perspectives. They are skilled at building powerful coalitions and determining whose buy-in is critical to their success. Instead of thinking of key stakeholders as targets, they position them as fellow "thought partners," whom they invite to participate in defining the process for achieving their goals (Conger 1998). Their ability to position themselves from a place of curiosity enhances their collaboration with others and ensures the creation of win-win solutions for everyone involved.

Based on the principle of reciprocity, influential leaders actively seek to determine the values of people in their targeted network groups and focus on providing help in ways that will be most valued by them. Those who are smart influential leaders and networkers will leverage character traits of accountability, trustworthiness and commitment in order to extend their spheres of influence and build a strong base of support (McIntosh and Luecke 2011). They understand that being well connected and well respected are key to gaining expertise, information and resources.

PART III

Leadership Best Practices

11

Align for Results

> If we are facing in the right direction, all we have
> to do is keep on walking.
>
> —Buddhist proverb

In Part 1, we looked at what it takes to be an effective leader, how to identify high-potential leaders and how to accelerate their development. In Part 2, we discussed critically important leadership competencies— coaching, motivation, communication, delegation and influencing others. A leader cannot be successful without using at some point these leadership behaviors. In Part 3, we review best practices for leaders that complement perfectly the competencies discussed in Part 2. Leaders must align their teams to make sure each member performs well and in accordance with the master plan. Leaders must be prepared to live through significant transitions when they become leader for the first time or when they progress to a more senior role. Effective practices are required to ensure success at this critical junction. New employees will join the leaders' teams at some point, so leaders need to be knowledgeable on the best way to onboard them and get the new team members productive fast. The final chapter of Part 3 looks at contemporary ways to grow leaders with an eye on formal, informal and social modalities.

LINE OF SIGHT

As a leader, one of your tasks is to work on the creation of a business plan. Establishing the plan is a well-defined process that encompasses a review of past developments, current performance and future goals. Creating the plan itself is relatively straightforward. The challenge for companies, particularly large ones, is putting that finely crafted plan into practice. How do you take that ambitious outline of the executive leadership team's intentions for the near future, spread it throughout the organization and breathe life into it?

If it sounds like a difficult exercise, that's because it is. And it is the focus of this chapter.

A leader's role goes well beyond simply knowing the organization's strategic goals. Great leaders understand how they and their teams contribute to achieving those goals, and can inspire those around them to take the steps that lead to their attainment. And in general, this is an area in which companies and their leaders need to improve.

Problems arise as the business plan and its components are passed down the line: what was clearly envisioned and understood by the plan's authors tends to be diluted and misinterpreted by managers and more junior team members. To remedy this, leaders need to establish a "line of sight" that reaches all parts of the organization. In practice, the line of sight, written or not, outlines the individual's contribution to the overall business plan and shows how it influences them in their regular day-to-day work. It is the connection between you—whoever and wherever you are in the organization—and the next level above to the strategic plan, mission and vision of the organization.

Establishing a line of sight may sound boring and rather functional. Yet it can't be either of those things if it is meant to be successful. Establishing a line of sight—one that works, at least—involves making it concrete and putting a little bit of excitement and passion behind it. Think of it as a straight line that connects the client to the organization and to the work and contributions that each employee makes. There are common characteristics of a line of sight that lays the foundation for companies to align for results. The line of sight:

- Connects employee and company objectives. Individual employees and teams recognize the alignment of the company's business plan with their individual performance goals.

- Engages individuals' skills and passions so that employees see how they add value to the overall value of the organization.
- Provides value to clients and to the community. Employees clearly see how the company's work benefits those outside groups.

Creating a line of sight proved to be a simplified process at consulting firm Deloitte, which has a vision to be "the world's most trusted advisers." Such an ambitious vision makes for a significant statement, but it needs to be credible and "materialized" for those inside and outside the organization. "You need to see coherence," says Alan Booth, a Toronto-based associate partner with Deloitte. "The vision [statement] has to be simple and easy to remember. If it is too long-winded, complex, or too vague, people won't [remember it]." So how do organizations create the line of sight so critical to align its overall vision (we could say here "mission," "strategic plan" or "critical objectives" and it would work just as well) with individuals and teams? How can an organization create a connection between an employee or a leader and a statement such as "the world's most trusted advisers"? At Global Knowledge, we have found that a three-step process works best for leaders in communicating the contribution of employees in the line-of-sight process for alignment:

1. **Make the connection.** Leaders need to create clarity about the organization's strategic framework and align the organization's purpose to individuals' objectives. It is not sufficient to simply explain the overall goals; leaders must also make those goals real and tangible for everyone from directors and vice-presidents on down to the frontline employees.
2. **Add value.** Leaders must identify ways that their teams add value. They have to explain to colleagues and employees why what they do is critical to the organization, drawing on their own passions to inject the line of sight with excitement and bring it to life, and to determine how exactly the team will add value.

   Where this gets tricky is creating a line of sight for employees who may never deal with the end client at all, typically because they are in support functions such as HR, maintenance or accounting. In those cases, it is even more important for leaders to emphasize and connect the value-added component of the employees' role in the organization and its strategic goals.

3. **Tell a story.** Leaders need to use the power of storytelling to bring abstract or barely known components of an organization to life. Storytelling requires leaders to go beyond the plan, objective or challenge and bring the line of sight to life with a personal touch. A leader talking with the IT or HR department, for instance, might outline the department's contribution to end clients by referencing real-life examples, such as the HR department's introduction of an effective training program that allows frontline workers to better serve the needs of customers or the IT team's new mobile technology application that allows physicians to provide better care for patients.

The storytelling skills leaders need to employ to create a line of sight for employees are very similar to the four Ps and KUBA (know, understand, believe, act) rules discussed in Chapter 8.

"We talk a lot about the values of the organization; things like integrity are big with us," says Christopher Hodgson of Scotiabank. "We don't compromise on key principles. We look at how people interact, how they deal with each other and how they try to come up with better solutions and that would be very different from other organizations that they have come from. We have worked hard to break silos down." The compartmentalization of the bank in four operating business units—their existence in distinct "silos"—is a constant battle for the Toronto-based bank. "We are really trying to work across and not down, and that is something we drive through balanced score cards, through performance reviews, through our compensation process. All of those things are integrated, and we try to support that through very broad communication and showing the executives working together too—in town halls, things like that."

Leaders can utilize an alignment framework like the one Global Knowledge uses with clients. (See Figure 11.1.) It lists the organization's vision, goals or priorities and links them to the objectives of departments, teams or individuals, illustrating how they align with those above and below.

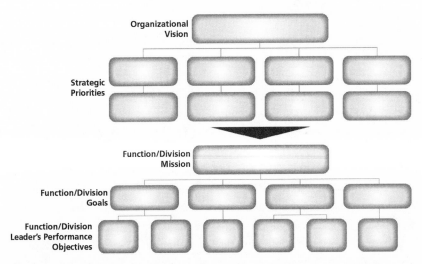

Figure 11.1: Alignment Framework for Organization and Individual Goals

As the figure indicates, the process of aligning organization and individual goals begins by setting a clear, value-laden statement describing how the organization wants to be in the future—its organizational vision. The next step is to set strategic priorities, the key themes that emerge directly from the vision statement. These provide the focus when establishing vision-driven objectives. From these themes, functional or divisional leaders can formulate a division mission statement that sets out the function or the division's purpose. Function or division goals are then formed by considering everything that has come before. Of primary importance, however, is the consideration of the strategic priorities for the organization. Function or division goals should link back to these priorities. Performance objectives at the function or division leader level are determined next. Because these goals are in alignment to the organization's priorities, in effect, the leaders' fulfillment of the objectives indirectly supports the overall success of the organization.

This process does not ensure that every task and priority will align perfectly with the organization's priorities, but if a leader sees, after going through the exercise, that there is little connection between his or her team's goals and those of the organization, it is time for the leader to review the team's goals to improve the alignment and line of sight. Think of it as a blueprint to show how top-level goals are put into practice at all levels.

In the case of the UK's Royal Mail, John Duncan, Human Resources group director, made a clear connection between critical strategic initiatives, such as the program "World Class Mail," and the HR plan. Each HR function can show a clear contribution to the strategic initiative. This contribution is illustrated clearly in internal communication documents; it is also communicated in many other ways on a regular basis. For Royal Mail, creating a line of sight and aligning for results are essential parts of a never-ending process. The organization issues an internal document every two weeks and operates an internal television channel that features fifteen- or twenty-minute segments. These programs allow employees to hear directly from senior leaders about what is going on in the organization, how goals are being achieved, what new initiatives have been introduced and what the company's expectations are. Thus, the "story" is being told many times and through different media.

The UK postal service has ambitious long-term goals, explains Duncan. "We are changing the business model, and in tandem we are going through this modernization and privatization exercise that will potentially see a new ownership model. There is a lot of change going on—letter mail is in decline, parcels and direct marketing are on the increase—so we are in the midst of a massive transformation initiative at the same time as we are managing this £9-billion, 150,000-person organization."

Moya Greene, CEO of Royal Mail, explains in an interview with McKinsey & Company (2012) how she spends her time, including on ensuring alignment between the employees and where the organization is going.

Given the heavy demands on her time, Greene partitions her agenda into "big blocks of time" that she vigorously monitors. Analyzing how she spent her time, she found that about 15 percent was spent managing and understanding her employees, 25 percent went to changing how the company was operated, 15 percent was devoted to changing "the conversation" inside the company and making Royal Mail more customer-focused and 10 percent went to strategic realignment—showing employees how the "new" Royal Mail would make money through nontraditional avenues such as parcels, media and the sale of data to commercial interests. The remaining 35 percent of her time went to general organization, recruitment, working with the board and crisis management.

LEVERAGING THE PERFORMANCE MANAGEMENT SYSTEM

Most organizations today operate a performance management system, which can go by various names, including "accountability system" and "performance appraisal system." Whatever it is called, it is really a system in which an organization sets expectations, conducts performances reviews, addresses gaps and provides coaching throughout the year. Unfortunately, performance management systems are perceived negatively in too many organizations as the pass-or-fail review mechanism determining whether one receives a salary increase, bonus or promotion.

I would like to stress that organizations that view performance management systems primarily as an instrument to conduct employee reviews are starting from the end of the process rather than the start. The primary raison d'être of a performance management system is to determine the contribution of individuals to the group plan or team plan. When it is used in this way, it becomes a vehicle to "cascade down" the overall objectives of the organization's business plan. (See Figure 11.2.)

If, for example, the organization is establishing the top-level goals of reducing the cost of operations and improving the quality of the relationship with customers, the impact on individuals at all levels will be affected. But what do they have to do differently on a day-to-day basis? A performance management system can act as a tool in the hands of top leaders to provide the necessary goals and linkages to those further down in the organization to ensure that all employees achieve the goals individually and as a group/department/business unit—in other words, creating a line of sight.

Management of The Ottawa Hospital created a very simple, powerful and compelling organization vision to align its thousands of employees with its clients, namely, their patients. For a few years now, the hospital has asked employees to think of every patient as a loved one, or more concretely, every patient should feel as though he or she was treated like a

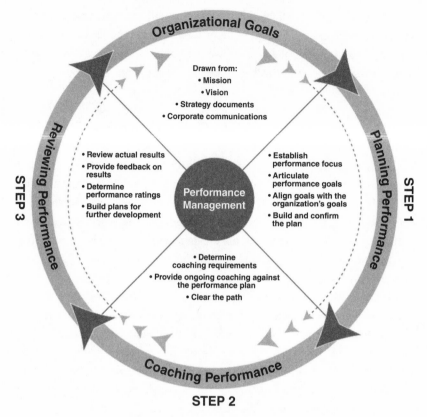

Figure 11.2: The Performance Management Cycle

loved one. This goal is communicated to the patient community through the hospital's You're in My Care campaign.

The Ottawa Hospital's vision is: "Provide each patient with the world-class care, exceptional service and compassion we would want for our loved ones." It is an admirable, powerful and effective goal, but how do you cascade it through the organization and measure its achievement? The Ottawa Hospital regularly measures its achievements through powerful measurement software and regular meetings of the hospital's leadership group to ensure goals are being met.

"The same scorecard appears at every meeting that we do, and the software we purchased ensures alignment of those goals," explains hospital

CEO Jack Kitts. For example, the hospital aimed to get employees washing their hands as close to 100 percent of the time as possible; it set a formal goal of 95 percent. "Each month, each manager of a unit puts in their score," Kitts explains. Hand hygiene is just one of twenty-five measures each hospital unit records and reports on. "Now every ninety days, the management team gets together offsite to reaffirm our goals, we display the results by unit so that all of management has the opportunity to look at the results and [we] benchmark internally to try to improve."

The hospital's efforts to align goals and achievement don't stop there. At quarterly meetings, which the hospital calls its Leadership Development Institute, the leadership team reviews "where we need to improve and what we need to do. We also recognize the indicators that we are doing well," says Kitts. "The alignment of the goals, and the understanding of what the goals are, have been incredibly important."

Today, Kitts and his leadership team believe that they have gone a long way to aligning employees and departments with the hospital's main goal, but that they are still a long way from completion. "I would say we are 75 percent of the way there. I would say we went from 25 percent to 75 percent. I think the next [improvement] is going to be much heavier lifting."

A BUSINESS STRATEGY

At its core, performance management systems outline and explain how individual performance advances the corporate agenda. In this sense, performance management systems stop acting like HR systems and begin working as vehicles to execute business strategy—think of them as line-of-sight enablers.

There's little doubt that performance management systems begin at the top. Obviously, if the CEO doesn't see the system as a driver of strategy, the chances of having an effective system drop significantly. The executive leadership team must clearly define the organization's strategic priorities and communicate them throughout the organization. The strategic priorities are the make-or-break, action-oriented targets that move your organization toward its vision—whether that vision involves boosting sales revenue, accelerating speed to market or improving customer retention rates.

Once the top priorities are defined, the executive leadership team establishes specific measures for those priorities. These metrics are incorporated into the senior executives' performance objectives. Using the performance management system, accountabilities cascade down to the next level, where managers discuss with their bosses specific goals and accountabilities that align with corporate goals. Managers then do the same with their direct reports, translating departmental goals, all the while maintaining alignment with corporate goals. This practice will have multiple effects on achieving the business strategy if applied at all levels of the organization and in all business units and departments. Just as the water cascading from top to bottom gives rise to a waterfall's full power, the alignment and definition of goals to all levels will too.

It's essential that an employee participate fully in determining how he or she can realize those priorities. It's also critical that all expectations be based on outcomes, measurement and time frame. Another common way to define clear expectations is by referring to SMART—specific, measurable, action-oriented, realistic and time-bound—criteria. More companies are beginning to publish the performance goals of executives and managers for all to see, as direct reports are impacted by those goals and so can adjust their own goals accordingly. In particular, tools such as corporate dashboards and balanced scorecards, which track progress on business and cultural strategies, are gaining in popularity because they offer multiple performance views that all can see. The cascading model works not only for the what (the business objectives) but also for the how (the organization values and competencies). Darren Entwistle, president and CEO of the telecommunications company Telus, illustrated it well in a recent interview (Bingham and Galagan 2012) with the American Society for Training and Development's *T+D* magazine.

Telus utilizes four leadership values to measure leaders' achievement of the how. The company evaluates its leaders against those values and their subattributes, which are tailored to each individual depending on that person's position within the Telus hierarchy.

Rather than starting with a statement such as "Here's how we think you've done," Telus begins by asking people to do a self-assessment against the company's values and attributes and compare it with the perception of the manager they report to.

The company doesn't stop there. It combines some of the feedback received and interjects social-networking thinking by challenging its leaders to ask their peers and those who report to them for their views of their leadership skills as measured against the company's leadership values. It's a process Telus carries out regularly. "This is not something you do only once or twice a year," Entwistle says. "You do this on a monthly basis. And you focus on the areas where the deltas [variances] are greatest."

Where the assessment process finds gaps between peoples' leadership and the Telus leadership values, the company creates a customized career development plan to provide its employees with the required leadership skills to continue their progression in the company. Telus has invested approximately $100 million "in recognizing the how."

The president and CEO of Telus explains that it is important to recognize the what formally; to make it real, Telus performs audits of how values are being recognized and pays attention to the balance of recognition between the what and the how.

Entwistle notes that the telecommunications company pays out $200 million in annual bonuses, or $1 billion over five years, "not a trivial amount of money." Another aspect of its bonus program that sets Telus apart is that it pays 50 percent of that bonus based on performance, the achievement of recognized objects, and the remainder on how its staff display and live up to the company's leadership values. Or, as he explains, "We pay 50 percent for the 'what' and 50 percent for the 'how.'"

Telus has recognized that the what can be transitory or change from year to year, while the how is both recognizable and recurring. While the what may change, getting to that goal the "Telus way" is repeatable. "So in terms of smart money, I want to invest in the how," Entwistle explains.

THE THREE PHASES OF THE PERFORMANCE MANAGEMENT CYCLE

One of the most appreciated benefits of a robust performance management program is the avoidance of lengthy, formal meetings. Rather, successful organizations make conversations about performance a regular, informal, event conducted as projects are being carried out. Such conversations and ongoing coaching are excellent tools for managing people. Further, it's in the context of such conversations that barriers to progress are discovered. In other words, if you really want to make your program strong, you must exercise it regularly.

So, how to get started? Most organizations can get a performance management system up and running in fewer than 100 days. To realize a system's true potential, however, it probably takes closer to three years, with all employees completing the process of goal setting, coaching, monitoring and performance review. For most employees, performance management systems are much different from what they're used to, and before getting started, employees should complete training in the three phases of the performance management cycle: planning, performing and reviewing. Note that here "employees" refers to all employees and leaders in the organization, in line with the recommendation that performance management must be done at all levels. In the description of each phase below, the actions can vary depending on whether you are the leader or the employee in the conversation.

Planning Phase

The planning phase demonstrates how performance management helps employees contribute to strategic priorities and department or functional area goals. Employees learn to:

- Identify most important areas of responsibility and develop measurable goals
- Identify competencies needed to accomplish their objectives and live the values of the organization
- Create individual development plans to improve skills in target competencies
- Head or participate in a discussion to reach agreement on performance plans

Performance Phase

In the performance phase, employees learn how they can effectively monitor their performance in order to meet or exceed established goals. They begin to:

- Monitor performance through specific tracking tools
- Lead or participate in interim performance reviews
- Provide or ask for feedback on important competencies
- Provide, seek and receive coaching

Reviewing Phase

In the reviewing phase, employees get instruction in how to conduct or participate in review discussions and plan for future development. They learn how to:

- Make the best use of leaders' time by taking full responsibility for gathering data and providing ratings
- Assess collected data and determine performance levels
- Prepare and lead or participate in a performance review discussion based on performance data and demonstration of targeted competencies

The impact of performance management is largely driven by its practicality. The system must be useful and usable. When it is, a performance management system helps the organization achieve target business results and maintain its desired culture. It crystallizes employees' understanding of how they are contributing to the organization's goals, what's expected of them, how they are doing and how they can continue to grow, develop and add value to the business. When employees understand the impact of their actions, they find their work more motivating.

Performance management programs also provide a unique mechanism for ongoing feedback and development, a critical component of engagement and retention. After setting goals together, managers and employees can track progress and ensure that performance stays in alignment with goals and changing work conditions. Continuous feedback facilitates performance by helping employees refocus behaviors when they get off track. During performance reviews, managers can provide more detailed feedback relative to goals in order to help employees identify strengths and developmental needs. In this way, new performance goals can be set to leverage employee strengths and provide opportunities to address developmental or career goals. And, ultimately, the company benefits from an aligned, accountable and engaged workforce better prepared to execute corporate strategy.

COOL TECH TOOLS

New Internet-based tools have made it easier than ever to harness employee performance. More than just electronic forms, many of these high-powered solutions feature intuitive automation that helps align organizational strategy with individual performance, streamline reporting and administrative functions, standardize performance review reporting and improve system compliance.

Most importantly, the technology provides executives, managers and employees with enhanced capability to drive execution. Senior leaders can instantly ensure that manager and employee performances are in sync and on track with organizational goals. Managers can better coach those who report to them because performance data is at their fingertips. Employees can see how their goals line up with those of their bosses. And individuals are better equipped to take charge of their own development.

Some solutions also enable a company to deploy common organization goals to all employees. For instance, if identifying a cost reduction is a company-wide objective, this objective can be distributed across the enterprise. So when you're identifying your specific individual goals, you can express how you plan to do your part in cutting costs to meet the company objective.

But while many software solutions can automate tasks to simplify administration, it won't make a bad performance management system better. Before investing in a technology solution, make sure it will provide:

- Simplified alignment of organization-leader-individual performance goals
- Real-time access to performance management data so all can access and monitor results
- Checkpoints that encourage frequent, informal leader-associate performance discussions
- Seamless integration with other human resources management systems

---

THE USE—AND MISUSE—OF PERFORMANCE REVIEWS

They are some of the most dreaded words in the business world: "annual performance review," "employee appraisal," "job review."

Whether it is painstakingly carried out annually by the HR department or consists of a semiformal chat in a manager's office, the performance review can give rise to equal parts angst, confusion and distrust. And that's just on the manager's side of the desk. Why is this? And why are employees anxious about the review process? It could be because they feel reviews are arbitrary and that they have no real input, or that their contributions are seen as meaningless.

It should be no surprise that a large number of people in any given organization see little value in HR-driven annual performance reviews. And who can blame them? The term alone sends the wrong message on two counts. First, the emphasis is backward—on the past instead of upfront goal setting and employee engagement, where it belongs. Second, waiting an entire year to measure and discuss performance is nonsense. Still, this is how most organizations have done things, whether through stubbornness or because of "it's the way we always have" inertia. Even Fortune 500 stars do it.

Forced Rankings

In the 1990s, General Electric's then CEO Jack Welch popularized a system in which, if an employee was not an A or B performer, or was not advancing toward becoming one, that employee was out. Great in theory, lousy in practice. A forced ranking approach may mandate managers to remove individuals regardless of circumstances, even if they are good performers with plenty of potential. It can also allow weak leaders to hide behind the system instead of taking proactive steps to address an individual's performance problems.

A Bad Combination

Another problematic approach is to talk about performance and compensation at the same time. Performance is too important a topic to be confused with the delicate question of pay. And compensation is so important to the employee that it tends to distract from any and all other topics being discussed. From an employee perspective, the discussion can become stressful and emotional; from a corporate perspective, fair compensation relative to company performance can be misconstrued by the employee. Smart companies link performance and salary, but hold focused discussions around each topic separately.

Multi-Rater Surveys

More companies are using 360-degree assessments for performance management. These are surveys completed by the people who work with the individual who is being rated—supervisors, peers, direct reports and sometimes vendors and customers. There are two major problems with this approach. First, it's too time-consuming, especially when numerous performance appraisals are due at the same time. In performance review season, as most managers know too well, conducting and submitting a team's reviews easily becomes a logistical nightmare. But more importantly, when the results of such surveys impact performance ratings, it means they are linked also to salary reviews and real money is on the line. In this situation, raters' feedback tends to be skewed. Instead of objective feedback related to performance and development, the raters' views can be tarnished by prejudice. Multi-raters are excellent tools for developmental purposes, and that's exactly how companies should use them—but not for performance management.

The good news is that organizations are starting to recognize these performance-rating pitfalls. Over the past decade, more companies are moving to a business-oriented performance management model that emphasizes shared ownership between employee and manager, aligns individual goals with corporate objectives and engages employees to perform at a higher level.

Put simply, the modern performance management model hardwires individual employee performance into the company's business plan.

WHAT THE EXPERTS SAY
Line of Sight

Given the competitive nature of organizations today and their increased emphasis on lateral leadership and associated employee contributions in decision making, it is no wonder that organizations have stepped up their efforts to help employees understand and articulate the organization's missions and their contributions to achieving its goals. For employees to understand the direction and objectives of their organizations, they need to be able to see how their job fits with the "big picture." Boswell and Boudreau (2001) were early contributors to what has become known as the line of sight, defining it as "a mechanism for ensuring employee understanding of an organization's objectives and how to contribute to those objectives." The authors argue that employees who understand what is expected of them and how to contribute will be better equipped to make the right decisions and do what is in the company's best interest. Looking at it from another perspective, line of sight relates to a shared mindset or vision and assumes that if employees see themselves as effective contributors to the company's goals, they should be more likely to perform at a higher level. Boswell and Boudreau caution that employees seeing themselves as effective contributors is not enough—that, in fact, employees may not be accurate in their assessments of the strategic objectives of the organizations or may not understand precisely how best to contribute. The authors argue that a clear strategy is needed to create this line of sight between employees and the organization. From the results of their study that surveyed and conducted focus group meetings with HR professionals from four organizations, each from different industries, on the critical issues related to line of sight, Boswell and Boudreau developed a model for how leading companies create, measure and achieve strategic results through line of sight. Their model involves specific strategies for these four processes:

1. Defining and detecting line of sight
2. What moves line of sight
3. How line of sight differs among employees and organizations
4. Consequences of line of sight

Defining and detecting line of sight involves strategies related to employee perceptions of alignment, feeling part of organizational success, belief in strategy and/or values, articulation of mission, listing of contributions to mission, and ranking of importance of objectives and behaviors, and the outcomes produced. Human resources management-related and general organizational practices, including communication, incentives, employee involvement and empowerment, leadership styles, learning maps, open-book management and cross-training, are identified as strategies that may foster or enhance line of sight. Boswell and Boudreau's model identifies several ways that line of sight differs across employees, groups and organizations, among them demographics (e.g., tenure, education), type of work/worker, culture or business cycle, mergers and acquisitions and reasons for alignment. It recognizes both individual- and organizational-level outcomes to line of sight, including morale/satisfaction, commitment/retention, performance/ success, accomplishment of goals, and timely and improved decision making. Overall, the model has largely positive implications for both the individual and the organization, but the authors point out that the potentially less attractive consequence of increased stress and decreased work-life balance exists for employees. Although the majority of participants had similar views about the general issues and importance of strategic alignment of employees within their organizations, they each acknowledged difficulties with measuring line of sight. The results suggest that while employee perceptions of employees may not accurately capture whether true alignment exists, perceptions nonetheless are important because they have the capacity to influence employee attitudes and motivation. The study identifies threats to alignment, such as organizational instability, decentralization and the use of contingent workers.

In a more recent article, Boswell, Bingham and Colvin (2006) draw on empirical evidence, theoretical perspectives and examples of exemplary organizations' practices to highlight the critical relationship between aligning employees with organizations' larger strategic goals and attaining strategic success. Specifically, the article focuses on how line of sight is created, how it is enhanced (or stifled) and how it can be effectively managed. The authors are in agreement with others (Boswell and Boudreau 2001; Gay and D'Aprix 2006) that in today's current business environment, marked by intense global competition, turbulent markets and changing business conditions, organizations cannot disregard nonexecutive employees as unimportant to strategic success. Boswell, Bingham and Colvin argue that although line of sight is of greatest importance at lower organizational levels, where employees have the most contact with customers and products, it remains the weakest among these employees, perhaps because executives lack confidence in the abilities of such employees to accurately understand the organization's strategic imperative. In terms of communicating a line-of-sight message, the authors recognize that organizations must have a clear vision of where they believe the organization is headed, as well as the strategic imperative necessary to facilitate success. They emphasize that direct one-to-one communication aimed at specifically linking employee roles and behaviors to organizational goals is key to identifying inconsistent perceptions and behaviors related to strategic objectives, and provide immediate opportunities for clarification. They argue that increased network-like communicational designs are imperative to ensure strategic objectives are effectively cascaded throughout the organizational hierarchy.

In terms of employee contributions to line of sight, Boswell, Bingham and Colvin acknowledge that work practices are diverging from defined work roles and seeking greater degrees of flexibility, cooperation and participation in decisions that affect an organization's overall success. The anticipated benefits to these changes do not come without increased risk as well, with benefits being fully realized only if employees accurately understand and behave in ways consistent with the organization's strategic goals.

The article compares the value of both extrinsic and intrinsic motivators to employee development of line of sight. Boswell, Bingham and Colvin argue that line of sight is critical to linking organizational-level incentive systems to individual performance. They recognize IBM's personal business commitments as an example of best practice in terms of providing employees with a clear understanding of the link between employee behaviors and strategic objectives that has resulted in increased employee empowerment and motivation—and impact on IBM's bottom-line performance. The authors point to stewardship theory, which depicts employees as collectivistic, pro-organizational and self-serving, as a perspective that suggests the value of intrinsic factors in employee development of line of sight. They argue that where stewardship is present, line of sight is more likely to be present and to produce actions aligned with the organization's strategic objectives. The authors raise challenges associated with facilitating employee line of sight, including the risk of having highly aligned individuals become so committed to the end itself that they lose sight of the means through which the goal is attained, and they warn of the potentially disastrous outcomes for organizations of a poorly developed strategic intent combined with highly aligned employees.

In a simple and straightforward way, Gay and D'Aprix (2006) describe the important role communication plays, as does a four-step plan, in creating a line of sight between employees and business strategy. The authors emphasize that a clear line of sight between employees and business strategy means that employees know and believe in the strategy, are committed to contributing to it and know what they need to do to help achieve it. The authors outline their four-step strategy to create this line of sight:

1. Develop and validate core messages.
2. Align leaders and define their roles.
3. Commit to proof points.
4. Measure success.

According to Gay and D'Aprix's strategy, senior leaders work collaboratively to develop the core messages that address each of the issues needing to be developed, and commit to using them as a blueprint by all communicators in the organization. In order to validate the messages, assess the current state and give employees a voice, helping them feel connected to the business and its goals, employee data is gathered through both quantitative (opinion and engagement surveys) and qualitative (focus groups and listening sessions) methods. The authors emphasize the importance of creating a compelling message that clearly lays out the case for change, the current state of the business and the future vision. They point to one organization's creation of a visual, interactive "journey map" that included typical on-the-job scenarios that leaders, managers and employees worked through in terms of how they act at present and how they would act in the future in ways that would be in line with the new strategy. Aligning leaders and defining their roles is crucial given that leadership and management communication is the key driver of employee engagement. Gay and D'Aprix distinguish the role of leaders versus managers in creating a line of sight for employees, pointing to senior leaders as being responsible for setting the vision, bringing it to life for employees and building context around the messaging. Managers, on the other hand, are responsible for making the business strategy meaningful to employees by connecting it to employees' job responsibilities, performance and group objectives, as well as acting as advocates for employee "voice back" through the organization. The authors point out that leaders and managers will often require leadership training and learning experiences related specifically to the new business strategy. In order to gain real commitment from employees, leaders and managers need to commit to ensuring employees can see "proof points" within the organization that support the new business strategy, including seeing processes that reinforce the importance of specific strategy goals and hearing success stories that recognize other employees for behaving in line with the strategy. An effective line of sight requires that the organization establish clear outcomes and measures of success. Gay and D'Aprix identify a few key questions that will help identify which critical methods/metrics to use:

- How will we know that our employees have a clear line of sight with the business?
- How can we measure if employees know, believe and are committed to the strategy?
- How will we measure behavior change?
- How will we know that leaders are doing an effective job of connecting employees to the strategy?
- Which business measures will this impact (i.e., profitability, productivity, customer satisfaction)?

The authors emphasize the importance of holding managers accountable for their role in helping employees develop a line of sight using, for example, incentives, individual coaching and development plans, or setting up a buddy system with a best-practice executive.

Performance Management

Performance management allows an organization to clearly identify and articulate its performance objectives and expectations and to establish a system that measures expectations. In a practical guide for implementing best practices related to managing performance, the Ontario Network of Employment Skills Training Projects (ONESTEP 2012) indicates that a comprehensive performance management system involves measuring outcomes across the organization. The guide recognizes that in order to measure performance effectively, organizations need to align, adapt and achieve. Alignment indicators should encompass measures related to the business strategy and line of sight, including opportunities in the sector, needs of clients and employee line-of-sight progress. Adaptive measures ensure that progress related to alignment is monitored, so the organization and its employees are able to adjust performance to meet performance objectives. Achievement measures that include timely feedback and effective rewards help ensure the organization's attainment of its goals. A critical function of an effective performance management system is to motivate and focus individuals to perform at their optimal levels of competence during a defined period. C.S. Schoonover (2011) identifies specific guidelines for goal cascading, as well as specific roles and responsibilities to support a fair contract for performance. (See Tables 11.1 and 11.2.)

Table 11.1: Guidelines for Goal Cascading

Organization Driver	What Needs to Be Defined?
Vision and mission	What do we want to be? How do we achieve it?
Values	What are our beliefs?
Competencies	What are we good at?
Culture (people, practices, climate)	Who are we?
Internal/external influences	What is the context in which we work? How do we know about and respond to changes?
Organization strategy (to gain competitive advantage)	How can we use our competencies to succeed?
Performance objectives	What has to happen for us to succeed?
Performance measures	How can we tell how well we did? How are we going to give feedback to continually improve?
Staffing and development strategy	What should our HR strategy be? How can we attract, retain and develop employees?

Table 11.2: Roles and Responsibilities in the Performance Management Process

Manager's Responsibilities	Employees' Responsibilities
Select and ensure alignment of goals and competency criteria between employees and the organization.	Suggest new and revised goals to improve performance.
Establish and record clear, specific performance criteria with employees.	Provide input on actions and behaviors to support goals and targeted competencies.
Engage employees in a collaboration to manage goals and competencies.	Reach an agreement with the manager about means and interactions to support targeted goals and competencies.
Provide intermittent feedback and coaching on performance.	Solicit feedback from the manager and others related to performance targets and career development.
Document a clear, no-surprise appraisal.	Define areas to discuss and clarify with the manager in the year-end review.
Conduct a full discussion of performance, including accomplishments, opportunities and development needs.	Participate actively in year-end discussions; explore career and development planning.
Translate strategies from the business planning process into team and individual goals.	Provide feedback on opportunities and limitations related to the team's ability to meet business expectations.

The specific guidelines for goal cascading involve methods that outline the appropriate number of goals, goal types and goal criteria. The authors provide these indicators:

1. Coaching support to focus on critical goals to ensure their relevance and alignment with business strategy
2. Refining and tailoring goals and action plans to individual needs and preferences
3. Ongoing dialogue to update goals and related actions to accommodate changes in business strategy's direction and tactics

In terms of key responsibilities of the manager and employees, Schoonover emphasizes the importance of having clear, well-articulated and accountable roles and responsibilities. The manager's primary role is as a coach who provides to employees consistent support related to individual performance and growth. The manager is required to:

1. Select goals and competency criteria and ensure there is alignment between employees and the organization.
2. Establish and record clear and specific performance criteria with employees.
3. Engage employees in a collaboration to manage goals and competencies.
4. Provide feedback and coaching on performance.
5. Document a clear appraisal.
6. Conduct a full discussion of performance, including accomplishments, opportunities and development needs.
7. Translate strategies from the business planning process into team and individual goals.

The employees' role is to take charge of their performance and development, and to seek ways to make positive contributions to the team and organization. The guide identifies several responsibilities. Employees are expected to:

1. Suggest new and revised goals to improve performance.
2. Provide input on actions and behaviors to support goals and competencies.
3. Reach agreement with the manager about means to support targeted goals and competencies.
4. Seek feedback from the manager related to performance targets and career development.
5. Define areas to discuss with the manager in the year-end review.
6. Participate in year-end discussions, including exploring career and development planning.
7. Provide feedback on opportunities and limitations related to the team's ability to meet business expectations.

Schoonover recognizes alignment as a *"reciprocal* set of interactions with *transparent, fully communicated* updates on business strategies and related changes in goals *cascaded frequently* and with *open, upward communications . . . that reach and are acknowledged* by top management" (emphasis in original). This feedback loop is considered one of the most important characteristics of a successful performance management system.

12

From Doing to Leading, and Other Leadership Transitions

> In the end, it is important to remember that we cannot become what we need to be, by remaining what we are.
>
> —Max DePree

People are not all typically born to be leaders. Well, that is, not unless their family name happens to be the same one that adorns the sign over the company's front door. The vast majority of leaders gain their position when someone above them in the organization decides that they should shift from doing a certain job to working with and leading others to get the work done. The change doesn't come with a special key to a marble and gold-plated washroom, as it does in a memorable episode of *The Simpsons*, but it does come with a lengthy list of responsibilities and the very real possibility of failure if the newly promoted individual is treated with benign neglect from above.

Letting new leaders "figure it out as they go" is all too often a reality in today's flat management structures, but it is also a sure recipe for failure. Instead, new leaders need to be provided with an understanding of their accountabilities, one that identifies ways that they need to develop, and shows them how to prioritize activities, allocate time, overcome roadblocks and earn respect and credibility. Developing approaches to ensuring that a new leader is successful is the main topic of this chapter. We will also look at other leadership transitions.

New leaders first of all need to understand what leadership is—and isn't—about. Linda Hill (2003) identifies several myths shared by new leaders. Professor Hill writes that, often, people pursue a leadership role because it will give them more authority. They soon realize that authority is not all it's cracked up to be. Successful leaders do not manage through authority alone (see Chapter 10 on influential leadership). Instead, leaders perform through others. Hill writes about one newly minted manager complaining that he did not become a boss but a "hostage." In other words, he realized that he depended on his team rather than on his own efforts for success. Authority or power may have been the go-to leadership tool of choice fifty years ago, but it will not work on its own today. Leaders need credibility to influence and lead others.

The Harvard professor also identifies another lingering myth about leadership: that existing one-on-one relationships with members of your team are insufficient to get the job done. The team has to jell into a functioning unit, rather than be managed as individuals in separate one-on-one relationships. Another myth is that leaders have control over people. In fact, new managers need individuals in their team to be committed, not compelled or controlled.

Hill notes that becoming a leader is similar to becoming a parent. You can read all the recommended books on parenting, but the reality is that, for the first-time mom and dad, the role of parent is new, unique for them and different. More importantly, it keeps changing every day, month and year. It is the same with leadership. It's a sudden change, just like parenting, and it is sure to evolve with time.

Taking on a leadership role can be a jarring transition. Newly appointed leaders may now be in charge of people whom they have worked beside for years. Alternatively, they may find themselves in charge of a team that they have never been introduced to before. Either way, they have to learn new skills and techniques and, just as importantly, they need to unlearn many of the habits that made them successful in their nonmanagement work life.

New leaders also have to rethink the nature of the satisfaction they derive from "a good day's work." No longer will that feeling come from the successful completion of a task. As a team leader, it will be the performance of the team, and how the leader grows them and makes them successful.

A radically different set of measures constitute success when moving from employee to leader.

Hill identifies three imperatives for new leaders. They must:

- Manage themselves
- Manage their network
- Manage their team

So first the new leader must undergo a personal transformation from doer to leader through self-awareness. Managing the network, Hill's second imperative, is the process by which a leader manages up and sideways to ensure that the necessary resources and support are provided for the team. Managing the team, the key role of a new leader, is the third imperative—and the primary focus of Part 2 of this book.

So what can be done to support new leaders in their transition from doer to leader? At Global Knowledge, we identified four key elements necessary to make the transition to leadership:

1. **Shifting the mindset.** New leaders now need to perform through their teams rather than as individuals. What accountabilities do they now have that they didn't have before? New leaders need to list and identify accountabilities that support their direct-report employees and team members, such as planning, delegating and providing feedback. They also need to determine accountabilities that support the organization, as well as ensure that team objectives are well established and the right systems are in place. Power comes with responsibility. Part of the process of changing the mindset requires that new leaders understand the impact of their behaviors on the team. As peers, they had a limited impact on the team; as leaders, they have far more impact and influence—for good and ill.

2. **Identifying opportunities for development.** Now that they have become leaders, what skills do they need to acquire and behaviors, learn? Typically, these are leadership skills (communicating effectively, motivating, delegating and coaching employees to raise their performance), as well as more traditional business skills (budgeting, systems planning and systems integrating). A good way to acquire these skills, apart from

taking courses, is to be paired up with a mentor or management "buddy" who can provide advice and tips and can deal with the concerns that routinely arise during the early transition period.

3. **Allocating time as a people leader.** How do they spend their day as new leaders? How much time do they spend with employees to coach and direct them? How long do they spend planning the work, gathering resources and overseeing the work? In fact, it is not really the time that you want to manage, it's the activities and the way you prioritize them, consciously or not. To help new leaders, we developed a priority quadrant (see Figure 12.1) whereby you determine whether a particular task is urgent or important. If it is high on both scales, you do it. If it is urgent or important (but not both), you can delegate. If it is neither, you can eliminate.

   New leaders are now in a position where they have to constantly decide what tasks and decisions are priorities and what can be delegated or eliminated. Very often, new leaders get overwhelmed because everything looks like a priority: they are reluctant to delegate, don't know how to postpone and feel obliged never to decline even nonessential tasks.

4. **Earning respect and establishing credibility.** We discussed what makes credibility in Chapter 10. It may sound strange, but being good at their former jobs is a good place for new leaders to start. "First be

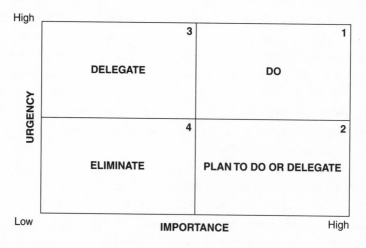

Figure 12.1: Priority Quadrant

a good doctor" was the critical first step for administrators of hospital staff, according to Jack Kitts, CEO of The Ottawa Hospital. That is, it is difficult for a new leader to have credibility with employees if they do not view that person as credible or as an expert in his or her own field or, at the very least, as having a working knowledge of what the team does. As well, new leaders can earn and keep respect and credibility only if they "walk the talk" and "practice what they preach." "As a leader, you suddenly have more visibility, and you can't ask members of your team to meet deadlines . . . if you, 'the boss,' do not make them regularly as well," says Kitts.

Robert Hogan, whose business is focused on the traits that individuals need to have (or, conversely, should not have) to be successful leaders, has over time created a list of must-haves for effective leaders. "First things first: they have to have good people skills, and they have to be rewarding to deal with," he says. "The second thing is they have to be smart enough to learn the job. The third thing is they have to be willing to do the job. We call it RAW: rewarding to deal with, able to learn and do the job, and willing to do the job.

"Finally, they have got to have the capacity for growth. As you go up in the organization, the jobs get more and more complicated, and they have different requirements. Performance at one level of the organization is absolutely no guarantee of performance at the next level," he explains. "So entry-level managers have to really get along with the work group. Middle-level managers have to be able to mediate between the work group and the demands that are coming down from on high. So, at the lower level, you have to work *in* the business; at the top level, you have to work *on* the business. That is what you need at the top level, you need to be able to think strategically."

LEADING VERSUS MANAGING

The terms "managing" and "leadership" are often used interchangeably and, in some cases, there really is little difference in practical terms. The literature on the subject, however, does find some separation between managing and leadership. It has been said, for example, that "managers administer

239

and leaders inspire," and that "leaders do the right thing, and managers do things right." According to yet another saying that attempts to clarify the distinction, "You manage process, you lead people." But the fact of the matter—and the critical point to be made—is that the individual who has been given senior responsibility within the organization has to develop the attributes of both a manager and a leader.

Harvard professor John Kotter, author of *What Leaders Really Do*, spelled out the differences between managing and leading that formed the foundation of people-based management—or what I call "leadership" in this book. Prior to Kotter's influential work, organizational theory was much more process-based than people-based.

One way to view the settling-in process for new leaders is to see it as a time of information seeking and developing relationships. The information-seeking component includes learning about their new environment, their team, the new challenges and expectations, and the new leaders in their team and among their peers and those above them. As for developing relationships, Michael Hyatt, author and speaker, and former chairman and CEO of Nelson Publishing, notes that among the typical shortcomings of new leaders is the failure to communicate effectively, the inability to build strong relationships and the absence of clear expectations. He advises new leaders to "meet and greet"—to create new relationships directionally: up and down (management and your employees), laterally (peers) and diagonally (experts or influencers in the organization and people outside the organization who have a key impact, such as customers, suppliers and stakeholders).

Hyatt urges new leaders to listen more and talk less, a topic we discuss in Chapter 8. He also advises new leaders to find out what success looks like. A new leader needs to be extremely clear with his or her new boss and know implicitly what actions constitute success. What are the superior's expectations?

When leaders find themselves having to select other leaders, they should not make the mistake of choosing only on the basis of technical skills or performance—leadership skills are an important criterion. Yet this is a mistake organizations continue to make time and time again (see Chapter 1).

New managers often are confused about short-term versus long-term actions: "Do I focus on what I need to do today or worry about tomorrow?"

It's a generalization, of course, but first-line managers more often have to worry mostly about the short term, whereas senior leaders spend far more time on future-oriented tasks. New leaders need to know they are both an agent of change and a change agent. Decisions by others will influence them, but they also need to influence those in their team and ensure that they lead change within their team.

THE MISSING HALF

The Manager–Leader debate began in 1977, when Harvard Business School professor Abraham Zaleznik published an article titled "Managers and Leaders: Are They Different?" Business schools reacted vehemently to the content and positions taken by Zaleznik. He argued that the scientific take on management, characterized by time-and-motion studies, was missing half the picture, that made up the human aspect at work—the inspiration, the vision and people's motivation and desires. The article became a seminal one and sparked one of the most important changes in leadership study and practices. Toyota's management philosophy, called "the Toyota Way," is a modern application of the "two halves" that Zaleznik described. The Toyota Way is a brilliant model encompassing manufacturing/quality principles and people development: the management and the leadership.

Harvard Business School Professor John Kotter first published "What Leaders Really Do" in 1990. He took key concepts from Zaleznik and came up with important additions. First, Kotter argued that both leadership and management are necessary and complementary in today's organizations. Second, he added specific behaviors and tasks that illustrate what managers and leaders do when they manage and when they lead. The heart of his critical work can be summarized like this: "Managers promote stability, while leaders press for change, and only organizations that embrace both sides of that contradiction can thrive in turbulent times."

Source: *Harvard Business Review,* December 2001 preview of reprint of John P. Kotter, "What Leaders Really Do," *Harvard Business Review,* 1990. http://hbr.org/2001/12/what-leaders-really-do/ar/1.

THE POWER OF SELF-AWARENESS

The new leader's period of adjustment is a good time to conduct a self-assessment of his or her natural leadership style, as well as the style of the people the new leader works with. The shift from doer to leader is not just a transition, it is (as Linda Hill says) a transformation. During this period of change, leaders need to reflect on what is happening to them and gather feedback in the initial six months or so to learn how they are adjusting.

At Global Knowledge, we train new leaders to appreciate the importance of communicating effectively. Communication is so much more important for those new to the leadership role. Suddenly, as leader, they are much more visible than they were before. Members of the team suddenly are paying close attention to what he or she says and does. Not communicating is not an option. In fact, the new leader who neglects to communicate with the team by verbal or written means is still sending a message, but it's not a positive example of leadership.

A leadership transition is stressful. It has been compared to other significant life events, such as getting married, having children or buying a first home. Just as these examples suggest, the stress is not necessarily a bad thing, but it does exist and must be recognized and dealt with. What's causing the stress? In a word, change. The political and power relationships are different, as the leader deals with new stakeholders. The level of complexity is changing; most likely it is growing in intensity. The dynamic of human relationships is changing too, particularly if the transition is from non-leader to leader. The requirement and pressure to delegate rises as the leader rises through the organization. The leader's network is also changing from internally to externally focused and must be developed and nurtured to grow along with the leader.

Leaders also tend to look at time differently than do non-leaders. As part of the transition from doing to leading, they need to decide where to allocate their efforts. Should more time be apportioned for communicating and influencing, establishing strategy or building a team? Should less time be given to administration and dealing with external clients? In other words, recently promoted leaders often find themselves shifting into their new role with little real guidance on what constitutes success. If there was any one thing I would encourage those taking on a new leadership role to do, it would be to establish with those higher in the organization clear objectives. Make clear with *your* leader your performance objectives, the key measures and what he or she is going to be looking at.

ROSS'S QUESTIONS

According to the participants in his leadership courses, Ross Rennie is a rock star. Ross is in my team, and he is not only great at developing others, but he has stories to tell, having been an executive in a financial institution for many years. I asked him, "What are the typical questions new leaders ask you or ask of themselves?" His response clearly illustrates the various problems new leaders face during this time of significant change. And, Ross said, "They are not much different from the questions I was asking myself when I became a leader years ago." The typical questions are:

1. What is my role?
2. How do I move from friend or colleague to manager?
3. How do I balance *doing* the work with *managing* the work equation?
4. Should leadership training be provided before or after I become a leader?
5. What are the key skills required to be an effective leader?
6. How do I manage people who are older and have more experience than me?
7. What are the generational differences influencing people's motivation?

LEADERSHIP TRANSITIONS

So far in this chapter we have talked mainly about the leadership transition that takes place when an individual contributor becomes a leader. But most leaders go through a number of transitions as they progress in their career. A good illustration of multiple transitions is made in the book *The Leadership Pipeline*, by Ram Charan, Stephen Drotter and James Noel. The authors describe clearly the typical transitions leaders can go through as they climb to the CEO level of a large organization. Of course, these levels and transitions vary depending on the size of the organization and its structure and, of course, not all leaders will get to that level.

These are the passages, as the authors call them, that a leader can experience as he or she is promoted:

1. From managing self to managing others
2. From managing others to managing managers
3. From managing managers to functional manager
4. From functional manager to business manager
5. From business manager to group manager
6. From group manager to enterprise manager

We can easily imagine that the higher up in the organization the leader is moving, the more complex the job becomes. But the fundamentals remain the same: at the time of transition, the leader must pay attention to shifting the mindset, identifying opportunities for development, allocating time as a people leader and earning respect and establishing credibility.

IN THE BOSS'S OWN WORDS

Scott Williams is president of Global Knowledge Canada, having joined the organization thirteen years ago when the company he was then working for was acquired. In this candid interview, he explains the various leadership transitions and the challenges he experienced in his rise through the ranks.

J.B.: Which leadership transitions have created the most vivid memories and why?

S.W.: The first and the last ones. The first one because it was anxiety inducing, and the last because it was the most difficult one. Those in between I don't remember as well. I didn't feel as stressed about becoming president, but it was much more complex. [Williams is referring here to when he became a leader for the first time and

(continued)

---

then when he became president of Global Knowledge Canada. His experience is perfectly aligned with the common challenges that I hear about from clients, and with the findings in the literature.] The first one because I was not prepared for it. I was an entrepreneur, and I became a manager when I hired my first few employees. I was not a manager before, and I had nobody in the company to prepare me for the leadership role. I had no role model. I was making it up as I went along.

J.B.: Why did it create anxiety?

S.W.: I was not sure if I was doing the right thing. Delegation, performance discussions and compensation issues were all management realities I had to deal with, but I had nobody to bounce ideas off. Even if I had my own managers before, it is interesting to realize how I was not self-aware about how to be a manager myself.

J.B.: You never know from whom you will get some help. Were there events that made you progress or somebody who helped you?

S.W.: I had a customer who had been an entrepreneur and was generous enough to coach me. He had made the same mistakes and knew how to help me. He had good business acumen; he knew how to solve cases in alignment with where we wanted to take the business.

I was lucky that I had hired a few experienced employees who agreed to coach me. One was a retired school principal who helped me on the management side. Even though he was much more experienced than me, he was at a period of his life where it was totally fine for him to help and leave the responsibilities to a younger person.

J.B.: Two years ago you became president of Global Knowledge Canada. What comes to mind when you think of that last leadership transition?

S.W.: Contrary to most executive leadership transitions in organizations on the market, which are well planned and supported by the board, mine was quite abrupt. I had no transition time with the previous president, so I had to figure it out by myself. Good or bad, it was a very clean and sudden break.

J.B.: What was challenging about living the transition this way?

(continued)

S.W.: It was difficult to embrace the role immediately. I felt an element of guilt regarding the previous person, who was my boss and a friend. It was difficult to celebrate also in front of my peers because I became their boss. The huge miss was that I did not have any "pass the baton" time, no learning period with my predecessor. I found it very difficult when I became president that suddenly I no longer had a peer group. This is why I asked my boss, the CEO, to be a coach and a mentor to me.

J.B.: What did you learn from that "thrown in the deep end" phase?

S.W.: Two dynamics were going on, the one regarding all the employees and the one with my senior management team. I was somewhat naive thinking it would be completely collegial like it was before. In some situations, I got a bucket of cold water thrown on me, making me realize that I had a different role. But on the other hand, I have a senior management team with a lot of experience, so I did not have to manage them too closely. We also had a common goal unifying us, which was to get the business back to success coming out of the recession. For all the employees, I wanted them to feel valued, that we believed in them; I wanted them to feel successful, that they are part of something worthwhile; I wanted them to know that we had a plan and somebody was in control. I think I did not do too bad on that aspect.

Because I had difficulty embracing the new role at the beginning, I was probably not open enough to talk with my team about my challenges. Maybe I am naturally feeling more like a number two than a number one. I don't want to take myself too seriously. I was not dreaming of becoming president, it just happened. I never felt that I had to get on the mountain top and receive cheers.

J.B.: Did you feel you had to become more strategic once you became president?

S.W.: Not that much, to be honest, maybe because I was already fairly strategic in my approach. What changed is that I was now expecting the people reporting to me to be strategic, which was not the case before.

WHAT THE EXPERTS SAY
From Doing to Leading

Organizations regularly need to restructure management for a host of reasons, such as improving organization performance, implementing changes, or mergers and acquisition. Transitioning executives and managers quickly into new or expanded roles is a tricky process, one that, if not carried out strategically, can be not only disruptive but also very costly to both the organization and individuals involved. A review of two articles that focus on interventions for leader assimilation reveals alarming statistics related to the challenges organizations face in transitioning leaders into new roles. Levin (2010) writes that executives report role transitions as being one of the most challenging and stressful life events they experience, second only to divorce and slightly more challenging and stressful than the onset of health-related problems. He also reports on one study that found that 92 percent of externally hired executives and 72 percent of internal transfers took at least ninety days to reach moderately high levels of productivity following a new role transition, and six months (62 percent new hires and 25 percent of internals) to get up to speed and comfortable in the new role (Institute of Executive Development and Alexcel Group 2008). The author points to the alarming findings by Master (2009) in which the executive search firm Heidrick and Struggles reports that, of 20,000 of its own executive placements, 40 percent of senior-level executives were pushed out, failed or quit within the first eighteen months in the new role. In a second article reviewed, Manderscheid (2008) points to studies that emphasize the vast numbers of leader transitions taking place in organizations today. He reports on one study in particular (Watkins 2003) that found that at least 25 percent of the managers or leaders in a typical company take new jobs each year, estimating that more than half a million managers enter new positions in Fortune 500 companies alone. Considering that the study is some ten years old, we can expect that number to be significantly higher today.

Research on transitioning leaders into new roles (Levin 2010; Manderscheid 2008) agrees that failures in leader assimilation are most often linked to errors made in the first 90 to 100 days and that the traditional sink-or-swim mentality is no longer an option. While Levin acknowledges that many organizations provide some degree of onboarding, he suggests that it is limited to a focus on visions, strategic priorities and operating policies, and that it neglects the learning and challenges associated with the new working relationships with members of the new direct-report team. Levin argues that without specific, clear strategies and interventions in place, the "feeling each other out" process necessary for productive collaboration drags out and can have significant impact on the bottom line. In addressing this gap in the literature, he proposes a facilitator-led five-step structured intervention to accelerate the assimilation period and learning curve of new leaders and their new teams. Defended by transition and newcomer socialization theory, the intervention objectives include:

1. Promoting mutual learning between new leaders and their direct reports regarding personal styles, values, preferences, motivators, aspirations and background—all important for building mutual respect and trust.
2. Defining and establishing mutual expectations for how new leaders and their direct reports will work together.
3. Reaching shared understanding of important business, organizational and operational challenges and opportunities for future success.
4. Developing an initial set of shared priorities and action items, and an action plan for moving forward.

Levin's five-step facilitator-led intervention consists of the following steps:

1. Launch
2. Leader preparation and team member interviews
3. New leader feedback meeting
4. Team feedback and working session
5. Follow-up meeting with the new leader and full team

During the launch, the facilitator establishes with the new leader and his or her executive report the intervention purpose, desired outcomes, approach and specific methods to be used and the ground rules. Interviews with team members are set, and the new leader is given a preparatory assignment that involves questions, the answers to which his or her direct reports would benefit from knowing. The author suggests the assignment include questions such as:

1. What factors or reasons led you to this new role?
2. What are some of your initial impressions of the new organization and new role?
3. What are your initial hopes and expectations for the new team and the organization?

Levin also recommends asking these questions of the new leader's direct reports:

1. What is your current role here, and how long have you been in this role?
2. What are the key challenges and opportunities facing your team or organization?
3. What are your suggestions or recommendations for meeting these challenges and taking advantage of the opportunities identified?

The facilitator uses the interview data to conduct a thematic analysis that is shared with the new leader during a feedback meeting. The knowledge the new leader gains will prove valuable when he or she returns to the larger group. It includes insights about the new leader's personal values, expectations of the direct reports and advice on how to work effectively with the new leader.

The intervention concludes with two follow-up meetings, the first one with the new leader only and the second one with the full team. Levin acknowledges that he has not conducted any formal research to evaluate the effectiveness of the intervention but does report that of sixteen of the executives who have engaged in the process facilitated by him, three-quarters of them remained in their new roles for two years, one-third remained in their new roles for at least five years and many of them reported that the intervention helped them transition and assimilate faster into their new roles, compared with their prior role-change experiences. Further validating the notion of a facilitated intervention for leaders in transition, Manderscheid (2008) reports on the observations and interview data of a study that looked at three cases and that found that such intervention helped accelerate learning, adaptation and relationship building. It also helped leaders learn about team culture and better understand expectations related to team and leader dynamics and organizational norms. Manderscheid provides useful guidelines for organizations wanting to do a new-leader assimilation intervention, including:

- Give priority to external hires.
- Ensure the new leader and team are properly informed of the intent, process, potential risks and outcomes of the intervention.
- Alert both the facilitator and leader to possible internal changes or issues that could derail the process, so adjustments can be made.
- Use an outside facilitator to increase the likelihood of honest feedback to the new leader.
- Have the facilitator follow up with the new leader to remind him or her to follow through on commitments made during the intervention.
- Conduct the assimilation process thirty to ninety days into the new-leader hire.

Manderscheid supports his belief that priority should be given to external new leaders by referring to several studies, including one (Watkins 2003) that assessed the challenge of coming in from the outside as much harder than, say, being promoted from within the organization. He attributed the high failure rate first to the outside executives' lack of familiarity with the new organization's structure and informal networks of information and communication, and corporate culture and, second, to the lack of acceptance by current employees for whom the new hire is unknown and consequently viewed as less credible than someone promoted from within.

Besides looking to leader transition facilitator-led interventions involving the participation of the new leader's direct reports, it is important to examine studies that explore the specific types of individual learning and competencies that lead to an efficient and timely transition to new roles, especially when it comes to individual contributors moving to a management role. In an exploratory study in which eight individual contributors in a Fortune 500 global consumer products company who had recently transitioned to operations manager roles were interviewed, Polarek (2007) sought answers to these questions:

1. What do new managers consider the most important skills and competencies to develop as a manager?
2. How do they learn these skills and competencies?
   a. What resources have been most influential? Why?
   b. Who has been most influential? Why?
3. What support did the organization initiate to provide these resources and to help develop these relationships?
4. Is there a difference in the perceptions of new managers who are meeting expectations and new managers who are exceeding expectations?

The author reports on the themes that emerged from the interview data, including:

- Unstructured, learner-driven informal learning guided by internal employees, in place of structured, teacher-driven formal learning
- "Trial and error" or "learning on the job" experiential learning, influenced by context and relationships
- Other influencing factors, including task variation, opportunities to consult experts inside and outside the workplaces, changes in duties and work that stimulates learning, and opportunities to facilitate informal communication, problem solving and innovation

Polarek points to research that recognizes informal learning as representing up to 90 percent of all learning in the workplace. Based on the themes that emerged from the study, the author made these recommendations:

1. Make direct managers aware of their important role in a new manager's informal learning.
2. Teach direct managers to be active management coaches and model.
3. Encourage new managers to connect with existing informal networks.
4. Find ways to make informal learning more structured and deliberate.

This experiential learning of how to be a manager by observing the behavior of more experienced direct managers has been coined a "cognitive apprenticeship." Cognitive apprenticeships provide new managers with "thinking out loud" modeling of desired behaviors as well as coaching to help them get to the desired performance.

Emerge Leadership Group (2008) provides a brief summary of a model developed in the 1970s by two professors at Harvard University, Gene Dalton and Paul Thompson, to describe and measure individual contribution and impact in organizations, to highlight the critical transition process from individual contributor to leader. These stages, identified as "stages of impact," are:

1. **Learner—helping and learning.** Usually a new hire who is learning a new position accepts direction from others and learns basic skills, while demonstrating future potential.
2. **Specialist—developing expertise.** The individual demonstrates full competency in the assigned role and works with minimum supervision.
3. **Leader—contributing through others.** The individual at this stage directs the work of others. He or she may be the leader of direct reports or the informal leader of a team. The focus shifts from narrow (specific expertise) to broad (organization expertise) as the individual builds strategic relationships and develops others.
4. **Strategist—leading through vision.** At this stage, the new leader is creating and deploying overall business strategy through a team of direct supports responsible for major functions of the organization. The focus is strategic, not tactical. He or she provides organizational direction, develops new ideas and represents the organization to the market.

Emerge Leadership Group notes that the transition from a stage 2 specialist, acting as an individual contributor, to a stage 3 leader who contributes through others is the most difficult. Expert individual contributors, considered the cream of the crop, are the individuals assumed to be the ones who will make the best leaders and, to this end, are given basic management skill development, though many of them do not get the assistance needed to move from stage 2 to stage 3. The Emerge Leadership Group reports that its research shows that most organizations err by focusing most of their transition support on stage 2, the mastery of management skills, and neglect stage 1, which is meant to provide the foundational transition development. This, then, is what leads management to voice complaints like "We give them all this skills training and they still can't make the transition to management." The group refers to research by Harvard professor Linda Hill that suggests that the problem with most transitions is that they go after the symptoms and never tackle the root cause of the transition problem. Pointing to the high failure rate of transitions, the Emerge Leadership Group reports on one of its own recent studies of more than 100 companies that found that 48 percent of all managers are seen as operating as individual contributors instead of as managers. The group identified a process that it believes helps ensure the successful transition to manager roles. The process calls for three actions:

1. Develop a personalized plan that establishes a time frame and creates accountability.
2. Use an assessment tool to determine the gap between an individual's current and required behaviors to fully function as a stage 3 leader.
3. Take on a project that addresses a high-value business need that requires more than what he or she can accomplish on his or her own.

Leaders of individuals making stage 2 to stage 3 transitions need to support the individual's transition plan, remove barriers, offer resources and provide coaching.

Becoming a leader for the first time is likely the most critical transition a leader will experience in his or her career. A real moment of truth, as I like to call it. This transition and any other leadership transition, no matter the level, need to be supported to maximize the probability of success. Thanks to popular authors and professors like Michael Watkins and Linda Hill, more HR professionals and leaders are conscious of the importance of intervening and providing support. Supporting leaders when they experience transition is not just being nice; it is a real investment to avoid losing time and money, and to support business results.

13

Onboarding

> The President of the United States gets 100 days to prove himself; you get 90. The actions you take during your first three months in a new job will largely determine whether you succeed or fail.
>
> —Michael Watkins

Most of us have had some personal experience with onboarding—the induction procedure put into effect on the first few days of a new job—and chances are it was an ordeal we would rather forget. Likely it was a traditional orientation program, a day or two filled with an endless stream of information about the new company's policies, procedures, benefits and administrative issues.

Thankfully, onboarding has changed. The more modern onboarding process that organizations are adopting takes care of that administrative stuff, but it also sets out the plan for a new employee's early success. Onboarding has received a lot more attention lately from organizations for a very good reason: the quicker a new hire settles into the role and begins working productively, the sooner he or she is making a positive contribution. From that perspective, onboarding can be viewed as an essential business process intended to shorten the period necessary to get new employees to reach the "breakeven point" and begin adding net value to the organization.

Unlike a traditional orientation program, today's onboarding process can be regarded as a transition involving a structured or phased journey for the new hire, rather than simply a one-time event that everyone must endure before starting the "real" job. It is a more holistic, structured and strategic process. Used to its potential, onboarding can speed a new employee's development from the time the candidate receives the offer letter, and then on through the employee's first ninety days and beyond.

The modern process of onboarding is described as holistic because it focuses on knowledge, values and motivations, skills and competencies, relationship building and other key linkages between the organization and employee. Yes, it's important to master the computer system and find the bathroom, but onboarding can and should also forge a strong connection between the new hire and the organization, linking the two in terms of business goals, individual and organizational performance, planning and measurement, talent and succession management and a host of other human capital management strategies.

Onboarding used to be thought of as an "HR thing." Today, HR still has a role to play, but so does everyone else in the organization. While leading research in the field still shows that one person or group of people needs to have ultimate accountability for onboarding the new employee, the overall process is now a shared responsibility jointly held by HR, the employee's manager and peers, and the employee.

When the onboarding process is understood by line managers as a structured way to get their new employees productive faster, they typically are much more enthusiastic and supportive of it than they would be if viewing it as an HR procedure carried out before the employees start actually working. In fact, the content of this chapter should interest three different groups: the HR professionals who are often taking the lead in designing and implementing an onboarding program; the leaders who want to see their new employees become productive faster and stay in the organization; and the leaders who are new themselves and are part of an onboarding program.

Why all the attention to onboarding? Part of it has to do with the modern, flatter organizations of today. Jobs are more complex and wider in scope than previously. New employees are expected to hit the ground running and be better when they get to full speed—they're expected to do more, innovate more, respond faster. At the same time, turnover of existing workers remains a concern: critical institutional knowledge and wisdom are continually exiting the organization. Newcomers to the organization have to learn fast to make up for what is being lost. A prime example of this is a key sales role, where it might take six months before the new employee really understands the organization's culture, products and customers. Any sales manager worth his or her salt can tell exactly when a new hire reaches the breakeven point where his or her contribution goes from negative to positive (Watkins 2003).

Identifying, selecting and ultimately hiring employees is a costly process. Failure to successfully integrate them so that they are happy and productive members of the workforce is far more costly. According to the Aberdeen Group's (2006) Onboarding Benchmark Report, 90 percent of new employees decide within their first six months whether they will stay at the company. If a new employee decides "this place is not for me" after a six-month tenure because the organization has not done the job of onboarding properly, it is a small but significant financial setback. Not only did the organization bear the cost of attracting and training the employee, but that employee was likely not productive during most of his or her employment, and worst of all, the organization has to go through the time and expense associated with hiring yet another new employee. Although onboarding is mainly about helping the new employee become productive, it is also about retaining talent: "The most important ingredient for successful retention, fostered by an ongoing orientation program, is giving employees a sense of being valued and important" (Sharpe 2000).

So what are the end goals of an effective onboarding process? For most organizations, they are:

- Shorten the time it takes for new employees to reach the breakeven point and begin adding net value to the organization.
- Help the new employee become competent, confident and productive faster.
- Optimize discretionary effort by accelerating and preserving new employee engagement.
- Secure new talent and improve overall retention rates.
- Install, right from the start, a culture of organizational effectiveness.
- Cement early loyalty through fusing the organization brand.
- Enhance overall customer value and satisfaction.

According to Michael Watkins, expert on accelerating transitions and author of the international bestseller *The First 90 Days*, the average time it takes the typical mid-level employee to reach that breakeven point is

6.2 months. Other research like the Mellon Learning Curve Research Study (Williams 2003) has found that the average time for new external hires to achieve full productivity can range from 2 months for clerical staff to 5 months for professionals, and as long as 6.5 months for executives. Shortening that process and moving that breakeven point closer to day one is the end goal of onboarding.

A HOLISTIC PROCESS

The holistic onboarding process introduces the new employee to experiences that seek to engage and connect the whole person with the whole system. It provides not only opportunities for knowledge transfer and skills development but also experiences that help align personal vision and values with organizational vision and values. It connects individual job objectives with organizational strategy, and fosters relationships between the individual and the work community.

Holistic onboarding can also be looked at from the 70-20-10 learning paradigm (the rule of thumb that 70 percent of what we learn comes through doing, 20 percent from others and 10 percent from formal learning). Observing this rule, 10 percent of onboarding might take the form of enrolling the new hire in formal courses, 20 percent might involve pairing the new hire with a company "buddy" in order to learn by watching others and 70 percent might focus on exposing the employee to projects in order to learn about the organization's culture and products.

An Integrative Process

For individuals, onboarding offers up a wide stream of parts, information, processes and activities designed to acclimatize, engage and equip a new employee. From the operational level, the onboarding process can be viewed as a key component of the business strategy, linking back to the company's business goals; individual and organizational performance planning and measurement, talent and succession management; and other human capital management strategies. For organizations intent on building brand identity, for example, the onboarding process might play a prominent role in strengthening the company brand and cementing loyalty from the very start.

A Shared Responsibility

As mentioned, research shows that responsibility for onboarding needs to ultimately reside with one person or group, but the overall process can be shared by many. Because many people play a part in the success of a new employee, the process might involve joint ownership between HR, the new employee's manager as well as peers, and ultimately the new employee too. The link between the onboarding process and productivity needs to be understood by all employees, existing and new, in order to promote a culture of high performance and organizational effectiveness.

While it is a shared process, in most cases accountability for the onboarding process rests with the HR team, while the ultimate accountability for ensuring that the new employee engages with the process and achieves speedy results rests with the manager. Table 13.1 illustrates some of the differences between old-style onboarding and the new, holistic model.

Table 13.1: Onboarding Evolution

	Traditional Orientation	**Modern Onboarding**
Intended result	New hire learns HR policies and procedures	New hire achieves early productivity and organizational effectiveness
Responsibility for process	HR	Organization treats it as integrated business procedure
Duration	Single training event	Phased transition
Structure	One size fits all	Flexible, individual and role-based
Instructional method	Tell and teach	Exploration, engagement and relationship building
Content	Information	Based on KUBA: know, understand, believe and act
Location	Classroom	Multiple modalities and blended learning approaches
Participation	New hire and HR staff	Treated as shared organization task

"It is important that we as leaders invest in our people," says Sylvia Chrominska, former group head of Global Human Resources and Communications at Scotiabank. "If someone new comes into my organization, I try to meet with them frequently and I tell them, 'Don't feel that you are out there alone, and no question is a stupid question. If you are at all feeling uncomfortable, then by all means come to me.' One of the things I can do from my vantage point is to provide context as to why things are the way they are." She echoes the KUBA principles when she says, "I have always advocated in the bank that you can't simply tell people what to do, you have to tell them why we are doing it and how they fit into the bigger picture."

Getting new employees familiar and comfortable with the new organization's culture as quickly as possible is a key goal of the Royal Mail. The UK's postal agency has adopted a few new practices as part of its onboarding process. "The one that I found quite interesting was an organizational diagnostic where the candidate coming in describes the culture of his current company and a number of executives provide a perspective on the culture at Royal Mail," explains John Duncan, Human Resources group director. "What that diagnostic does is identify gaps between the executive's current corporate culture and the one he is going to. It could be problematic. I can really see how this would have benefit in that people know the environment they are going into and can be prepared perhaps to make some adaptations in the way they would approach new responsibilities."

LONG-TERM OUTCOMES OF ONBOARDING

Organizations surveyed about onboarding perceive that the process can improve retention rates, time to productivity and overall customer satisfaction. When conducted correctly, new employee onboarding leads to:

- Higher job satisfaction
- Organizational commitment
- Lower turnover
- Higher performance levels
- Career effectiveness
- Lowered stress

A MODERN AND STRUCTURED APPROACH

Global Knowledge attempts to shorten the period it takes for a new hire to become competent, confident and productive, and to add value to the organization. We intend the new hire to move as quickly as possible from being a net cost to a net benefit to the business. Our approach, most often completed within ninety days, is designed to be carried out in four distinct phases:

1. **Phase 1—Anticipate.** This phase starts when the new employee accepts the letter of offer. It can include a preview of what the first days and weeks on the new job will be like and is designed to reduce the anxiety that comes from a lack of information prior to day one. Other elements of this first phase include the distribution of a booklet titled *All about Onboarding at Our Company*, an Anticipate Activity Tool Kit, and optional e-learning modules.

2. **Phase 2—Align.** The align phase starts the new employee's first day. It involves presenting to the new hire the organization's goals and its specific expectations. Rather than leave the new employee to figure things out on his or her own, this phase ensures that that person begins to build an internal network by getting to know others in the organization. The objective is to have the new hire feel more connected, aligned and supported. Critically, this is also the period when new employees start to view themselves as part of the organization.

3. **Phase 3—Accelerate.** Whereas phases one and two are intended to be foundational stages, the accelerate phase is designed to speed up the new employee's confidence and capability through activities that assist him or her to further develop a network and job skills. This section contains a focus on performance management, with activities prescribing coaching sessions to ensure that the employee is focused on achieving the goals of the team, department or company.

4. **Phase 4—Activate.** The final phase of the onboarding process begins after the employee is fully capable of completing the basic tasks associated with the role. The new hire will continue to expand his or her internal network in new ways, for example by participating on work committees or special projects. This is also the time that expectations are set for the employee as he or she graduates from the onboarding

process. The coach or manager works with the employee to identify the performance objectives to focus on after graduation.

THE FOUR Cs

Onboarding has four distinct levels—the Four Cs—according to a Society for Human Resource Management (SHRM) paper titled "Onboarding New Employees":

- Compliance: covers teaching employees basic legal and policy-related rules and regulations
- Clarification: refers to ensuring that employees understand their new jobs and all related expectations
- Culture: a broad category that encompasses providing employees with a sense of organizational norms, both formal and informal
- Connection: points to the vital interpersonal relationships and information networks that new employees must establish

The SHRM paper also details four short-term outcomes of onboarding:

1. Self-efficacy, or self-confidence in job performance
2. Role clarity, or how well a new employee understands the role and expectations
3. Self-integration, or meeting and establishing working relationships with peers and superiors; one estimate suggests that 60 percent of managers who fail to onboard successfully cite failure to establish working relationships as a primary reason
4. Knowledge of fit within an organizational culture; understanding the organization's unique politics, language, goals and values is critical to employee commitment and satisfaction, and to low turnover

---

WHAT THE EXPERTS SAY
Onboarding

Making the transition from individual contributor to leader is a difficult one and continues to have its challenges well into the early stages of a new leader's career. What the new leader and the organization don't need is the uncertainty, delay and human and financial costs associated with a poorly managed onboarding process. Onboarding has been described as the "direct bridge between the promise of a new employee talent and the attainment of actual productivity" (Snell 2006). A well-managed and automated onboarding process reduces costs, speeds up time to productivity and improves retention of a new hire because of greater employee satisfaction. Besides the straight business advantage of onboarding, Snell (2006) points to global considerations such as high recruitment rates, multiple levels of corporate policy and culture, and multilingual/multicultural barriers. An effective streamlined onboarding process enables a new leader to gain access to the information, tools and materials needed to perform his or her function efficiently and quickly.

Snell reports on alarming statistics indicating that 64 percent of new executives hired from outside the company will fail in their new jobs, pointing to the criticality of a comprehensive introductory onboarding process. The author reports on a research survey of onboarding practices of large corporations that found that more than one-third of organizations did not have a formal process to monitor and coordinate the completion of onboarding activities, and that fewer than half of the respondents were satisfied with the onboarding process at their company. Snell emphasizes that optimal onboarding has a number of benefits:

- Reduced time to contribution and competence
- Improved productivity and performance
- Stronger bonds among colleagues
- Enhanced job satisfaction and loyalty
- Improved employee engagement and retention

The author identifies critical components necessary for the design and management of a successful onboarding process:

1. Process analysis
2. Implementation
3. Integration
4. Reporting

Traditionally, a review of the onboarding process involves the new hire, the hiring manager and the HR department and involves an evaluation of the following activities:

- Payroll and benefits
- Parking space and permit
- Office assignment and setup
- Security-related documents, badges and keys
- Training setup and delivery
- General orientation, including introduction to employees and colleagues
- IT-related setups (computer, phone, e-mail account)

Although Snell insists that implementation, integration and reporting processes are best handled through technology platforms, he emphasizes that socialization activities are integral to successful onboarding. The author recommends aligning onboarding with other processes related to the cyclical talent management system, such as workforce planning, selection, performance management and succession planning.

Reese (2005) reports that effective onboarding programs are still the exception and not the rule at Fortune 500 companies and that now, more than ever, organizations need strategic onboarding programs that involve a high level of human interaction and are tailored to individuals' needs. The author notes that while companies invest considerable financial and management resources to recruitment and leadership development, there is a disproportionate investment made in onboarding. Reese identifies common pitfalls in designing an effective program for incoming executives in particular, with some failures directly related to lack of proper orientation, but most failures can be traced back to the recruiting processes. Common pitfalls identified include:

- Mismanagement of expectations during the recruiting process
- Poor cultural fit
- Resentment from colleagues
- Lack of feedback
- Lack of credibility in new role
- Failure to think strategically about onboarding experience

- Dropping the ball on short-term deliverables
- Failure to learn the unwritten rules

With these pitfalls in mind, the author identifies key elements of a successful onboarding program, including the recognition that the formal process begins during recruitment and should be thought of as a bridge for the company to deliver on the expectations and commitments made during recruitment. Reese provides a general guide for the time frame of an onboarding program for incoming leaders, with these elements:

1. 7 days before new leader starts: onboarding program agenda and deliverables and administrative matters completed
2. 30–120 days: new leader is integrated into peer group and organization
3. first 90 days: new leader develops key networks
4. 90–120 days: new leader establishes teams
5. first 90 days: new leader solicits feedback from direct supervisor and HR to evaluate progress and develop game plan to address development needs
6. 90–180 days: new leader delivers on expectations and commitments

The author provides a best-practice checklist for an onboarding program:

1. Create a strategic plan that includes a consistent and agreed-upon onboarding strategy
2. Field a team that includes the new hire, an HR professional and a senior-report supervisor
3. Define deliverables that include acceptable time frames
4. Ensure participation of key constituents, including incumbents, subordinates and supervisors
5. Integrate new employee into peer group, including other new executives who have successfully integrated within the last year
6. Communicate the culture, including exposing the new leader to established leaders who best embody the organization's culture
7. Implement a mentoring program to address issues related to introductions, networking, resources, internal politics, communication and problem solving

8. Provide feedback, in part by setting up a formal process to gather and analyze the feedback
9. Ensure any necessary intervention to address development needs
10. Confirm to the new hire his or her own responsibility as part of the onboarding process

Besides improving the effectiveness and retention of new hires, an effective onboarding program has the added benefit of attracting top candidates to fill available positions.

To remain competitive globally, companies are increasingly looking outside their own organizations for fresh leadership. Dai, De Meuse and Gaeddert (2011) trace the evolution of onboarding, compare current onboarding best practices with traditional new employee orientation and provide clear and detailed descriptions of six strategy areas to be taken into account when implementing an external executive onboarding process. The authors back up their focus on external hires by pointing to research (Sessa and Taylor 2000) that found that when given the choice, selection committees chose external over internal candidates 75 percent of the time. Dai and colleagues argue that the reason onboarding appears to be having little impact on improving executive hiring success rates is that the onboarding process employed is simply an extension of the socialization practices and new employee orientation techniques that have been around for decades. The authors point to studies that looked at the satisfaction of new executive hires with their onboarding experiences, identifying one study (Pomeroy 2006) that found that only 30 percent rated their experiences as satisfactory, whereas 32 percent rated their experiences as poor or below average, and a second study (Wells 2005) that found that only 39 out of 100 senior-level managers and CEOs were satisfied with their company's efforts to integrate them into their new organizations.

Based on a review of management and leadership literature, Dai, De Meuse and Gaeddert (2011) identify six areas that appear to directly impact the derailment of new executives and the achievement of strategic goals, and then propose how strategically implemented onboarding can help newly hired executives transition smoothly into a new organizational environment and accelerate their successful performance. According to the authors, the following six strategic areas, listed in sequence, need to be addressed when onboarding external executives:

1. Acknowledgment and adjustment for predecessor's position imprint
2. Establishment of clear performance and contribution expectations
3. Recognition that parts of leadership are not transportable
4. Provision of outside hires with "inside views"
5. Preparation of the organization for change
6. Setting in place an effective senior leadership team

In terms of the predecessor, the authors point to the stress that successors experience as their performance is measured against, for example, a highly successful retired executive. They note that successors who didn't match the position imprint were more likely to turn over than those whose performance closely matched the predecessors' performance. Here, they propose that onboarding enhance the new hire's awareness of potential position imprints and help him or her understand the "dos and taboos" of the new position. Dai, De Meuse and Gaeddert (2011) emphasize the importance of making sure newly hired executives have realistic expectations in terms of performance objectives and timelines. They refer to the article "7 Hidden Reasons Employees Leave" (Branham 2005) that identifies unrealistic expectations as the number one reason employees disengage and quit. The authors emphasize that part of the onboarding process should include ensuring that the selection process includes ongoing management of person-to-role fit so that the new hire is kept abreast of what is expected of him or her, short and long term. In terms of transportable versus nontransportable skills, Dai, De Meuse and Gaeddert point out that, although many types of leadership skills related to general management (e.g., decision making and operating skills) are transportable from one company to another, other, more company-specific skills (e.g., social relations with other team members) are less transportable. They propose that onboarding should help build new hires' least transportable leadership skills. The authors recognize that companies oftentimes search for fresh outside leadership when they are in financial difficulty or are looking for a strategic change. Unfortunately, this strategic decision making has a flip side, as "outsiders" may not understand company culture, traditions, customer base, employees and sources of problems, making it imperative that the onboarding process includes getting the new hire up to speed in terms of accumulating these "inside" views so that effective changes can be made quickly. If the strategic plan for hiring externally is based on organizational change, it is critical that the onboarding process includes helping the new executive assess the readiness for changeability, before initiating change. Dai, De Meuse and Gaeddert argue that because relationship building is one of the least transportable leadership skills executives possess, and yet to be successful, new leaders need to garner critical mass support for their initiatives, onboarding should support the new hire with networking across the organization. Although the authors endorse the six strategic areas of onboarding listed above, they recognize that a one-size-fits-all process will fall flat—that no single, fixed onboarding activity can be applied to all situations. Instead, they argue that for onboarding to be effective, it needs to be tailored to the organization and the executive. In addition, they recognize these organizational moderators as impacting the salience of these onboarding issues:

1. The structure of the senior management team (i.e., hierarchical vs. lateral leadership)
2. Organizational life cycle (i.e., entrepreneurial vs. mature)
3. Temporal mental model (i.e., fast-paced and short-term orientation vs. slow-paced and long-term orientation)

An interesting recent analysis of a 2008 study (Hemphill and Begel 2011) conducted by Andrew Begel at SoftCo, a Fortune 500 software company, describes some of the onboarding challenges associated with virtual teams. With virtual teams being a common feature at many global organizations, it is vital that organizations prepare to adapt their onboarding process to this new reality. As noted above, one of the most nontransportable leadership skills is relationship building. The everyday face-to-face, informal activities and communication that new employees engage in when working together in the same physical environment are greatly reduced or absent in virtual team environments. Hemphill and Begel (2011) point to literature indicating that the geographic separation of virtual teams hinders help-seeking by making it more difficult for team members to understand one another's area of expertise. Geographical distance also reduces opportunities for members to interact in ways that establish trust and knowledge about one another. This has critical implications for onboarding new hires, including leaders. The authors emphasize the importance of having one or more trusted insiders to act as mentor(s) during the early days and weeks of a new hire's appointment. It is difficult for virtual teams to engage in the kinds of informal communication that facilitates discussions about nonwork interests, conversations needed to establish the social ties necessary for mentorship relationships. An analysis of the results of the exploratory study at SoftCo found that:

1. Informal communication and teammates' visibility were especially influential in the teams' transition to virtual work and in onboarding a remote employee.
2. Remote new hires lacked awareness of performance expectations, and their teammates lacked awareness of the new hire's acquisition of skills and knowledge.

The difficulties inherent in onboarding into virtual team environments was apparent in some of the long-distance remote workers' comments: they were missing "the face to face" and "open office walk-up"; "You have to work pretty hard and be continuously proactive to compensate"; "I get all the e-mails about the movie nights and take your child to work day, but can't do anything about it"; "The problem I am facing is getting information about the processes"; "When you are doing it face to face, you can observe your colleagues . . . remote, the only thing you can do is say, 'I have this problem, what should I do?'" Drawing from the results of the study, supporting literature and academic knowledge, Hemphill and Begel propose several suggestions for onboarding with virtual teams, including:

1. Select high self-monitoring candidates, who tend to strive to understand the dynamics of their environments.
2. Develop an informal hierarchical structure, such as a point person, who takes charge of communicating with a remote team to reduce miscommunication.

3. Increase the frequency and nature of team interactions, including informal, scaffolded, one-to-one video conference interviews and even periodic traveling to have face-to-face communication.

4. Hold daily meetings, called "scrums," where all team members "meet"—connect virtually—to discuss their work, what they plan to do before the next scrum and any problems that have arisen.

5. Train new hires to be self-monitoring and proactive to make it more likely that they will seek information and be comfortable interacting with unfamiliar teammates.

6. Provide a team mailing list for remote employees to use when asking and answering questions instead of sending e-mail to individual team members.

14

Contemporary Development Solutions

Leadership and learning are indispensable to each other.

—John F. Kennedy

Learning is more than a one-way training event. New and ever more powerful communication platforms and technologies are transforming the way people learn and how organizations can develop them at every level. Classrooms, and even remote videoconference learning, are increasingly giving way to mobile learning, informal learning, an online community of practice, social media, electronic simulation and scenario-based online learning. Organizations can either make a determined effort to keep up with the communications revolution that new media represents—and embrace its incredible potential for skills and leadership development—or fall hopelessly behind.

In a 2012 survey, social media content company Brandfog found that companies large and small fail to utilize the potential of social media. It found the "vast majority of modern day CEOs and C-Suite executives are conspicuously absent from social media channels. As of January 2012, 61 percent of Fortune 500 brands were engaging with customers via Twitter, but less than 2.5 percent of Fortune 500 CEOs were actively participating on Twitter."[1] It appears that there is a positive impact on the perception of leaders who utilize social media compared with those who do not use it.

---

[1] *2012 CEO, Social Media & Leadership Survey,* 2, http://www.brandfog.com/CEOSocialMediaSurvey/BRANDfog_2012_CEO_Survey.pdf.

CEOs GO SOCIAL

The results of a 2012 Brandfog survey on the utility of social media for business leaders are as follows:

- 81 percent of respondents believe that CEOs who engage in social media are better equipped than their peers to lead companies in a Web 2.0 world.
- Respondents said that social media–wielding CEOs build better connections with customers (89 percent) and were more engaged with employees (85 percent) and investors (66 percent).
- A majority of those surveyed said social media–wielding CEOs were perceived as better communicators and as brand ambassadors, and were more transparent.
- 86 percent of respondents rated CEO social media engagement as either somewhat important, very important or mission critical.
- 94 percent of respondents said CEO participation in social media helps communicate the company's values and shapes its reputation.
- 78 percent of respondents said they are more likely to want to work for a company whose leaders are active in social media.

Simply said, CEOs, the tools are there for you to use, and your various constituents want it. So engage, go social.

Source: *2012 CEO, Social Media & Leadership Survey,* http://www.brandfog.com/CEOSocialMediaSurvey/BRANDfog_2012_CEO_Survey.pdf.

FORMAL, INFORMAL AND SOCIAL LEARNING

The term "social media" has been succinctly described as an "umbrella term that defines the various activities that integrate technology, social interaction, and the construction of words and pictures."[2] (And to the latter I would add video and audio.) Many people today use the term to describe platforms such as Facebook or Twitter. As well-known as those two services are, they are, in fact, just the visible portion of a figurative iceberg, just

---

[2] http://econsultancy.com/ca/blog/3527-what-is-social-media-here-are-34-definitions.

a fraction of a far larger whole. In companies, these social media platforms can take the form of wikis, microblogging, blogging, online discussion lists and comments, as well as common areas to post files or presentations for further input and comments. Social business platforms such as Microsoft's Yammer and IBM's Connections are gaining wide acceptance too.

As all-encompassing as the definition above is, it doesn't describe the frenzied activity in the social media world. Here are some stark facts. Three out of four Americans used social technology as far back as 2008. More than two-thirds of the global Internet population visit social networks. Time spent on social networks is growing three times faster than the overall growth of the Internet and accounts for more than 10 percent of all time spent online. Social media has also taken the keys out of the hands of information's gatekeepers, namely, the mainstream media establishment. As media mogul Rupert Murdoch said: "Technology is shifting the power away from the editors, the publishers, the establishment, the media elite. Now it's the people who are in control."

So what does that mean for an organization intent on developing its talent pipeline? There are plenty of new and emerging tools available, but the basics really haven't changed all that much. Telus Corp.'s Dan Pontefract, author of *Flat Army*, utilizes the term "connected learning" to describe the increasingly digital learning ecosystem of today's world. Although the mode of delivery may change as technologies come and go, the basics of connected learning never change. (See Figure 14.1.)

The swirling mix that makes up connected learning today (and tomorrow) features a mix of formal, informal and social learning, which may utilize several modalities (such as blogs, websites, video conferences and virtual instruction). Pontefract defines the three modes of learning or development as:

- **Formal.** A self-contained and scheduled learning event, typically but not always tracked, providing a comprehensive and at times logical or sequential approach to a topic. "Let's be clear, formal leadership training is not going away, nor should it," Pontefract says. "You can't have an organization think that there is no room for classroom or formal e-learning."
- **Informal.** An opportunity without conventional structure, atypical in relation to formal learning, providing guidance, expertise or acumen

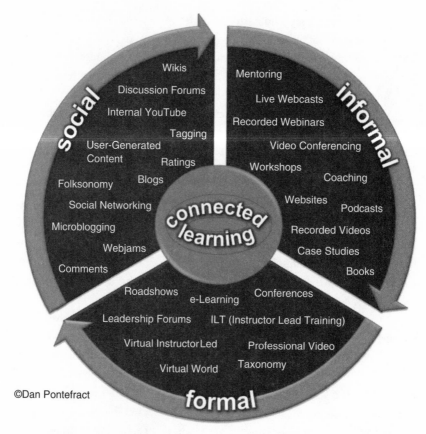

Figure 14.1: Connected Learning

Source: http://www.danpontefract.com/learning-2-0-is-dumb-use-connected
-learning-instead/.

typically in a nonformal environment. It may occur as a town hall meeting, coffee chat or coaching session.

- **Social.** An exchange of ideas, knowledge or information typically
characterized by friendly interaction through online services that provides supplemental understanding often via personal and professional
networks.[3]

---

[3] Dan Pontefract, *Flat Army* (San Francisco: Jossey-Bass, 2013), 197–205.

I love the analogy Jay Cross, author and informal learning guru, gives for formal and informal learning: "Formal learning is like riding a bus, the driver decides where the bus is going; the passengers are along for the ride. Informal learning is like riding a bike; the rider chooses the destination, the speed and the route."[4]

It is fascinating to realize the impact of social media and the information available on learning and leadership style. It will be more and more difficult for leaders to be command-and-control when, in many cases, employees have as much access to information as they do. Employees used to cocreating and freely accessing information are expecting leadership styles to align with their democratic and open world. We certainly saw the impact of social media on political leaders with the Arab Spring in the Middle East and Africa.

Pontefract urges leaders to take up social media to connect and collaborate so that leadership and learning are not just command-and-control or sage-on-the-stage events. The same trends that are changing the way people learn should also be changing the way leaders lead. He urges leaders to produce weekly blogs discussing what they did over the course of the week (and perhaps leave it open for comments and feedback from others in the organization). "It is little things like that that open up the behavior from cultivate and coordinate to connect and collaborate that lend [themselves] to the idea that learning is part formal and informal . . . And just like learning, leadership is part formal and informal."

Leaders who enthusiastically embrace the three forms of learning can transform the process from one of merely pushing information and knowledge to others inside and outside an organization to a push-and-pull process. A real-life example is a leader tweeting or blogging a thought, message or opinion and subsequently engaging in online discussions through various means (instant messaging, blogging, and so on). Participants in this process are in fact cocreators of knowledge as they share ideas, opinions and information. Leaders need to understand that they can take advantage of these new media only if they get involved with them.

---

[4]Connie Malamed, *Informal Learning: An Interview with Jay Cross,* The eLearning Coach, n.d. [2010]. http://theelearningcoach.com/elearning2-0/informal-learning-an-interview-with-jay-cross/.

"At some point we thought that bosses had the most information, just as we once thought that teachers had the most information," says Sylvia Chrominska of Scotiabank. "Now we all have access to lots of information, so now the ask of the teacher, or the ask of the boss, is very different."

At Telus, Pontefract believes that willingness to embrace social media as a learning and development tool has much more to do with leadership style and outlook than a leader's age or what generational cohort he or she may belong to: "If you think that leadership is about command and control at age twenty-five because you saw the forty-five-year-old do it, it's learned." Younger leaders do have the advantage of having grown up with emerging social media technologies and are generally more comfortable trying out new modes of communication. There is no evidence that younger leaders are better wired to take advantage of emerging technologies or that older leaders are doomed to analog obsolescence in a digital world.

I believe that striking the right balance between the formal, informal and social modes of learning is critical. The mix may depend on the level of experience and knowledge of employees in the organization. Research suggests that formal learning is most effective for those employees who are either newer to the organization or have less experience, while informal learning is most beneficial to the more experienced people within the organization. But to maximize the learning and growth for leaders and employees and to meet various learning preferences, the three need to be present.

COMMUNITIES OF PRACTICE

At Global Knowledge, we have found that one of the most effective ways to learn informally is to be part of a community of practice. This goes by other names, such as user groups, blogging and microblogging. Whether it is called "learning 2.0" or something more hip and current, learning based on a community of practice brings together a group of people who share a concern, a set of problems or passion about a topic, and who deepen their knowledge and capacity for action through interacting and communicating with others on an ongoing basis. Communicating about a common topic is as old as the caveman. What has changed is that it can now be conducted without a committee, project team or management group.

Instead, the online tools give birth to and support communities of practice. When it comes to the technologies that are driving the social media revolution and creating powerful learning and development tools for organizations, Pontefract urges companies to focus on function rather than ubiquitous brand names. "I'm agnostic, I believe in the technology descriptions, not technology companies or products," he explains. "You don't say Twitter or Yammer, you say microblogging. That is a huge piece of being an open leader, being a connected leader. As is instant messaging. A connected leader would not turn off instant messaging and show themselves as unavailable all day. Showing your status is a sign of a connected leader and helps people see what you are doing and where you are."

Just as organizations should be brand or technology-provider agnostic, when it comes to social media platforms for tasks such as blogging or instant messaging, they should not presume that new is necessarily better for learning and development. "Companies can get lost in the behavior or the tools themselves versus the results that they produce," says Tom Gram, senior director of Learning Services of Global Knowledge. "Sometimes there is a value judgment that underlies all of this, that learning through social media is better than learning through other mechanisms. I don't know if there is a better or a worse. It [social media] provides a vehicle to accomplish things through different ways that are sometimes faster, or allow collaboration to get better ideas in there and potentially produce better outcomes.

"I get a little concerned when we start to put people into camps—[for example, that] those that use social media are better learners or are more advanced in their approach to communication than others," he adds. "All those early concerns about social media are still true: the jury is still out to a certain degree on whether they absolutely produce better productivity within organizations."

Leaders need to recognize that they can't do everything. They can't be tweeting and blogging and consulting thousands of sources constantly. Instead, leaders should view the three categories of learning (formal, informal and social) and pick their battles according to their needs. What do they need to stay up-to-date, to grow and to progress professionally? The three categories of learning, especially the informal and the social, present leaders with a gigantic buffet of choices of how to learn and stay up-to-date; they need to select those that will contribute to their growth and fit their style. And perhaps most importantly, they need to leverage all three categories—which blog to read and contribute to, which RSS feed to subscribe to, which professional association events to attend and courses to take? Sticking simply with options that provide formal learning, say, would mean that a leader is ultimately missing out.

It is no different really from the 70-20-10 rule, which illustrates how we know what we know in the workplace (see Chapter 4). We need some of each approach to become proficient in our professional roles, just as we need to embrace informal and social learning as well as more formal modes of learning.

THE FOUR MYTHS OF SOCIAL LEARNING

It is not unusual that, with something as popular as social media, a wealth of facts and opinions are shared and made available—on social media, of course. But at some point we need to clarify and demystify that which is becoming more myth than reality. The following four myths are probably the most common ones about social learning.[5]

Myth 1: Social Learning Is New

In the late 1970s, psychologist Albert Bandura established the most well-known theory of modern social learning, which proposes that people can learn in a social context. Among other things, his theory states that:

- Learning can occur by observing others' behaviors and the resulting outcomes.
- Learning can occur cognitively without a corresponding change in behavior.
- Modeled behavior is reinforced by producing desirable outcomes (for both the observed party and the learner).
- Three variables in the social learning context—the learner, the behavior and the environment—can influence each other.

---

[5] http://www.blackboard.com/sites/social/thought-leadership/myths.html.

These points about the advantages of social learning, including learning by example and the reinforcement of knowledge that comes with the "human connection," are as valid today as they were when Bandura published his theory.

We now know that social media technologies support and significantly impact learning. This, of course, has consequences for facilitators, teachers and instructors, the traditional providers and supporters of learning. Their roles are no less important today than they once were, and they still need to be positive role models, but they also need to become accustomed to a less controlled environment and the plethora of ways available to engage learners.

Myth 2: Social Learning Is the Same as Social Media

Popular social media platforms such as Twitter, Facebook, LinkedIn and Pinterest allow, like never before, people to meet (virtually) to share interests and information, and build relationships. The downside is that they can also be immense time stealers as people meander and follow topics that do not necessarily advance their interests or those of their organization.

When incorporating social media platforms into a learning environment, it is often useful to include objectives, strategies and guidelines for their use, through, for example, direction from the instructor or a lesson guide. Learning in a social environment does not necessarily have to be that structured—it can happen without a designed leader or moderator, and without a defined instruction plan, with topics chosen or discovered by student participants.

Internet-based social platforms allow students to connect irrespective of distance and allow for informal sharing of ideas and skills, which are the basics of social learning. While social learning and social media can and do operate on their own, social media tools can be used to spur social learning, as social learning strategist and designer Tom Spiglanin has noted. Dan Pontefract makes a similar distinction: "Social media is a tool; social learning is an action. And online social technologies have enabled frictionless social-learning opportunities."

Myth 3: Social Learning Is Just for Fun

Probably the biggest benefit and change that social learning brought to us is the ability to share: share among individuals and institutions, anywhere, anytime. That in itself exponentially increased our capacity to learn and exchange important content and information.

Cathy Davidson, professor of interdisciplinary studies at Duke University, teaches a course called "This Is Your Brain on the Internet." While part of the course material consists of readings from journals and websites, her innovative approach is to have most of the course design and content and be peer-led.

Davidson (2011) realized that social learning provides freedom to the learners and allows them to retain more. With fewer rules and restrictions, students submitted papers that were more creative and meaningful than typical conventional term papers.

Although social media is commonly used for gossiping and exchanging relatively insignificant information on day-to-day activities, it is certainly feasible to take advantage of social media tools to support and maximize learning. Davidson indicates that research shows the benefits of social media in learning, particularly related to socialization and interaction. As a professor, she also notices a better quality of writing and content from students' writings when they are public, as with blog posts, in comparison with traditional assigned papers that only the professor would read.

Myth 4: Social Learning Doesn't Have Broad Appeal

No matter how the digital world evolves, social learning is here to stay.

Social learning is not the flavor of the month; it is too ingrained in our education and learning systems to be considered just a trend. Its modalities and tools will certainly change, but the new learning approach created largely by the learners themselves is here to stay and attract more and more people, mainly due to its high added value for the users.

According to digital analytics company comScore, the time spent using social tools increased by more than 62 percent (from one out of thirteen minutes to one out of eight) between 2011 and 2012. Usage of the Internet for nonsocial purposes dropped by more than 500 million hours during that time. Ben Elowitz, founder and CEO of Wetpaint, argues that the interactive, "connected social web is alive, moving, proactive and personal, while the document web is just an artefact—suited as universal reference, but hardly a personal experience." Social media also creates and strengthens relationships, which raises levels of engagement, which can boost learning.[6]

WHAT THE EXPERTS SAY

Over the last few years, we have seen the emergence of a new kind of worker who recognizes the power and competitive advantage of using the Internet, and social media in particular, to work and learn more quickly, easily and in new ways. Dubbed "Smart Workers" by Jane Hart, founder and director of the Centre for Learning and Performance Technologies, these workers are gaining an advantage by decreasing their time spent in formal learning environments, such as classrooms, and increasing their time spent engaged in informal learning, supported by technology (Hart 2012). With the ever-changing and competitive nature of organizations, and with management becoming increasingly cognizant of their bottom line, organizations are no longer willing to spend millions of dollars on training and developing their managers through traditional, formal learning channels.

Hart (2012) traces the history of workplace learning from the formal learning approaches, including classroom learning, e-learning and blended learning and, more recently, to informal social learning approaches. Although classroom learning provided the social experience, it hasn't kept up with the demands associated with flexibility, speed, twenty-first-century learning styles and budget deficits. At their peak, e-learning and blended learning were praised for accommodating the need for flexibility and faster-paced learning, but learners gradually became disenfranchised and less enthusiastic because they found themselves spending much of their time with nothing but a computer, with little opportunity for human interaction.

Furthermore, workers were no longer content with having their learning managed by learning management systems, resulting in what has been coined the "consumerization of IT," where learners make use

---

[6] http://www.blackboard.com/sites/social/thought-leadership/myths.html#myth-1.

of social media Internet tools, often bypassing learning-and-development and IT departments. This consumerization of learning means that more and more people are doing their own thing in order to address their learning and performance requirements (Hart 2012). In a blog article titled "I come not to bury training, only to put it in its place," Harold Jarche (2012b) promotes informal social learning, writing that "the increasing complexity of our workplaces means we have to accept the limitations of training and education as we have practiced them" and that there is a "growing need to help people be more creative and to solve complex problems, on a daily basis and in concert with others." To stay relevant and provide services that match the ways that individuals and teams are working, learning and development departments are evolving and building new roles in organizations, including helping individuals become Smart Workers, in particular Smart Managers. In an earlier blog post titled "Informal learning, the 95 percent solution," Jarche (2012a) writes that formal training is "like a hammer that sees all problems as nails" and that "these nails only account for 5 percent of organizational learning."

Drawing on her study titled "Top 100 Tools for Learning," Jane Hart identifies eight key features of how Smart Workers are making use of social media for working and learning. According to Hart, Smart Workers or Smart Managers:

1. Recognize they learn continuously as they do their jobs
2. Want immediate access to solutions to their performance problems
3. Are happy to share what they know
4. Rely on a trusted network of friends and colleagues
5. Learn best from others
6. Keep up-to-date with their industry and profession
7. Constantly strive to improve their productivity
8. Thrive on autonomy

According to Hart, Smart Workers understand that learning continuously while they do their jobs is crucial to their survival and ability to develop. The necessity to learn actively to stay current and adapt to change is not totally new; we probably have all come across the words of Alvin

Toffler: "The illiterate of the 21st century will not be those who cannot read and write, but those who cannot learn, unlearn, and relearn." And how about going back even further to Charles Darwin, who said, "It is not the strongest of the species that survives, nor the most intelligent, but the one most responsive to change." The major differences between Darwin's time and today are the multiplicity of ways to learn, the pace at which we need to learn to stay up-to-date and the expectations that learning is part of the day-to-day work.

In his article titled "The Other Side of Learning: Performance Is Everything," leadership development consultant Dr. Conrad Gottfredson (2011) emphasizes that the nature of twenty-first-century learners is "resistant to learning options that are delayed and removed from the here and now" and that "today's work environment doesn't tolerate learners stepping out of their work flow to learn unless it is absolutely vital to do so." Gottfredson describes twenty-first-century learners as "self-directed, adaptive and collaborative in their approach to learning" and says that if organizations don't efficiently prepare them to effectively perform in the present time, they "are predisposed to simply walk away and look elsewhere for the shortest path to successful performance." Summarizing her number one feature—that the Smart Worker learns continuously—Hart (2012) points out that smart learning and development thinking have positive consequences. The Smart Worker:

1. Values the informal, social learning that takes place continuously as people do their jobs
2. Integrates learning in the workflow
3. Helps workers make effective use of the social web

Hart notes that Smart Workers seek immediate access to solutions to their performance problems. In other words, they want to find quick solutions to problems by accessing resources that individuals have created and shared for others to use, including:

- How-to materials at sites such as wikiHow
- Videos and screencasts at sites such as YouTube
- Presentation slide sets at sites such as SlideShare

When learning, Smart Workers are focused on performance outcomes—in other words, on what they will be able to do rather than what they will know after using the materials.

When looking for solutions to performance problems, Smart Workers focus on:

- How they will use the content
- Performance outcomes
- Short and simple material
- Resources that are readable in mobile devices
- Thinking in terms of job aids instead of formal courses

Smart Workers don't want to memorize a bunch of material *just in case* they need it; rather, they only need to know *where* to find it, *when* they need it. Hart points to a report on a survey of younger-generation workers age eighteen to twenty-nine. Some 75 percent of them said workplace training would be more valuable if it was available remotely through handheld mobile devices, and 63 percent said training sessions would be more valuable if they were shorter and less time-consuming.

The iPad is considered by many to be the ultimate current mobile device. In a recent blog post, Jeff Bullas (2011) reported that the iPad was the fastest-selling technology hardware device in history, with 15 million sold in eleven months. Bullas reports that 87 percent of owners use it every day, while 24 percent use it more than two hours a day. Further, 75 percent use it for accessing the web, 63 percent for e-mail, 41 percent for social networking, 29 percent to research products and services and 13 percent for work.

Smart Workers also make use of social media for working and learning by routinely and willingly sharing what they know with others. The more organizations encourage employees to create and share resources with one another and with people outside their organizations, the more resources there are in the pool to tap from when they need them (Hart 2012). Hart identifies concerns organizations have about sharing resources, which may impact their decision to encourage sharing, including ensuring:

1. Materials are of professional quality
2. Materials are accurate
3. The privacy and security of an organization's content

However, a growing number of organizations are developing ways to help teams create and share content with one another, including Dare 2 Share (which shares podcasts and other resources, such as blogs, RSS feeds, documents and portals) and Intelpedia (a grassroots collaborative resource-building program developed by Intel engineer Josh Bancroft). In an interview with Socialmedia.biz (Lasica 2010), Bancroft reported on the success of the project, noting that in the four-years-plus that Intelpedia has been operating, no inappropriate use of the system was reported. Built on MediaWiki, the open-source wiki software that powers Wikipedia, Intelpedia's strength is for knowledge sharing across departments.

Another feature identified by Hart of how Smart Workers make use of social media is the degree to which they rely on a trusted network. The center points out that although this concept is not entirely new in the workplace, what *is* new is how much quicker and easier it is to access a much wider group of friends and colleagues through online social networks.

Based on a survey, Hart (2012) notes that people use social networks to:

- Ask questions of colleagues and answer their questions
- Share and receive ideas, resources and experiences
- Solve problems and brainstorm together
- Keep up-to-date with what their colleagues are doing and thinking
- Learn from their colleagues in many different ways

Hart notes that besides public networks there exist many private, specialized communities where people can meet with colleagues for more focused discussions and networking. She points to her own website, where people can discuss the concept of social learning and how it supports performance, as well as the wider use of social media in organizations.

Hart notes that the private networking tool Yammer provides quick and easy networking within organizations, as well as facilitating the creation of groups and external networks. The Yammer website indicates that more than 200,000 companies, including 85 percent of the Fortune 500 companies, use Yammer to foster team collaboration, empower and engage employees, boost productivity and socialize intranets. Companies can set up basic enterprise social networking for free and expand their networking options later, for a minimal cost of $3 to $4 per user per month.

Curtis Ogden at the Interaction Institute for Social Change provides the following summary of the differences between network and hierarchy thinking. Network thinking represents:

1. Adaptability instead of control
2. Emergence instead of predictability
3. Resilience instead of redundancy
4. Contributions before credentials
5. Diversity instead of divergence

With respect to emergence and predictability, the author notes that we cannot predict what will emerge from continuous learning, but that cocreating and sharing at the individual, organizational and market levels will make organizations more resilient. The redundancy of network connections helps support the spread of social learning, offers different ways of communicating or finding something and provides more opportunities for learning complex ideas. The fourth feature reflects that smart thinking and development help individuals build an external network of friends and colleagues and help groups and teams set up internal group spaces so they can support one another.

The fifth feature Hart stresses is that Smart Workers understand that they learn best with and from others. David Pollard, former chief knowledge officer of Ernst and Young, coach for entrepreneurs and writer of the *How to Save the World* blog, points to the limits of what you can find online or alone by identifying a list of skills that social learning provides, including social skills and the capacity to get along with others, as well as competencies and capacities that require real-world practice (empathy, facilitation, conversation, collaborative skills, consensus, invitation, conflict resolution and storytelling) (Pollard 2011).

Tutoring, one-to-one coaching and mentoring have been high on the agenda in many organizations, but social media has taken it to the next level. Although there are external providers that offer individual coaching and mentoring, Hart (2012) suggests that organizations use their own experts to pass on their knowledge by becoming mentors or consider "reverse mentoring," where older workers share their experiences with newcomers in exchange for support and help using social media tools. Social media technologies provide the opportunity for building online mentoring-group learning communities that help Smart Workers get immediate solutions to their performance problems. Smart Workers develop their own informal group space (e.g., on Facebook or LinkedIn), where they can hold discussions and share what they know with each other.

Smart Workers' sixth feature is keeping up-to-date with what is happening in their industry or profession. John Seeley Brown (2012) refers to "entrepreneurial learning," which involves the Smart Worker constantly looking around for new ways, and new resources, through which to learn new things. It isn't enough to show up at an annual conference or two and read a few magazines. Hart identifies several things Smart Workers do to keep up to speed on what is happening in their industry or profession. They:

1. Keep in contact with a network of trusted colleagues they have built inside and outside the organization
2. Attend regular webinars to keep up with ideas and meet like-minded people
3. Regularly read favorite industry and analyst blogs, making use of an RSS reader to subscribe to blog feeds, manage subscriptions and be alerted to new blog posts as they become available
4. Use feeds to keep up with industry website news, job and contract positions, podcasts and wiki updates

In summary, the sixth feature points out that smart thinking and development helps individuals make effective use of the social web, including helping them with their personal knowledge management and setting up filters to deal with information overload.

The seventh feature is that Smart Workers use social media to improve productivity. Smart Workers are always on the lookout for better tools. Seth Godin, author, marketing guru and public speaker, sums up this feature in his blog post "Time for a workflow audit," where he suggests: "Go find a geek. Someone who understands Gmail, Outlook, Excel and other basic tools. Pay her to sit next to you for an hour and watch you work. Then say, 'Tell me five ways I can save an hour a day.'" In summary, the seventh feature points out that smart learning and development encourages the use of personal tools and devices and helps with workflow audits to identify new tools and devices that will aid productivity.

The eighth and final feature identified by Hart suggests that Smart Workers thrive on autonomy, through organizing and managing learning by helping individuals and teams to self-organize.

Social learning is often confused with other concepts, such as participation, and the difference between individual and social learning is seldom stressed. This confusion makes it difficult to determine and measure whether social learning has in fact taken place and, if so, to what extent, between whom, when and how. Hart (2012) attempts to clarify the conceptual basis for social learning by arguing that social learning has taken place only if the process demonstrates that:

1. A change in understanding has occurred in individuals involved.
2. Learning is situated within wider social units or communities of practice.
3. Learning has taken place through social interaction.

As you have read, there are so many contemporary ways to learn and grow, and to develop leaders to meet business needs. Ignoring them would be a major miss. Leveraging new ways to learn that are part formal, informal and social will pull you in the right direction to accelerate your leadership development.

Conclusion

The older I get, the less I listen to what people say and
the more I look at what they do.

—Andrew Carnegie

Over the course of this book, I have shown the step-by-step process necessary to accelerate leadership development in your organization, both from
the perspective of the HR professional charged with developing the next
generation of leaders and from that of the manager intent on acquiring the
tools to become a great leader him- or herself.

This is a good time to take stock of what we have covered. Part 1 of
the book dealt with the twin challenges of leadership development and
succession management. The processes meant to meet these challenges
should not be carried out haphazardly, as they are so often in today's businesses, too many of which suffer from lean HR management structures
and time-pressed leaders. Instead, they need to have rigor and structure
in order to contribute to the success of the organization. They must be
purposeful, with a dedicated, repeatable approach. What the organization
requires in a leader has to be clearly identified and aligned with business
goals and strategy. In other words, we want leaders with these sets of
skills, experience and knowledge to achieve specific goals in the business.
Aligning that success profile with the organization's business goals makes
the process robust, gives it a sense of urgency and ensures that management
is sufficiently behind it.

It is not enough, however, simply to create accurate success profiles of
future leaders. Organizations also need to create detailed sets of criteria to
identify high-potential candidates. Similarly, what makes a high potential

in any given business cannot be vague or subject to the arbitrary wishes of any one manager; rather, there must be a clear set of skills and qualities. Every individual is different and unique, but the characteristics that organizations can use to predict the leadership potential of each candidate should not be.

Once those proto-leaders are identified, organizations need to determine what skills they already have in their tool kits and what needs to be added. That's the subject of Chapters 3 and 4, on development needs and solutions. The latter includes the real-life 70-20-10 rule, which reminds us that most people learn primarily by doing, less by observing and least of all by classroom learning, conferences or e-learning.

If there is a recurring theme to Part 1, it is that the preparation of leadership succession must be purposeful, articulated and measureable.

Leadership can be described in terms of a theory, an approach, a school of thought, or even as a trend. Part 2 shows that, in a day-to-day work environment, leadership in action consists of behaviors. In this section, I developed and explained the fundamentals of leadership in action. The modern leader is a coach for his or her team, preparing its members to be successful. Communications skills are the foundation of leadership. You cannot succeed without them. A highly motivated team will perform better and produce superior results compared with a similar team that may be more technically competent but less motivated.

Today's leaders are busier than ever before, so delegating deliberately and providing feedback are critical, must-have skills. They are necessary not only to manage the workload but also to quicken the development of team members around them. An effective leader spreads the work around and, moreover, distributes skills and knowledge to those who report to him or her. Increasingly, leaders operating in today's complex organizations with informal teams and matrix structures must learn to lead and motivate people over whom they have little or no formal authority. It bears repeating Alan Booth's sage observation: "You cannot rely on brute force. The streets are littered with leaders who only use authority as leadership." Influential leadership is the new competency of twenty-first-century business.

Part 3 contains a series of moments of truth, highlighting organizational best practices for today and tomorrow. Leaders face such moments whenever they are handed business goals and business plans and are required to align their teams with those goals and make the strategies come to life. Achieving this alignment is a critical, real-life test of leadership that will augment success or lead to the failure of the team and, ultimately, the organization.

Leadership can also mean transition. Individuals may move from employee to leader, and leaders may assume new and greater levels of responsibility. At such moments, they need support from those higher in the organization to maximize their chances of success and to avoid failure—which can occur all too frequently.

In our personal and work lives, technology can be both a gift and a curse. It can streamline and speed up business processes, but it also blurs the line between working and not working. We see today the use of technology in people development. Many of today's most successful companies have created an effective blend of the old and new by leveraging recent and emerging technologies and learning modalities with more traditional practices and solutions. When organizations go about developing and growing leaders, they should look at utilizing new systems and tools whenever possible. Contemporary ways of learning are accessible to all.

If you take away just one concept from this book, let it be this: leadership development can be accelerated with focus, structure and rigor, while maintaining simplicity and practicality of the development solutions.

Now the decision to act on the development of leaders is all yours. You will most likely meet doubters and naysayers who try to diminish the importance of leadership development. And yes, there is always an outlier organization that performs well financially with questionable leadership—or despite it. This is no different from the case of your old uncle who lived well into his late nineties despite smoking and drinking all his life. Science has now demonstrated that, if we exercise, eat well and avoid smoking, we maximize our chance of living long lives and in good health. Your uncle beat the odds. Are you willing to take the same risks? Similarly, the tried-and-true leadership best practices that are at the heart of this book have shown that organizations will greatly improve their odds of meeting business goals when strong leaders are consistently and continually recognized, nurtured and promoted.

It's up to you to improve the odds. Let's get started!

References

CHAPTER 1

Amit, K., Popper, M., Gal, R., Mamane-Levy, T., and Lisak, A. 2009. Leadership-shaping experiences: A comparative study of leaders and non-leaders. *Journal of Leadership and Organization Development* 30: 302–15.

Boyce, A.L., Zaccaro, J.S., and Wisecarver, Z.M. 2010. Propensity for self-development of leadership attributes: Understanding, predicting, and supporting performance of leadership self-development. *Leadership Quarterly* 21: 159–78.

Dragoni, L., Oh, I.-S., Vankatwyk, P., and Tesluk, E.P. 2011. Developing executive leaders: The relative contribution of cognitive ability, personality, and the accumulation of work experience in predicting strategic thinking competency. *Personnel Psychology* 64 (4): 829–64.

Gentry, A.W., and Sparks, E.T. 2012. A convergence/divergence perspective of leadership competencies managers believe are most important for success in organizations: A cross-cultural multilevel analysis of 40 countries. *Journal of Business and Psychology* 27 (1): 15–30.

Groves, S.K. 2007. Integrating leadership development and succession planning best practices. *Journal of Management* 26 (3): 239–60. doi: 10.1108/02621710710732146.

Hendricks, W.J., and Payne, C.S. 2007. Beyond the Big Five: Leader goal orientation as a predictor of leadership effectiveness. *Human Performance* 20 (4): 317–43.

Hogan, Robert. 2003. *Personality, Leadership, and Organizational Effectiveness.* Presentation document. Hogan Assessment Systems, http://annex.ipacweb.org/library/conf/07/hogan.pdf.

—. 2012. History of Personality. Hogan Assessment Systems, http://www.hoganassessments.com/.

Hogan, Robert, and Kaiser, Robert. 2005. What we know about leadership. *Review of General Psychology* 9 (2): 169–80.

Jokinen, T. 2005. Global leadership competencies: A review and discussion. *Journal of European Industrial Training* 29 (3): 199–216.

McCallum, S., and O'Connell, D. 2009. Social capital and leadership development: Building stronger leadership through enhanced relational skills. *Leadership and Organization Development Journal* 30 (2): 152–66.

CHAPTER 2

Achtenhagen, L., Melin, L., Mullern, T., and Ericson, T. 2003. Leadership: The role of interactive strategizing. In *Innovative Forms of Organizing: International Perspectives*, ed. A. Pettigrew, R., Whittington, L., Melin, C., Sanchez-Runde, F., Van Den Bosch, A.J., Ruigrok, W., and Numagami, T., 49–71. London: Sage.

Atwater, L.E., Dionne, S.D., Avolio, B., Camobreco, J.F., and Lau, A.W. 1999. A longitudinal study of the leadership development process: Individual differences predicting leader effectiveness. *Human Relations* 52: 1543–62.

Bass, B. 1990. *Bass & Stogdill's Handbook of Leadership.* 3rd ed. New York: The Free Press.

Beard, Alison. 2012. Life's work: Bela Karolyi. *Harvard Business Review*, 90 (7–8): 164–68.

Bobbio, A., and Manganelli Rattazzi, A.M. 2006. A contribution to the validation of the motivation to lead scale (MTL): A research in the Italian context. *Leadership* 2: 117–29.

Brackett, M.A., Rivers, S., Shiffman, S., Lerner, N., and Salovey, P. 2006. Relating emotional abilities to social functioning: A comparison of self-report and performance measures of emotional intelligence. *Journal of Personality and Social Psychology* 91: 780–95.

Brackett, M.A., Warner, R.M., and Bosco, J. 2005. Emotional intelligence and relationship quality among couples. *Personal Relationships* 12: 197–212.

Brown, M.E., Treviño, L.K., and Harrison, D.A. 2005. Ethical leadership: A social learning perspective for construct development and testing. *Organizational Behavior and Human Decision Processes* 97: 117–34.

Button, S., Mathieu, J., and Zajac, D. 1996. Goal orientation in organizational behavior research: A conceptual and empirical foundation. *Organizational Behavior and Human Decision Processes* 67: 26–48.

Chan, K., and Drasgow, F. 2001. Towards a theory of individual differences and leadership: Understanding the motivation to lead. *Journal of Applied Psychology* 86: 481–98.

Chemers, M.M., Watson, C.B., and May, S.T. 2000. Dispositional affect and leadership effectiveness: A comparison of self-esteem, optimism, and efficacy. *Personality and Social Psychology Bulletin* 26: 267–77.

Ciulla, J.B. 1998. *Ethics: The Heart of Leadership.* Westport, CT: Praeger.

Colvin, G. 2003. Corporate crooks are not created equal. *Fortune* 27: 64.

Conger J.A., and Fulmer R.M. 2003. Developing your leadership pipeline. *Harvard Business Review* 81 (12): 76–84, 125.

Corporate Leadership Council. 2005. *Realizing the Full Potential of Rising Talent.* Washington, DC: Corporate Leadership Council.

Côté, S., and Miners, C.T.H. 2006. Emotional intelligence, cognitive intelligence and job performance. *Administrative Science Quarterly* 51: 1–28.

Duckworth, A.L., Peterson, C., Matthews, M.D., and Kelly, D.R. 2007. Grit: Perseverance and passion for long-term goals. *Journal of Personality and Social Psychology* 92: 1087–1101.

Dweck, C.S. 1999. *Self-Theories: Their Role in Motivation, Personality, and Development.* Philadelphia: Psychology Press.

Fay, D., and Frese, M. 2000. Conservatives' approach to work: Less prepared for future work demands? *Journal of Applied Social Psychology* 31: 171–95.

—. 2001. The concept of personal initiative: An overview of validity studies. *Human Performance* 14: 97–124.

Feldman, R.S., Philippot, P., and Custrini, R.J. 1991. Social competence and nonverbal behavior. In *Fundamentals of Nonverbal Behavior*, ed. R.S. Feldman and B. Rime, 329–50. New York: Cambridge University Press.

Frese, M., Fay, D., Hilburger, T., Leng, K., and Tag, A. 1997. The concept of personal initiative: Operationalization, reliability and validity in two German samples. *Journal of Organizational and Occupational Psychology* 70: 139–61.

Gardner, W.L., and Schermerhorn Jr., J.R. 2004. Unleashing individual potential performance gains through positive organizational behavior and authentic leadership. *Organizational Dynamics* 33: 270–81.

George, B. 2003. *Authentic Leadership: Rediscovering the Secrets to Creating Lasting Value.* 1st ed. San Francisco: Jossey-Bass.

Hafsteinsson, L.G., Donovan, J.J., and Breland, B.T. 2007. An item response theory examination of two popular goal orientation measures. *Educational and Psychological Measurement* 67: 719–39.

Hooijberg, R., Hunt, J.G., and Dodge, G.E. 1997. Leadership complexity and development of the Leaderplex Model. *Journal of Management* 23: 375–408.

Hoyt, C., Murphy, S., Halverson, S., and Watson, C. 2003. Group leadership: Efficacy and effectiveness. *Group Dynamics: Theory, Research, and Practice* 7: 259–74.

Judge, T.A., Colbert, A.E., and Ilies, R. 2004. Intelligence and leadership: A quantitative review and test of theoretical propositions. *Journal of Applied Psychology* 89: 542–52.

Keltner, D., and Kring, A.M. 1998. Emotion, social function, and psychopathology. *Review of General Psychology* 2: 320–42.

Lahteenmaki, S., Toivonen, J., and Mattila, M. 2001. Critical aspects of organizational learning research and proposals for its measurement. *British Journal of Management* 12: 113–29.

Lopes, P.N., Salovey, P., Côté, S., and Beers, M. 2005. Emotion regulation abilities and the quality of social interaction. *Emotion* 5: 113–18.

Lopes, P.N., Salovey, P., and Straus, R. 2003. Emotional intelligence, personality, and the perceived quality of social relationships. *Personality and Individual Differences* 35: 641–58.

Mayer, J.D., and Salovey, P. 1997. What is emotional intelligence? In *Emotional Development and Emotional Intelligence: Educational Implications*, ed. P. Salovey and D.J. Sluyter, 4–30. New York: Basic Books.

Mayer J.D., Salovey, P., and Caruso, D.R. 2008. Emotional intelligence: New ability or eclectic traits? *American Psychologist* 63: 503–17.

McCormick, M.J. 2001. Self-efficacy and leadership effectiveness: Applying social cognitive theory to leadership. *Journal of Leadership Studies* 8: 22–33.

Mehta, S. 2003. MCI: Is being good good enough? *Fortune* 27: 117–24.

Murphy, S.E. 1992. "The Contribution of Leadership Experience and Self-Efficacy to Group Performance under Evaluation Apprehension." PhD diss., University of Washington.

—. 2001. Leader self-regulation: The role of self-efficacy and "multiple intelligences." In *Multiple Intelligences and Leadership*, ed. R. Riggio, S. Murphy and F. Pirozzolo, 163–86. Mahwah, NJ: Lawrence Erlbaum Associates.

Nowicki Jr., S., and Duke, M.P. 1994. Individual difference in nonverbal communication of affect: The Diagnostic Analysis of Nonverbal Accuracy Scale. *Journal of Nonverbal Behavior* 18: 9–35.

Paglis, L.L., and Green, S.G. 2002. Leadership self-efficacy and managers' motivation for leading change. *Journal of Organizational Behavior* 23: 215–35.

Rosete, D., and Ciarrochi, J. 2005. Emotional intelligence and its relationship to workplace performance outcomes of leadership effectiveness. *Leadership & Organization Development Journal* 26: 388–99.

Savage, C.R. 2002. The role of emotion in strategic behavior. In *The Wisdom in Feeling*, ed. L.F. Barrett and P. Salovey, 211–36. New York: Guilford Press.

Slater, S.F., and Narver, J.C. 1995. Market orientation and the learning organization. *Journal of Marketing* 59: 63–74.

Sosik, J.J., Godshalk, V.M., and Yammarino, F.J. 2004. Transformational leadership, learning goal orientation, and expectations for career success in mentor-protégé relationships: A multiple levels of analysis perspective. *Leadership Quarterly* 15: 241–61.

Tobin, D.R. 1993. *Re-Educating the Corporation: Foundations for the Learning Organization*. Brattleboro, VT: Oliver Wright.

Treviño, L.K. 1986. Ethical decision-making in organizations: A person-situation interactionist model. *Academy of Management Review* 11: 601–17.

VandeWalle, D. 1997. Development and validation of a work domain goal orientation instrument. *Educational and Psychological Measurement* 57: 995–1015.

Volberda, H.W. 1996. Toward the flexible form: How to remain vital in hypercompetitive environments. *Organization Science* 7: 359.

Walumbwa, F.O., Avolio, B.J., Gardner, W.L., Wernsing, T.S., and Peterson, S.J. 2008. Authentic leadership: Development and validation of a theory-based measure. *Journal of Management* 34: 89–126.

Watson, C., Chemers, M., and Preiser, N. 2001. Collective efficacy: A multilevel analysis. *Personality and Social Psychology Bulletin* 27: 1057–68.

Zaccaro, S.J., and Klimoski, R.J. 2001. The nature of organizational leadership: An introduction. In *The Nature of Organizational Leadership*, ed. S.J. Zaccaro and R.J. Klimoski, 3–41. San Francisco: Jossey-Bass.

CHAPTER 3

Bar-On, R. 1997. *The Bar-On Emotional Quotient Inventory (EQ-i): A Test of Emotional Intelligence*. Toronto: Multi-Health Systems.

Dasborough, M.T., and Ashkanasy, N.M. 2005. Follower emotional reactions to authentic and inauthentic leadership influence. In *Monographs in Leadership and Management*. Vol. 3, *Authentic Leadership Theory and Practice: Origins, Effects and Development*, ed. W.L. Gardner, B. Avolio and F.O. Walumbwa. Oxford: Elsevier/JAI Press, 281–300.

Daudelin, M.W. 1996. Learning from experience through reflection. *Organizational Dynamics* 24 (3): 36–48.

Goleman, D. 2005. *Emotional Intelligence*. New York: Random House.

Harms, D.P., and Crede, M. 2010. Emotional intelligence and transformational and transactional leadership: A meta-analysis. *Journal of Leadership and Organizational Studies* 17 (1): 5–17. doi: 10.1177/1548051809350894.

Hogan, R., and Benson, M. 2009. Personality, leadership, and globalization: Linking personality to global organizational effectiveness. *Advances in Global Leadership* 5: 11–34.

Hogan, R., and Kaiser, B.R. 2005. What we know about leadership. *Review of General Psychology* 9 (2): 169–80. doi: 10.1037/1089-2680.9.2.169.

Hogan, R., and Warrenfeltz, R. 2003. Educating the Modern Manager. *Academy of Management Learning and Education* 2(1): 74–84.

Mayer, J.D., and Salovey, P. 1997. What is emotional intelligence? In *Emotional Development and Emotional Intelligence: Educational Implications*, ed. P. Salovey and D.J. Sluyter, 3–31. New York: Basic Books.

Meindl, J.R. 1995. The romance of leadership as a follower-centric theory: A social constructionist approach. *Leadership Quarterly* 6 (3): 329–41.

Nesbit, L.P. 2012. The role of self-reflection, emotional management of feedback, and self-regulation processes in self-directed leadership development. *Human Resource Development Review* 11 (2): 203–26. doi: 10.1177/1534484312439196.

Palmer, B., and Stough, C. 2001. *Workplace SUEIT: Swinburne University Emotional Intelligence Test—Descriptive Report.* Melbourne: Swinburne University, Organisational Psychology Research Unit.

Smollan, R., and Parry, K. 2011. Follower perceptions of the emotional intelligence of change leaders: A qualitative study. *Leadership* 7 (4): 435–62. doi: 10.1177/1742715011416890.

Stein, J.S., Papadogiannis, P., Yip, A.J., and Sitarenios, G. 2009. Emotional intelligence of leaders: A profile of top executives. *Leadership and Organization Development Journal* 30 (5): 87–101. doi: 10.1108/01437730910927115.

CHAPTER 4

Avolio, B.J., Reichard, R.J., Hannah, S.T., Walumbwa, F.O., and Chan, A. 2009. A meta-analytic review of leadership impact research: Experimental and quasi-experimental studies. *Leadership Quarterly* 20: 764–84.

Bennis, W.G., and Thomas, R.J. 2002. *Geeks & Geezers: How Era, Values, and Defining Moments Shape Leaders.* Boston: Harvard Business School Press.

Burke, M.J., and Day, R.R. 1986. A cumulative study of the effectiveness of managerial training. *Journal of Applied Psychology* 71: 232–45.

Collins, D.B., and Holton, E.F. 2004. The effectiveness of managerial leadership development programs: A meta-analysis of studies from 1982 to 2001. *Human Resource Development Quarterly* 15: 217–48.

Fulmer, M.R., Stumpf, A.S., and Bleak, J. 2009. The strategic development of high potential leaders. *Leadership* 37 (3): 17–22. doi: 10.1108/10878570910954600.

Gabarro, J.J. 1987. *The Dynamics of Taking Charge.* Boston: Harvard Business School Press.

Hannah, T.S., and Avolio, B.J. 2007. *Developmental readiness: A construct to accelerate leader development.* Paper presented at the Leadership for Critical Response Organizations symposium conducted at the 22nd annual conference of the Society for Industrial and Organizational Psychology, New York.

Hannah, T.S., and Avolio, J.B. 2010. Ready or not: How do we accelerate the developmental readiness of leaders? *Journal of Organizational Behavior* 31 (8): 1181–87. doi: 10.1002/job.675.

Hill, L.A. 1992. *On Becoming a Manager.* Boston: Harvard Business School Press.

McCauley, D.C. 2008. *Leader Development: A Review of Research*. Center for Creative Leadership. http://www.breakoutofthebox.com/LeaderDevelopmentReviewOfResearch.pdf.

CHAPTER 5

Barnett, R., and Davis, S. 2008. Creating greater success in succession planning. *Advances in Developing Human Resources* 10 (5): 721–39. doi: 10.1177/1523422308322277.

Bleak, L.J., and Fulmer, M.R. 2009. Strategically developing strategic leaders. http://www.dukece.com/papers-reports/documents/Strategic_Leaders.pdf. Excerpted from Linkage Inc., *Best Practices in Leadership Development Handbook*. 2nd ed. San Francisco: Pfeiffer.

Campbell, M., and Smith, R. 2010. *High-Potential Talent: A View from inside the Leadership Pipeline*. Center for Creative Leadership. http://www.ccl.org/leadership/pdf/research/highPotentialTalent.pdf.

Corporate Leadership Council. 2005. *Realizing the Full Potential of Rising Talent*. Washington, DC: Corporate Executive Board.

Groves, S.K. 2007. Integrating leadership development and succession planning best practices. *Journal of Management Development* 26 (3): 239–60. doi: 10.1108/02621710710732146.

Hewitt Associates. 2005. *Research Highlights: How the Top 20 Companies Grow Great Leaders*. Lincolnshire, IL: Hewitt Associates.

Rothwell, J.W. 2002. Putting success into your succession planning. *Journal of Business Strategy* 23 (3): 32–37. doi: 10.1108/eb040249.

Saslow, S. 2004. *Current Challenges in Leadership Development*. Palo Alto, CA: Institute of Executive Development.

CHAPTER 6

Caproni, P.D. 2001. *The Practical Coach*. Upper Saddle River, NJ: Prentice Hall.

Ellinger, A.D., Hamlin, R.G., Beattie, R.S., Wang, Y.-L., and McVicar, O. 2011. Managerial coaching as a workplace learning strategy. In Professional and Practice-Based Learning. Vol. 5, *Supporting Workplace Learning*, ed. Rob F. Poell and Marianne van Woerkom, 71–87.

Finkelstein, L.M., and Poteet, M.L. 2007. Best practices in workplace formal mentoring programs. In *The Blackwell Handbook of Mentoring: A Multiple Perspectives Approach*, ed. T.D. Allen and L.T. Eby, 345–68. Malden, MA: Blackwell.

Janssen, O., and Van Yperen, N.W. 2004. Employees' goal orientations, the quality of leader-member exchange, and the outcomes of job performance and job satisfaction. *Academy of Management Journal* 47 (3): 368–84.

Locke, E.A., and Latham, G.P. 1990. *A Theory of Goal Setting and Task Performance*. Englewood Cliffs, NJ: Prentice Hall.

Longenecker, C.O., and Neubert, M.J. 2005. The practices of effective managerial coaches. *Business Horizons* 48 (6): 493–500.

Matthews, J. 2010. Can Line Managers Ever Be Effective Coaches? *Business Leadership Review* 7.2. http://www.mbaworld.com/blr-archive/issues-72/4/index.htm.

McCauley, D.C. 2008. *Leader Development: A Review of Research.* Center for Creative Leadership. http://www.breakoutofthebox.com/LeaderDevelopmentReviewOfResearch.pdf.

Neubert, M.J. 1998. The value of feedback and goal setting over goal setting alone and potential moderators of this effect: A meta-analysis. *Human Performance* 11 (4): 321–35.

Pfeffer, J. 1992. Understanding power in organizations. *California Management Review* 34 (2): 29–50.

CHAPTER 7

Archambault, J. 2013. "What Is the Predictive Value of Qualitative Elements on the Performance of Portfolio?" DBA candidate, thesis in preparation.

Basford, E.T., Offermann, R.L., and Wirtz, W.W.P. 2012. The impact of leadership level on follower motivation and intent to stay. *Journal of Leadership and Organizational Studies* 19 (2): 202–14. doi: 10.1177/1548051811436279.

Dent, F., and Holton, V. 2009. Employee engagement and motivation. *Training Journal,* November 1, www.trainingjournal.com.

Kahn, A.W. 1990. Psychological conditions of personal engagement and disengagement at work. *Academy of Management Journal* 33 (4): 692–724.

Pink, D.H. 2009. *Drive: The Surprising Truth about What Motivates Us.* New York: Riverhead Trade.

Thompson-O'Neal, Marguerite. 2012. "Unleashing the Power of Gen-X Leaders: Inter-Generational Succession Management." MA in leadership, Guelph University.

Wallace, L., and Trinka, J. 2009. Leadership and employee engagement. *Public Management* 91 (5): 10–13.

Wiley, W.J. 2010. The impact of effective leadership on employee engagement. *Employment Relations Today* 37 (2): 47–52. doi: 10.1002/ert.20297.

Xu, J., and Thomas, C.H. 2011. How can leaders achieve high employee engagement? *Leadership and Organization Development Journal* 32 (4): 399–416. doi: 10.1108/01437731111134661.

CHAPTER 8

Baldoni, J. 2004. Powerful leadership communication. *Leader to Leader* 32: 20–24.

Barrett, J.D. 2006. *Leadership Communication: A Communication Approach for Senior-Level Managers.* http://scholarship.rice.edu/bitstream/handle/1911/27037/Leadership%20 Communication%20-%20A%20Communication%20Approach%20for%20Senior -Level%20Managers%20-%20Barrett.pdf.

Bowman, G.W., Jones, L.W., Peterson, R.A., Gronouski, J.A., and Mahoney, R.M. 1964. What helps or harms promotability? *Harvard Business Review* 42 (1): 6–18.

Conger, J.A. 1998. The necessary art of persuasion. *Harvard Business Review* 76 (3): 88.

Flauto, F.J. 1999. Walking the talk: The relationship between leadership and communication competence. *Journal of Leadership Studies* 6 (1–2): 86–97.

Friedmann, J., and Maurer, S. 2003. Innovation: A wealth of contradictions. *Executive Agenda* 6 (3): 55–63.

Hackman, M. 2006. Communicating for leadership success. Executive Forum, www.execu-tiveforum.com.

Mast, C., Huck, S., and Zerfass, A. 2005. Innovation communication: Outline of the concept and empirical findings from Germany. *Innovation Journalism* 2 (7): 1–14.

—. 2006. *Innovationskommunikation in dynamischen Märkten: Empirische Ergebnisse und Fallstudien.* Münster, Germany: LIT.

Rogers, C.A. 1980. *A Way of Being.* New York: Houghton Mifflin.

Zerfass, A., and Huck, S. 2007. Innovation, communication, and leadership: New develop-ments in strategic communication. *International Journal of Strategic Communication* 1 (2): 107–22.

CHAPTER 9

Cannon, D.M., and Witherspoon, R. 2005. Actionable feedback: Unlocking the power of learning and performance improvement. *Academy of Management Executive* 19 (2): 120–34. http://www.jstor.org.ezproxy.library.ubc.ca/stable/4166182.

Dahling, J.J., Chau, L.S., and O'Malley, A. 2010. Correlates and consequences of feedback orientation in organizations. *Journal of Management* 38 (2): 531–46. doi: 10.1177/0149206310375467.

Foss, K., and Foss, J.N. 2005. *Credible delegation: The role of organizational design.* Copenhagen: Department of International Economics and Management, Copenhagen Business School, 1–39. www2.druid.dk/conferences/viewpaper.php?id=2682cf=18.

Osterloh, M., and Frey, B. 2000. Motivation, knowledge transfer and organizational form. *Organization Science* 11: 538–50.

Turner, R.N., and Hewstone, M. 2009. Attribution Biases. In *Encyclopedia of Group Processes & Intergroup Relations,* ed. John M. Levine and Michael A. Hogg. Thousand Oaks, CA: Sage, 43–46.

Zhang, S., Tremaine, M., Milewski, E.A., Fjermestad, J., and O'Sullivan, P. 2012. Leader delegation in global software teams: Occurrence and effects. *Electron Markets* 22 (1): 37–48. doi: 10.1007/s12525-011-0082-y.

CHAPTER 10

Barbuto, E.J., and Wheeler, W.D. 2006. Scale development and construct clarifica-tion of servant leadership. *Group and Organization Management* 31 (3): 300–26. doi: 10.1177/1059601106287091.

Conger, A.J. 1998. The necessary art of persuasion. *Harvard Business Review* 85–95.

Covey, R.S. 2009. How the best leaders build trust. *Linkage Leader.* http://www.linkageinc.com/thinking/linkageleader/Documents/Stephen_Covey_How_the_Best_Leaders_Build_Trust.pdf.

Fehr, E., and Gächter, S. 2000. Fairness and retaliation: The economics of reciprocity. *Journal of Economic Perspectives* 14 (3): 159–81. doi: 10.1257/jep.14.3.159.

Frisina Group. 2012. Accountability: A tool for leadership performance. *Influential Leader* 11 (May): 1–4. http://www.thefrisinagroup.com/wp-content/uploads/May-2012 -Newsletter.pdf.

Heady, C.A. 2008. *Become a More Self Aware Leader.* http://learningandperformancesolutions .com/pdf/ebook.pdf.

Johnson, K.L. 2003. Debriefing Jay Conger: Exerting influence without authority. *Harvard Management Update* 8 (12), 3–4.

McIntosh, P., and Luecke, A.R. 2011. *Increase Your Influence at Work.* New York: American Management Association.

Pontefract, D. 2010. My network is my net worth: A personal story. *Dan Pontefract* (blog), November. http://www.danpontefract.com/my-network-is-my-net-worth-a-personal-story/.

Taylor, N.S. 2010. Redefining self-awareness by integrating the second component of self-awareness. *Journal of Leadership Studies* 3 (4): 57–68. doi: 10.1002/jls.20139.

CHAPTER 11

Bingham, T., and Galagan, P. 2012. TELUS reveals its secret to success. *T+D*, September 7. http:// www.astd.org/Publications/Magazines/TD/TD-Archive/2012/09/TELUS-Reveals -Its-Secret-to-Success.

Boswell, R.W., Bingham, B.J., and Colvin, J.S.A. 2006. Aligning employees through "line of sight." *Business Horizons* 49: 499–509. doi: 10.1016/j.bushor.2006.05.001.

Boswell, R.W., and Boudreau, W.J. 2001. How leading companies create, measure, and achieve strategic results through line of sight. *Management Decision* 39 (10): 851–60. doi: 10.1108/EUM0000000006525.

Gay, C., and D'Aprix, R. 2006. Creating line of sight between employees and strategy. *Strategic Communication Management* 11 (1): 26–29. http://news-business.vlex.com/vid/ line-sight-between-employees-strategy-63638000.

McKinsey & Company. 2012. Interview with Moya Greene. Leading in the 21st Century series. September. http://www.mckinsey.com/features/leading_in_the_21st_century/ moya_greene.

ONESTEP. 2012. *Managing Performance: A Practical Guide for Implementing Best Practices.* Ontario Network of Employment Skills Training Projects. http://onestep. ca/Resources/Performance_Management_Guide.pdf.

Schoonover, C.S. 2011. *Performance Management Best Practices.* Schoonover Associates. http://www.schoonover.com/userfiles/Performance%20Management%20Best%20 Practices.pdf.

CHAPTER 12

Emerge Leadership Group. 2008. *The Critical Transition into the Leadership Role.* http:// www.crgassociates.com/pdfs/ELGWhitepaper.pdf.

Hill, L.A. 2003. *Becoming a Manager: How New Managers Master the Challenges of Leadership.* 2nd ed. Boston: Harvard Business Press.

Institute of Executive Development and Alexcel Group. 2008. *Executive Transitions Benchmark Survey.* http://www.crossroadsconsulting.net/pdf/ExecutiveTransitions MarketStudyReportpw.pdf.

Levin, M.I. 2010. New leader assimilation process: Accelerating new role-related transitions. *Consulting Psychology Journal: Practice and Research* 62 (1): 56–72. doi: 10.1037/a0018630.

Manderscheid, V.S. 2008. New leader assimilation: An intervention for leaders in transition. *Advances in Developing Human Resources* 10 (5): 686–702. doi: 10.1177/1523422308322269.

Masters, B. 2009. Rise of a headhunter. *Financial Times,* March 30, http://www.ft.com.

Polarek, L.N. 2007. *Optimizing the Transition from Individual Contributor to New Manager.* http://www.sesp.northwestern.edu/docs/Polarek_Capstone_Exec_Summary.pdf.

Watkins, M. 2003. *The First 90 Days: Critical Success Strategies for New Leaders at All Levels.* Boston: Harvard Business School Press.

CHAPTER 13

Aberdeen Group, 2006. *Onboarding Benchmark Report: Technology Drivers Help Improve the New Hire Experience.* Boston: Aberdeen Group.

Branham, L. 2005. *The 7 Hidden Reasons Employees Leave: How to Recognize the Subtle Signs and Act Before It's Too Late.* New York: AMACOM.

Dai, G., De Meuse, P.K., and Gaeddert, D. 2009. Onboarding externally hired executives: Avoiding derailment—Accelerating contribution. *Journal of Management and Organization* 17: 165–78.

Hemphill, L., and Begel, A. 2011. Not seen and not heard: Onboarding challenges in newly virtual teams. Microsoft Research, research.microsoft.com.

Pomeroy, A. 2006. Better executive onboarding processes needed. *HR Magazine* 51 (8): 16.

Reese, V. 2005. Maximizing retention and productivity with onboarding. *Employee Relations Today* 31 (4): 23–29.

Sessa, V.I., and Taylor, J.J. 2000. *Executive Selection: Strategies for Success.* San Francisco: Jossey-Bass.

Sharpe, C., ed. 2000. *Successful Orientation Programs: Career Development.* Info-Line, no. 8708. Alexandria, VA: American Society for Training and Development.

Snell, A. 2006. Researching onboarding best practice: Using research to connect onboarding processes with employee satisfaction. *Strategic HR Review* 5 (6): 32–35.

Watkins, M. 2003. *The First 90 Days: Critical Success Strategies for New Leaders at All Levels.* Boston: Harvard Business School Press.

Wells, S.J. 2005. Diving in. *HR Magazine* 50 (3): 54–59.

Williams, R. 2003. *Mellon Learning Curve Research Study.* New York: Mellon.

CHAPTER 14

Blackboard. 2013. Debunking 4 myths of social learning. http://www.blackboard.com/sites/social/thought-leadership/myths.html.

Brown, S.J. 2012. *Cultivating the Entrepreneurial Learner in the 21st Century.* http://dmlcentral.net/sites/dmlcentral/files/resource_files/jsb_transcript_slides.pdf.

Bullas, J. 2011. 29 statistics reveal how Apple's iPad is changing our lives. Centre for Learning and Performance Technologies, April 4. http://www.jeffbullas.com/2011/04/04/29-statistics-reveal-how-the-apples-ipad-is-changing-our-lives/.

Chief Learning Officer. 2012. Poll shows generational gap in workplace training programs. Chief Learning Officer, July 12. http://clomedia.com/articles/view/Poll-shows-generational-gap-in-workplace-training-programs/1.

Davidson, C. 2011. Collaborative learning for the digital age. *Chronicle of Higher Education,* August 26.

Godin, S. 2011. Time for a workflow audit. Centre for Learning and Performance Technologies, July 8. http://sethgodin.typepad.com/seths_blog/2011/07/time-for-a-workflow-audit.html.

Gottfredson, C. 2011. The other side of learning: "Performance is everything." *Learning Solutions Magazine,* April 26. http://www.learningsolutionsmag.com/articles/668/the-other-side-of-learning-performance-is-everything.

Hart, J. 2012. How the smart knowledge worker learns today. Centre for Learning and Performance Technologies. http://c4lpt.co.uk/new-work-place-learning/8-key-features-how-the-smart-workers-learn-today/.

Jarche, H. 2012a. Informal learning, the 95 percent solution. Jarche.com, January 4. http://www.jarche.com/2012/01/informal-learning-the-95-solution/.

Lasica, J.D. 2010. The story of Intelpedia: A model corporate wiki. *Socialmedia. biz: Social Solutions for Business,* July 8. http://socialmedia.biz/2010/07/08/the-story-of-intelpedia-a-model-corporate-wiki/.

Ogden, C. 2011. Network thinking. Interaction Institute for Social Change, December 14. http://interactioninstitute.org/blog/2011/12/14/network-thinking/.

—. 2012b. I come not to bury training, only to put it in its place. Jarche.com, July 18. http://www.jarche.com/2012/07/i-come-not-to-bury-training-only-to-put-it-in-its-place.

Pollard, D. 2011. The limits to what you can learn online or alone. How to Save the World, July 29. http://howtosavetheworld.ca/2011/07/29/the-limits-to-what-you-can-learn-online-or-alone/.

About the Author

Jocelyn Bérard is Vice-President Leadership and Business Solutions, International, for Global Knowledge. He has worked in the leadership and talent management field for twenty-five years, with clients in the United States, Canada, Europe and Asia. His business unit at Global Knowledge focuses on research and intervention initiatives with organizations to develop their leaders and improve their talent management. A sought-after speaker, Bérard has presented at numerous HR associations in Canada, Europe and the United States, including CSTD, HRPA, CRHA and SHRM, and is a frequent speaker at Global Knowledge Executive Speaker Series events.

Global Knowledge is an award-winning global organization known for its strategic solutions with a very strong focus on people development. The company is one of the world's largest learning and development firms with training centers around the world.

Index